'This book is about the events, most of them quite unpredictable, and my observations and memories from the day of the unforgettable autumn in 1939, the day Poland was invaded by Germany, till my arrival in London in the winter of 1957.

These include two years deportation to Kazakhstan as forced labour, ten years as a political prisoner in the Soviet labour camps, and four years eternal exile in Siberia.'

Urszula Muskus – died in England in 1972.

Peter Muskus is the grandson of Urszula Muskus. Born in 1951 near Leicester in the United Kingdom, he studied farming at Aberdeen University and after 21 years managing a dairy farm is now a self employed crofter. Resident with his wife and children near Nairn in the Highlands of Scotland where they have self catering holiday homes on an organically farmed croft.

Kate Allen is the Director of Amnesty International UK.

THE LONG BRIDGE
Out of the gulags

Urszula Muskus

Introduced by
Peter Muskus

Preface by
Kate Allen
Director, Amnesty International UK

SANDSTONEPRESS
HIGHLAND | SCOTLAND

Nakladem, Kola Lwowian, Rodziny I Przyjaciol, Londyn 1975
First printed in Polish by Lwow Citizens Association,
Family and Friends, London 1975.

First published in Great Britain in 2010
Sandstone Press Ltd
PO Box 5725
One High Street
Dingwall
Ross-shire
IV15 9WJ
Scotland.

www.sandstonepress.com

Consulting Editor: Robert Davidson
Copyright © Peter Muskus 2010
Preface Copyright © Amnesty International UK

The moral right of Urszula Muskus to be recognised as
the author of this work has been asserted in accordance with the
Copyright, Design and Patents Act, 1988.

Cover Image: Detail from a Gulag memorial located at the Sculpture Park,
Tretyakov Gallery (New), Moscow © Iain Masterton/Alamy

The publisher acknowledges subsidy from the
Creative Scotland towards this volume.

ISBN-13: 978-1-905207-55-8

Cover by Zebedee Design, Edinburgh

Typeset in Linotype Sabon by Iolaire Typesetting, Newtonmore.
Printed and bound by JF Print, Yeovil, Somerset

Contents

Contents

Preface

The Long Bridge is the story of a woman of great courage and determination, in an exceptionally eloquent account of extreme hardship and hope. It speaks to the profound and ongoing relevance of human rights. Indeed, eight years after Urszula Muskus' arbitrary arrest, the Universal Declaration of Human Rights (UDHR) was adopted as nations tried to avert any recurrence of the atrocities of the Second World War. The UDHR was the first document to agree common terms for what we know to be right and just and is the bedrock of Amnesty International. Yet it was to be fully another eight years before Urszula was released.

Sadly, it remains the case that where wars erupt, suffering and hardship invariably follow. Conflict is the breeding ground for mass violations of human rights including unlawful killings, torture, forced displacement and starvation. Urszula witnessed or experienced all of these, and yet one of the most striking and moving aspects of *The Long Bridge* is its revelation of an indomitable human spirit. As she says, 'oppression cannot imprison thought'.

Kate Allen, Director
Amnesty International UK
www.amnesty.org.uk

Introduction

This story is not mine, and so I have chosen not to write about Urszula in the introduction. I want you to meet her and come to know her through her own words. If you enjoy my grandmother's book and are curious to know more there is a postscript with notes on her background and later life. Instead, I will describe how the book came to be published and, since the story took place two or three generations ago a brief historical background is appropriate for those unfamiliar with European history in the mid 20th century.

Poland, as a country in central Eastern Europe, experienced several changes of boundaries and rulers over the centuries. In 1939 the Poles were in a strong position, with lands extending eastwards into the present day Ukraine (following the collapse of the Austro-Hungarian Empire in 1918 and defeating the Bolsheviks in 1921) but they were not ready for the might of the Germans when they attacked, nor able to resist the Soviets when they entered after the Molotov Ribbentrop Pact.

In the years following Lenin's death in 1924, Joseph Stalin rose to become leader of the Soviet Union. His economic policies of collectivisation and five year plans caused disrupted food production and famine. In the 1930s he expanded the hard labour camps, commonly known as gulags, in Kazakhstan and Siberia to which he deported those 'politicals' caught in mass arrests together with more common criminal types.

When the USSR invaded westwards in 1939, at the start of the Second World War, Stalin extended the mass arrests to the occupied territories to eliminate the professional classes, and install in power those he could more easily control. Urszula, whose husband was an ex-army officer and self-employed forestry surveyor, and her family were included. Her husband was arrested first and then she was deported with her children to the USSR for sixteen years.

Urszula died in her sleep while looking after a friend's house in Hayling Island in 1972. Living there on her own, she had been using the peace and quiet to complete the book that she had been working on for fourteen years. She had stopped typing in mid sentence and the chapters were laid out across the floor. The story was complete, but the tidying up and sequencing of the chapters had not been finished. Writing in such detail about sixteen years of her life, with no notes or diary, from two to thirty years after the event was a major achievement.

Three years after Urszula's death family and friends funded a small, private print run for the use of the Polish community in London and family in Poland. At that time it was illegal to distribute this genre of books in Urszula's home country so it had to be smuggled in.

I first read a translation of my grandmother's manuscript as a teenager, probably around 1968, before the final chapters were written. At that time it was a sheaf of scruffy papers, of different sizes, typed on different machines using different coloured ribbons. I was fascinated by my family history, my roots, because my father had said very little about his past, probably a defence mechanism against the hardships and horrors that he had experienced. I now had knowledge of the gulags at a time when many Socialists in the UK still believed that the USSR was a Utopia. Sadly I was not ready to ask my grandmother the many questions that have arisen, that I can no longer get an answer to.

The translation I had was by a Pole, whose English was less than perfect, so in later years I had the translation transferred to disc so that I could correct the more glaring grammatical errors, format the manuscript and print it for the family. I was never very happy with the ending and, on comparing it with the original Polish publication, realised that several closing chapters were missing. I asked my father to translate these last chapters.

I now had the complete story in English which I could print at home. Copies were put into our self catering holiday homes and I received very positive responses from all those who read it. So much so that, in 2000, I determined to have it published professionally and distributed widely. Submissions to publishers were all politely rejected. I persevered, but with a young family and other commitments time slipped by.

In 2005 I sought and received two professional assessments of the English-language version. Both were extraordinarily positive. The first spoke of Urszula as 'a woman of truly noble spirit and humanity, with the fine eye of a novelist'. The second 'regards it as a privilege to have read this memoir'.

All of this made me still more determined to properly publish my grandmother's book, this apart from the declaration by my daughter that she wouldn't read the story until it was published!

An agent agreed to take on the manuscript and he established interest from over twenty publishers at the London Book Fair, but all were eventually rejected. All avenues appeared to be closed until, in 2009, a chance meeting by my brother-in-law with an old friend, Iain Gordon, at the Nairn Art and Books Festival established that Iain was now a Director of Sandstone Press. Also knowing Iain I approached him and he read Urszula's book with enthusiasm. He recommended publication to his Board and, to my delight and relief, they agreed.

This impelled me to investigate every word, place and name and, in the course of this work, I have learned much and been in touch with many helpful and interesting people. They include the Memorial Society of Russia, a Kazakh journalist, a Polish translator, an American history professor and Amnesty International. On *katynfamilies.com* I found the story of Janina Nowak who was deported on the same train from Rawa Ruska as my grandmother and father, sent to the same collective farm and mentioned Urszula by name. A German friend located the address of Walter, the German POW who became her friend in the gulags in 1948, and, to my absolute joy, we found him alive and well at the age of 96.

Among these many communications I received an unforgettable email from a 27 year old Kazakh woman who helped me with my research. This she has done, but accompanied her corrections with this casually disturbing message:–

'It's quite sad, but I don't know that much history about that period of my country. It was forbidden and many documents were destroyed. All I knew is from Soljenitsyn's book about gulag and people who suffered there. I also read articles and some other stuff, but the thing is that after Kazakhstan became independent in 1990 and they started to dig out the truth it was not easy. We have the memory day for people who were in camps and prisons during Stalin's time, but we don't talk about that much. It's quite a political issue and of course there are not many victims left. Just recently I've read an article from a man who was born in these camps in Kazakhstan and it's quite horrible in a way that as a child he played with human bones that used to be remains of former prisoners who were buried there. My generation doesn't know anything about it and people don't talk that much. It's quite sad really. I'm happy that your Babusia survived and saw her family and wrote a book at the end.'

Aliya's plea for knowledge defines in a nutshell why I believe that Urszula's memoir needs to be published, and hopefully one day, in Russian. Few are aware that Stalin may be responsible for the deaths of 15 million people, and many in Russia still idolize him to this day.

There are many people I want to thank. First and foremost is my wife, Therese, who has supported me throughout this project. Robert Lambolle wrote a very eloquent and positive evaluation which gave me the encouragement to keep going. Robin Wade, the literary agent who believed the manuscript had potential and gave it a good go, ultimately having to give up without making anything for himself. Aliya Boranbayeva helped with Kazakh spelling. Professor Steven Barnes of George Mason University, Virginia USA, for locating the gulags. Nicky Parker and Amnesty International for their support. The many friends and family who encouraged me and helped with research and proof reading. Last but not least Robert Davidson at Sandstone Press for his sensitive editing and enthusiasm for the project.

Urszula lived her closing years out frugally but fully, intent on laying down her testimony before her time was done. When she died her pension had served her well enough and she was left with just £50 in her post office savings. As my sister, Ann, has put it, she was 'a woman with little baggage, just a book.'

Peter Muskus
Laikenbuie, Nairn, Scotland
July 2010

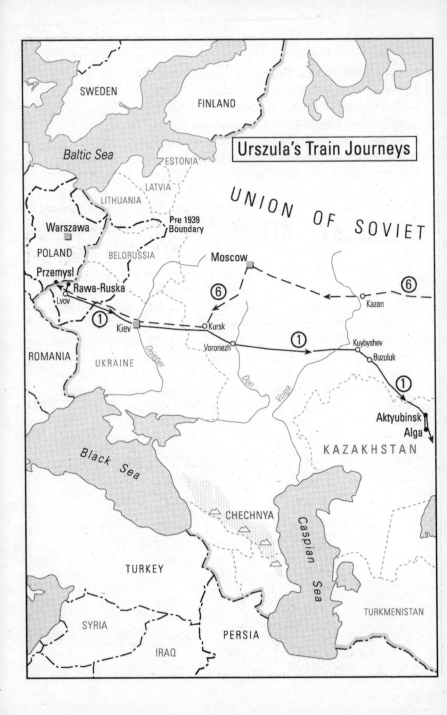

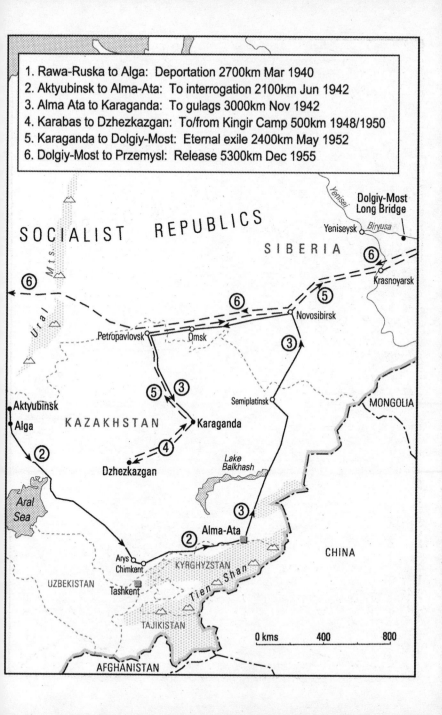

1. Rawa-Ruska to Alga: Deportation 2700km Mar 1940
2. Aktyubinsk to Alma-Ata: To interrogation 2100km Jun 1942
3. Alma Ata to Karaganda: To gulags 3000km Nov 1942
4. Karabas to Dzhezkazgan: To/from Kingir Camp 500km 1948/1950
5. Karaganda to Dolgiy-Most: Eternal exile 2400km May 1952
6. Dolgiy-Most to Przemysl: Release 5300km Dec 1955

SOCIALIST   REPUBLICS

Ural Mts.

SIBERIA

Yenisei

Dolgiy-Most
Long Bridge

Yeniseysk   Biryusa

⑥

Krasnoyarsk

⑥   ⑤

Novosibirsk

Petropavlovsk   Omsk

Aktyubinsk

Alga

⑤ ③

③

KAZAKHSTAN   Karaganda

②

④

Semiplatinsk

MONGOLIA

Dzhezkazgan

Lake
Balkhash

Aral
Sea

③

Alma-Ata

②

Arys
Chimkent   KYRGHYZSTAN

CHINA

UZBEKISTAN

Tashkent   Tien Shan

TAJIKISTAN

0 kms   400   800

AFGHANISTAN

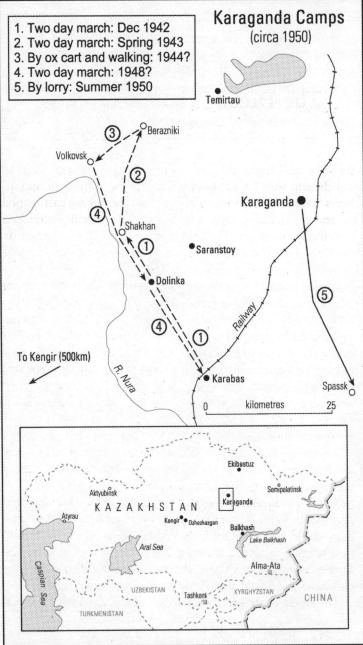

1. Two day march: Dec 1942
2. Two day march: Spring 1943
3. By ox cart and walking: 1944?
4. Two day march: 1948?
5. By lorry: Summer 1950

Karaganda Camps
(circa 1950)

Temirtau

③ Berazniki

Volkovsk

②

Karaganda

④

Shakhan

①

● Saranstoy

● Dolinka

④   ①

Railway

To Kengir (500km)

R. Nura

Karabas

Spassk

0   kilometres   25

Ekibastuz

Aktyubinsk

Semipalatinsk

K A Z A K H S T A N

Karaganda

Atyrau

Kengir ● Dzhezkazgan

Balkhash

Lake Balkhash

Aral Sea

Alma-Ata

Caspian Sea

UZBEKISTAN

Tashkent

KYRGHYZSTAN

CHINA

TURKMENISTAN

PROLOGUE
The Dream That Came True

I awoke, still under the impression left by a striking dream.

I dreamt that I was standing near some lofty wall and all ways were closed for me, whilst before me, facing east, gaped an enormous chasm over which a very long bridge stretched into the far distance. The bright blue sky became overcast by leaden clouds approaching from the west and it grew dark. Sunbeams broke through from time to time, and lit up the bridge here and there as they passed along it to the far side where they dwelt for a time, illuminating the very end.

Something impelled me onto the bridge where I found myself amidst a crowd of, mostly, women and children bowed under the weight of heavy sacks. Their faces betrayed disquiet as they looked around and, without realising how it happened, I suddenly found that I was holding my children by their hands, one on either side. Just as the heavy, leaden clouds merged with one another in the sky, so did I mingle with and become part of the crowd. I peered at the faces around me as I went along and an oppressive calm, barely touching my consciousness, slowly spread through my whole being. I was quite alone in the dusk, people were disappearing.

When I looked towards the end of the bridge I saw a tiny, very bright light. With all my heart I wanted to reach it as soon as possible, but some force slowed my steps whilst the brightness seemed to recede with the end of the bridge, farther and farther away. It was so dark at times that I could hardly see my children, and I held their little hands ever more tightly.

The single sunbeam resting on the end of the bridge was still

bright before me. There were rifts in the clouds here and there
and I vaguely felt them thinning as I went on. A dense cloud
rolled across the sky and darkness for a moment dwelt within
me. A ray of light broke through and, when I saw with horror
that my children had disappeared, I awoke. Under the strong
impression of the dream I could not regain full consciousness
until suddenly I heard knocking on our door. It was 13 April
1940.

CHAPTER 1
September 1939

The blessed summer was ending and to its wealth now came the bounty of autumn. The barns and granaries were full, while large stacks of straw lay in front of them. Some of the inhabitants of Rawa-Ruska lived on its outskirts and tilled the farms around this Polish county town. Seen from afar, it was as if surrounded by sturdy walls of tightly packed straw and hay.

The harvest was astonishingly large that year – the elder folks said there had not been a harvest so large since 1914. The trees in the orchards drooped under the weight of their fruit, and the apples became ruddier and redder as if to tease the green pears which were unable to put on anything more than a jaundiced yellow. The plums, mature and coquettishly covered with a layer of down, hung invitingly ready, to be plucked. Asters, gladioli and roses . . . the last of the season . . . gladdened the eye with their hues and filled one's heart with the peace of a garden in bloom. There was no presentiment of the coming storm.

The produce of autumn filled the market square around the old sixteenth-century town hall. Wagons full of cabbages, their leaves tightly wrapped round the bald-headed tops. Gherkins lay in piles with their rounded tummies turned in every direction. Beside them heaps of brown potatoes simply asked to be stored away for the winter in cellars. On the stalls there were orange carrots, nestling against pale parsnips and heads of celery. Crimson tomatoes jostled flirtatiously with bright green peppers. Rotund melons and curvaceous pumpkins awaited the probing touch of the housewife. As if to stress the carefree atmosphere of the many-hued market scene, heaps of sweet maize lay with their smiling lines of little, golden teeth showing between the parted, pastel-green sheath which wrapped each so neatly. Here was the early autumnal earthy smell of a county town, the scent of fresh fruit and vegetables mingled with the honest sweat of man and horse whose labour was accomplished.

The schools were to re-open in three days and, if only for this reason, the streets and shops were crowded. The pupils of secondary and vocational schools were coming in to town from all around, filling the streets and squares with the youthful exuberance of merry, sun-tanned teenagers greeting one another with joyful shouts. They stood about in groups, showing their purchases while others conducted a lively barter in text-books and the like.

The younger fry licked their ice creams as they spoke of their summer holidays or passed on character studies of their teachers in the coming term and other vital school news. Mothers went about with these younger members of the school generations, buying items of school kit, satchels and the like. They would stop to chat with acquaintances similarly engaged and experiencing the same joys and hopes, troubles and worries that every new school year brings, a traditional ritual.

The streets became quiet in the evening when all the excitement and chatter went into the houses. Here, in the family circle, the youngsters once again inspected their books and school things, the new, shining shoes. Tired out by the events of the day they carefully stacked up everything by the bedside, again looked proudly at the evidence of their educational progress, and fell asleep in happiness and peace. The elder folk now made up their accounts, summed up what had been spent and how much they still had.

Finally, in the stillness of the night, the dogs began their nightly concert. They had howled strangely throughout the summer of 1939 but never so much and so mournfully as during the last three days of August. Sleep was impossible as long as the windows were open whilst the dogs, as if banded together, joined their voices in one long, unbroken cadence. Throughout the hours of darkness their weird wailing rose and fell, as if they were keening for the little country town of Rawa and its unsuspecting inhabitants.

Recalling this howling, I can still feel its impact. It provided a topic for small talk in the town.

'Did you hear those dogs howling and whining?'

'What's come over the dogs?'

'A sure sign of misfortune to come.'

Some said the dogs raised their heads when they howled, 'It means there'll be a great fire.' Others said they lowered their heads and interpreted this to portend some impending misfortune. Some, of course, simply said, 'Doesn't mean a thing. Nothing to worry about. The mutts feel like whining, so they whine.' The amateur psychologists pronounced, 'Even a dog must somehow express his longing.'

The new school year was beginning that day. Droves of children and teenagers hurried through the streets, assembling at each given school and then marching in procession to participate in the solemn inaugural Mass. Afterwards, the children strolled about, chattering and laughing.

Suddenly, the tranquil course of life in our little town, in the whole world, was shaken by terrible news. War! German aircraft, without any declaration, had attacked Poland and were bombing Polish towns. Lwow, fifty kilometres away, had been bombed. Things now moved very fast in Rawa. First sheer astonishment – for none had been prepared for such news. Then rumours and various surmises swept through the town. Passing from one person to another they gained in force and sowed fear. People hurried about uncomprehending and helpless.

'War! Why? It can't be. There must be some mistake. They

must be our own aircraft, training.' Groups assembled at every radio set. Unfortunately, the broadcasts fully confirmed the rumours.

Later in the day, people came from Lwow . . . people who had personally seen the damage and casualties caused by the German bombs. There was an immediate run on the shops where the public bought up all the food and clothes they could get. An emergency organisation was set up for defence against air attacks and poison gas, an auxiliary fire brigade, and Red Cross first aid posts.

German aircraft bombed Rawa on the next day. Part of the railway station was shattered and some twenty houses. Several persons were killed and a large number injured. The first refugees from central and western Poland arrived in Rawa and for these billets and soup kitchens were arranged. Hospital trains and ambulances arrived a little later and it at once became necessary to organise emergency hospital services. The people of Rawa gave themselves up wholeheartedly to this relief work. We slept little and ate hastily at odd moments. The teenagers who had started their new school year with such enthusiasm, now showed even greater zeal as they carried out their civic tasks and helped their elders in the kitchens, on guard duties, and in fire fighting. They were overjoyed when they could render even the slightest service. The emergency services were functioning quite efficiently within three days. The Germans bombed the town and its environs every day. It was lucky that many of the bombs did not explode.

The news which reached us from outside was every day more tragic and saddening. The Germans were advancing rapidly into Poland. The broadcasting stations were destroyed and the railway lines damaged. The able-bodied men left Rawa in small groups and with their little knapsacks marched off eastwards where, according to rumour, Polish troops were concentrating. Alas, they returned after two or three weeks, dusty, footsore, exhausted, and close to despair. We were between two fires. The Russians had invaded Poland from the east as allies of the Germans.

The German forces drew ever nearer to our town whilst the Polish forces retreated, some northward, some westward and others towards the east. On the night of the thirteenth day of the invasion, the Germans entered Rawa Ruska. Some of them stayed for a short rest, but the main body pressed on, and a stream of armour swept across the country, day and night, here and there liquidating the heroic but unavailing resistance of the Polish forces.

It was only now that we realised how unprepared Poland had been for this unexpected aggression. The Germans ordered the inhabitants of Rawa to carry out their normal duties while their officers chose their accommodation and the soldiers camped in our yards and squares. The staff had a short rest at our house, they took only a little folded drawing table and some measuring instruments. Some women had their rings and other jewellery stolen.

Apart from those quite isolated incidents, the German soldiers left the town's folk unmolested, but when the Gestapo came a few days later matters took a distinct turn for the worse. They brutally broke into houses, took everything they wanted, and were really nasty to everyone, but especially the intelligentsia and women.

The Jews were terror stricken, praying for hours in their synagogue. The SS broke into their homes and drove them out with rubber coshes to sweep and clear up the town.

Some Jewish babies were shot dead in the streets.

One of the leading Jews was forced to stand on top of a church tower while they took pot-shots at him. They finally tired of this 'sport' and allowed him to come down. His hair had turned white.

There were many other means of baiting and torturing the Jews. The world has already heard of them.

In the meantime, there was heavy fighting in the area

between Rawa and Tomaszow with many killed and wounded on both sides. Hour after hour the wounded were brought to town, and more and more buildings were requisitioned for use as first aid posts.

I will always remember one episode. A large transport of wounded soldiers had been brought in, and among them was a badly wounded Polish Officer of whose remarkable courage both Poles and Germans spoke with the utmost admiration. The doctors did everything possible to save his life and his condition improved so much that it was possible to send him to Zhovkva hospital within a week.

The doctors inspected the wounded man before his departure. The German chief MO at the head of his suite, stopped in front of the Polish Officer's bed and asked, 'Do you feel strong enough for the journey?' The officer answered, 'Yes.' The MO spoke kindly to him but suddenly looked at him keenly and asked, 'What will you do when you are discharged from hospital?' The answer was, 'I'll go on fighting the Germans.' The German bowed to him and said, 'May I shake hands with you?' They shook hands without pathos, and honestly.

The final arrangements for de-limiting the demarcation line between the German and the Soviet zone of occupation were now completed and thirteen days after the Germans entered Rawa, they officially handed over the town to the Russians. The ceremony took place before the Town Hall. German tanks lined up on one side of the square and Soviets on the other. Officers alighted and met in the middle, where they exchanged papers and shook hands.

As this was taking place, the German flag was lowered on the Town Hall tower, and the Soviet flag was hoisted. The inhabitants of the town stood around at a distance, silent and depressed. The Germans returned to their armoured cars and drove off along the road to Warsaw. As the soldiers drove off, they shouted to us, 'Auf Wiedersehen!' We'll be seeing you again.

During those three weeks or so, everything in Rawa had been turned topsy-turvy, shattered and trodden underfoot, morally and materially. It seemed as if swarms of predatory creatures had attacked Poland from the east and from the west, destroying, murdering, plundering all they could . . . and there was no saying which of the two invaders was worse. Enormous herds of cattle had been driven westward through Rawa, and equally enormous ones now passed through the town towards the east. It is difficult to describe how depressed we all felt and how premonitions of still worse to come saddened us.

During the short stay of the Germans in our town, we really had no time to ponder our situation. We were occupied not only with our usual work but also with relief work. The great numbers of refugees and wounded soldiers required constant help, accommodation and feeding.

Immediately after their arrival the Soviet soldiers went around the town in search of food because, apart from a few herring, they had brought nothing. In our shops, which were still well stocked, they did not conceal their astonishment that they could buy as much as they wanted. The rouble and the zloty became equal, so they paid the due price for goods. They were really polite to Polish people and keen to familiarize with us. Being far from their political commissars, they came to our houses for a chat. Taught by their country's deceitful propaganda that people outside the Soviet Union lived in poverty and humiliation they were now stunned by the wealth and freedom to be found in 'the rotten west'. They openly told us about their hard life in the Soviet Union and we could hardly believe that almost every one of them had family members in prison or distant exile.

I watched their attitude to the NKVD (Soviet Secret Police). Both officers and regular soldiers hated them and, from time to time fought for better accommodation, or food or other rations in front of us. Naturally the NKVD functionaries always won since they were a privileged and vicious caste.

In a short time their families arrived, squeezing us into the minimum of rooms, or turning us into the street. They bought up all possible goods and sent parcels to Russia. The shops became empty and finally closed, and we began to suffer from lack of food.

When the Soviet authorities installed themselves in Rawa, we were dismissed from our posts. Newcomers were appointed, people who had so far either done nothing or who had preyed on human misery, types that morally counted for very little. Communist propaganda was launched almost immediately, and compulsory mass meetings were held for our enlightenment at which everything in the past was declared evil and everything Communist exalted. The Communists sought to transform human minds by hook or by crook and soon organised a 'free election'. The polling halls were decorated and, with music on, they treated us to sandwiches. When we did not cooperate they forced us to participate with truncheons.

The chaos was indescribable. Great crowds of refugees crossed the 'frontier', returning to their homes in western and central Poland, then under German occupation. The Soviet authorities caught and arrested thousands of these refugees, who were then sentenced to penal labour camps in the Soviet Union for a term of from eight to ten years for the 'crime' of crossing the occupation demarcation line without a visa, or for espionage. All these poor people were deported immediately.

CHAPTER 2
My husband is arrested

Mass arrests started in the town. Both my brothers were arrested, and on 6th January 1940 the same fate met my husband. From February 1940 whole families were being deported to Siberia. The winter that year was exceptionally severe, even for that part of the world, and the thermometer stood at minus 42 centigrade. Many mothers lost their children on the way, as they froze to death in the goods wagons, crawling for weeks on end from Poland to Siberia.

I did not at first want to write about this terrible experience but today is the twentieth anniversary of that event in my life and my children's. We had lived, quietly and respected, in a small country town and we had never even thought of living in another land. Yet the very first day of the war proved decisive in the lives of millions of human beings. I am now living in a quiet, peaceful village, in England, at my son's home, and writing about the seventeen years of my Odyssey. Yet the memory of my husband's arrest is still vivid in my memory, and I feel compelled to record what happened. After all, it represented not only my own personal tragedy, but also that of millions of women in all the countries which had been seized by the Soviet Union.

In those times, for the inhabitants of the lands annexed by the Russians, every knock at the door aroused profound disquiet. It was at 11 o'clock in the morning that someone knocked urgently at our door. I looked at my husband and said, 'It must be them', went to the front door and opened it. Three Soviet soldiers with bayonets on their rifles, and two agents of the NKVD stood at the threshold. One of them informed me that they had come to make a search of our home. I asked whether they had a warrant but was told sharply it was none of my business. I was violently pushed from the doorway and they entered our flat. A soldier was put on guard whilst the rest made a thorough search, creating a scene of the wildest disorder.

I may mention that my husband was a forestry engineer and there were many maps and plans, apart from other office material in our home, including quite a lot of surveying instruments and other valuable equipment which had been hidden from the Germans. All this was now thrown higgledy-piggledy into packing cases which had been brought in. Finally, about 6 p.m., the agents finished their 'work' and had the cases loaded on to a truck. They told my husband to put on his coat and accompany them to the NKVD head-quarters where he would have to sign some formal documents.

Shortly after they left my sisters came to cheer me up. Deeply depressed we nevertheless decided to tidy my home but, to our great joy, my husband returned barely an hour later. I and my sisters begged him to go into hiding or to cross the demarca-tion line and seek shelter upon that part of Poland occupied by the Germans. After all, this 'frontier' was less than 15 kilo-metres away, he knew the terrain perfectly, all the roads and paths, and had many friends and acquaintances in the various villages nearby.

My husband refused categorically. He said he could not leave me and the children, and had no intention of hiding in his own country whether under Russian or German occupation. So he remained.

Some friends visited us in the evening and we listened to the radio. I had a bad headache, not surprisingly after the events of the day, and went to the bedroom to lie down, excusing myself to our guests.

Barely three hours later, there was again a loud knocking at our door. Two NKVD agents came in and demanded that my husband go off with them immediately. On his way out, my husband opened the bedroom door to say goodbye to me. As his captors made as if to follow him in, he stopped on the threshold and waved his hand to me as a farewell gesture and went out of my life under menace of the drawn revolvers of the secret police agents.

I dressed quickly and found my sisters were still in the other room. We now were certain that my husband had been arrested. The NKVD men came again after midnight to make a further search. I asked them what they were looking for, perhaps I could help them. I told them I'd give them whatever they needed . . . they had already taken whatever valuables we had. They chose some items that had been overlooked before and which had taken their fancy, and went off with their loot under their arms.

I tried to secure an interview with the Chief of the NKVD to find out why my husband had been arrested, but was refused admittance day after day until, finally, my importunity was rewarded and I was admitted into the presence of the great man. He coldly informed me it was the business of the police to know why they arrested anybody and that if I showed so much interest in their affairs, they could arrest me too . . . and I would then find out why people are arrested in the Soviet Union. It could not be helped. There was nothing I could do in the face of such tyranny by the secret police of Russia.

The children and I went to the prison every day . . . our group was not the only one and there were more and more of us day by day. We were, of course, not admitted within the prison walls . . . visitors are not allowed under the Russian system. We prowled about in the vicinity, dressed in our warmest things and though we could not really hope to see our loved ones, it seemed to us that our spending a few hours in this way might bring some consolation and . . . who knows? . . . perhaps a prisoner looking through the iron-barred windows might catch a glimpse of a mother or wife, a child, sister or friend. We were not allowed to leave any food or clothes for my husband. Week passed after week without any news.

Then one day in the morning, a Jew came to my flat (I did not know him personally but knew that he collaborated with the Soviet authorities) and he told me that he had seen my husband being led into the NKVD headquarters and that, if I went immediately, I might manage to see him. I lost no time, collected the children, took some cigarettes and food, and five minutes later was at the door of the secret police building. Some acquaintances of mine who were co-operating with the Russians saw my plight and helped me get into the building.

They led me to a small room where my husband was waiting to hear his fate. I went in and could not at first recognise him, unshaven since I saw him last, with sunken eyes, emaciated and with an unhealthy sallow face. His eyes lit up when he saw us and I fell into his arms with the children wriggling to join in. As he embraced and kissed me, I asked, 'What is it they've against you?' He whispered, 'They want me to collaborate with them and report if any Polish organisation is set up in the district here . . . you know me, I'll never agree, so be prepared for the worst.'

I slipped the cigarettes and food into his pockets just as we were being shooed out before the higher authorities found out we were making an 'illegal' visit. I must add that my husband was widely known and respected in the whole county of Rawa, not only by Poles but also by Jews and Ukrainians . . . even those who had joined the Russian ranks tried to help us as much as possible.

Again whole weeks passed without any news of my husband until, very early one morning there was again a furious knocking at the door. I hurriedly opened it and was astounded to see an old Jewish cab driver standing there. He was stuttering with profound emotion but I managed to catch the gist of what he wanted to say. As he was driving along the road, he had seen a

14

large crowd of prisoners being led off by guards towards the railway station and he recognised my husband among them. He at once whipped up his horse and came to inform me. He begged me to let him drive me and the children to the station . . . we might, perhaps, manage to see my husband.

We dressed hurriedly, packed a bag of food and underwear, and were immediately driven to the station by the kindly old Jew. There was a tremendous crowd at the station and on the platforms hundreds of prisoners were waiting under heavy guard for the train to come in. In spite of great difficulties, the children and I got on to the platform through a side door and luckily caught a glimpse of my husband through the waiting room window.

The prisoners near the window made way for my husband, and now we stood close to each other looking through the glass. A smile lit up his face with two great tears appearing in his eyes. I felt like screaming and crying and my hand itched to smash that window pane, but I kept myself under control and, smiling, said, 'Don't worry about us, we will manage somehow. You know what fine children we have. All will be well.'

A Russian soldier, a loutish type, came up and brutally pushed us away from the window. We were not allowed to approach it again so we stood some distance away with a crowd of women who had also come to see their loved ones being taken away. After a long wait the train came in and the prisoners, escorted by a dense screen of guards, were led to the train. Unshaven, some with long beards, dirty, with crumpled clothing, with little bags or bundles, they stumbled or shuffled on.

There was a slight hold-up as my husband's group came up. I ran up and threw him a bag of food which he caught. We looked into each other's eyes for a moment and sent a parting greeting . . . we parted, though I did not know at the time, forever.

Finally, all the prisoners were loaded into the train and it slowly pulled away. All of us on the platform raised our hands in farewell. The train drew away farther and farther, and I felt a sharp pain in my heart. The train disappeared behind a bend, and all of us, together with the children, sadly returned to our empty homes.

We found out that our husbands had been taken to Lwow. I went there from time to time in order to locate him and finally established that he was being held, together with one of my brothers, in Brygidki Prison. There was no news about my other brother. Years later I learned that he had managed to escape from prison and had been in hiding using a different name.

Thousands of women waited in queues about the prison to try and leave something for a prisoner. I stood in a queue for two days and one night on end when, at length and to my great joy, a small parcel of linen was accepted for delivery to my husband. I came back home by train, very tired and went to bed.

I was dreaming. I saw a tiny, very bright light when suddenly I awoke. Not fully aroused and with my dream still vivid in my mind, a loud knocking at the front door brought me sharply back to reality.

'They've come,' I said to myself. It was well that most of the things had been packed in readiness for this emergency, all the skiing clothes and the sound, strong boots. Convinced the Russians would deport us, I had been expecting them night after night.

I jumped out of bed and put on my dressing gown. It was ten minutes past midnight. I slowly went to open the door. The thundering at the door was going on all the time . . . someone was evidently battering at it with a rifle butt. Nobody could sleep through such a noise. I opened the door and said, 'Don't you know there's a bell at the door?' Two Red Army men stepped in with fixed bayonets. A plain clothes individual followed them and most politely asked me my name and other personal details. He then told me he had a search warrant.

We went into my room and he half-heartedly began to rummage among my things. The children started dressing. The plain clothes man pulled out some papers and, reading them, gabbled out that on the basis of the ordinance of such and such a date, I and my children, as particularly dangerous social elements, were to be transferred to another place of habitation. I was permitted to take one hundred kilograms of baggage per person.

It never occurred to me at the time that this new place of habitation would be many thousands of miles away, in Asia. I asked why this notification could not have been made by day, without frightening the children at the dead of night and waking up the neighbours with all that noise.

'What kind of people go about at night, do you know? I should think a big country like the Soviet Union can permit itself to do such things even in the daytime,' I added with wasted irony. The Russian told me to stop making propaganda. I knew, of course, that nothing could be done. Neither agonised despair nor scolding would help, and he was only carrying out orders. As I hurriedly finished off my packing the realisation suddenly came on me that henceforth I could count only upon my own efforts.

I began to cram the bed linen and blankets into the already prepared sacks. The children helped me most valiantly. I went into the kitchen and found one of the soldiers guarding the back door. Looking round, I said, 'What shall we need most?' He stepped up to me and whispered, 'Take as much food as you can . . . bread and salt.' He seemed sorry for me and, in spite of my troubles and the frantic hurry, I felt the warmth of his sympathy and was glad of it. Instead of pots and pans, all the food I could find was flung into the big basket.

The children slipped out to tell our relatives we were being deported, only to learn that they were also packing in preparation for a similar journey. It was sixteen years later that I found out their departures had been put off and how this had come to pass.

Everything was packed by 4 a.m. My daughter ran up to say goodbye to the piano, and played a few notes of 'the piece by Schubert that Daddy liked so much.' I looked around for the last time and saw my knitting needles lying on the table. I picked them up and put them into my handbag . . . they might be useful, I thought. The soldiers were urging us to hurry. A lorry was already waiting for us in front of the house.

Day broke, sullen and overcast. Despite the very early hour, there was much coming and going on the streets. Lorries stood before many of the houses and people were throwing their bags into them. Here and there could be heard the cries and sobs of women and children. The taut faces of those who had for a time been spared a nocturnal visit could be seen at the windows and in the chinks between the curtains. I looked up at the house we were leaving and saw my neighbours tearfully bidding us a discreet farewell. I waved to them in reply. There were some Russians standing outside the Secret Police building nearby and laughing as they watched us set off. The situation seemed to call for some active defiance and I called out, 'Long live Poland!' hoping they would understand Polish, and feeling all the better after this demonstration of undaunted patriotism.

The lorry set off to the station with the children and me sitting on our bags and baskets. Things were very lively at the station. Lorries were dashing up and driving away still faster after transferring their passengers to goods wagons, surrounded by lines of Red Army men. The town was by now fully aroused. People were hurrying from all sides to the station to see who was being deported. Weeping families ran up to take leave of their dearest ones. I saw some of our family in the crowd just as the children and I were pushed into the wagon and the doors were slammed shut and bolted.

We were the last to enter, and the wagon was already closely packed with people and their belongings. I heard my mother and sister calling out my name. Looking through a crack in the wall, I saw them both for the last time . . . they were crying bitterly. The crowd pressed against the lines of soldiers in an effort to come closer to the deportees but was brutally beaten back by the rifle butts of the soldiers. A stentorian voice announced that machine guns were trained on the crowd and the order to shoot would be given if the crowd did not stop. The soldiers forced the people far back away from the train and the shouting and sobbing died away, while we remained helplessly awaiting our fate, dazed and unbelieving.

We could barely see in the wagon, so little daylight could enter. Torn away from our homes and loved ones our hearts were heavy and we found it hard to speak but, having regard for the children, we tried to hide our feelings and our fears. There was only one woman who could not control her sobbing and tears. With forced gaiety, we spoke of the 'Mystery Tour' before us and wondered aloud to which interesting place we were going . . . it would be such a surprise! The children listened hopefully, though still a little doubtful. The security of their childish life could not be destroyed so quickly, but inexplicable things had happened and the atmosphere around them was hardly reassuring.

As usual in country towns we all knew one another, at least by sight. There was a mix of all professions and social classes, from the intelligentsia to unskilled manual workers, but mostly women and children. It was a very small goods wagon yet there were fifty of us, with piles of baggage in confusion on the floor.

We sorted out and arranged the things tidily in a spurt of energy and soon occupied our share of the cramped space more or less to our satisfaction. The lack of a sanitary convenience was a great privation. We banged on the doors and walls but nobody came to answer our calls until, finally, someone offered an old pail. Even so it was most embarrassing, and one painfully held out as long as possible, at length finding relief during the privacy afforded by somebody acting as a screen.

It was noon before the children reminded us that they had had no breakfast. Everyone took out some food from baskets or bags and we satisfied our hunger. We all felt cold . . . most of us had very little or no sleep during the night . . . and whether the time of year could be called late winter or early spring, it was certainly chilly enough. We decided to demand some hot water and milk for the children, but our shouts and banging were disregarded by our captors.

The train moved a little some hours later, and stopped at the goods ramp. Looking through the tiny window and the cracks in the walls, we saw Fr. Stoklosa, our young parish priest, some distance away. He stood erect and, as he blessed us with the sign of the Cross, we could see the tears trickling down his face. The train remained there hour after hour, and evening fell at last. We sat down, to save space, and for a time remained silent or spoke only in undertones. Some of the women said the Litany to the Virgin Mary. Others prayed individually. It became darker and darker . . . there were no lights. We all stood and sadly sang the old Polish hymn 'Under Thy Protection.'

The children dozed off but none of the adults could sleep though we were all very tired. It appeared that the Russians had arrested the husbands of nearly all the women in the wagon. I thought of my own husband and wondered how I would cope with the unknown yet menacing future, and I dwelt on the tragedy that had overcome my country, on the plight of a democratic and freedom-loving people hemmed in between two militaristic and totalitarian states. I could hear quiet sobbing here and there in the darkness. Two of the babies began to cry and would not be consoled. At length, at some time in the small hours, the train set off and did not stop until

11 a.m. The doors were opened and we were ordered to get out with all our belongings.

We looked around, and somebody told us we were just outside Lwow. A small group of people, quite a distance away, stood looking at us intently in absolute silence and without a single wave of the hand. After a long wait, a very long goods train rolled in on another track and we were ordered to get into the wagons. We now knew where we were being taken. The wagons were not on standard gauge tracks but on the wide gauge ones used in the Soviet Union.

The wagons were much larger and wider than the standard ones. Along both sides there were two board shelves, and in the middle of the floor there was a small opening. We entered with our things and took up our places. Shortly afterwards, new families were brought to our wagons. They were being deported from Lwow, and eighty-five persons were now crammed into the wagon.

The onlookers now came closer and closer. The soldiers tried to keep them away but after some hours became discouraged and let the people come up to the wagons. They nearly all had little parcels of food, bread and smoked meats, which they handed up to us. The children got hot milk, much appreciated. Quite a crowd of relatives turned up from Rawa on a passenger train to bid us farewell once again. From time to time somebody came up and asked, without showing any special interest, how many of us there were in the wagon . . . our names, where we had come from and our occupations. We told them and they assured us we would not be forgotten and should not lose courage, after which they melted away in the crowd.

All the visitors were driven away when dusk fell. The Russians checked and locked the wagons. The train moved off eastwards. As long as we were passing through the Lwow district, thousands of people could be seen in the distance waving to us. In the wagons we were deeply moved by this expression of sympathy and fellow feeling.

Before it became quite dark we set up a screen round the hole in the floor. Then, without undressing, we lay down on the shelves, but many people had to lie on the floor, side by side like sardines.

The train stopped only once during the night at some station and a little later we saw frontier posts with the Polish colours lying on the ground. We were leaving Polish soil and, with tears streaming down our cheeks, sang the Polish National Anthem to demonstrate our feelings.

We learned later that the inmates of all the other wagons did the same quite spontaneously. The train stopped again for a short time at the frontier station between Poland and the Soviet Union, at Podwoloczyska. The local population, mostly Ukrainians, at once boldly came up to the wagons and despite the protests of the guards handed us bread and hot milk. The villagers stood along the railway track and wished us well as the train moved on. Some of us threw out letters and cards addressed to our families. The villagers picked them up and nearly all of them were duly delivered in time.

We now began to organise our life in this prison-wagon. A spokesman was elected to represent us in relations with the guards and groups were set up for keeping the place tidy etc.

Once we entered the territory of the Soviet Union, the landscape changed fundamentally. The fields were no longer narrow ones separated by boundary paths or hedges as in Poland, but huge areas upon which all we could see were broken down machines and some heaps of rusty scrap iron. The cottages were clean but without any fences, whilst the few orchards we saw looked dilapidated. We were travelling through the Ukraine, the granary of the Soviet Union. The train stopped only at some major stations where we received hot soup and groats (hulled grain, especially oats) once in twenty-four hours. On such occasions, a few persons were allowed to leave each wagon with buckets to bring the food for the rest, and hot water . . . *kipyatok*, as the Russians call it . . .

so that we could make tea for ourselves. We stayed a whole day in the environs of Kiev, where I was one of those who went for hot food and water. The city looked colourful with the typical cupolas of the churches glittering in the sun and it was certainly a magnificent sight.

The train travelled on, carrying us farther and farther from our own country and our loved ones. We were too, ever nearer to the unknown fate awaiting us. We left the Ukraine and the train still went eastwards. As we entered the Russian plain the landscape changed again becoming flat and marshy. Spring was just beginning, great grey clouds swept across the sky and sleet continued to fall. The fields and the tumble-down houses without fruit trees near them looked sad and badly neglected.

There were crowds of people in the stations we passed through, and we noticed they were poorly dressed and looked under-nourished. Gazing curiously at our train some of the bolder spirits came up closer and chatted while exchanging information. We asked them what kind of life they had and why they were so poorly dressed. They told us that life was very hard and there were frequent arrests. Textile materials were not to be had, and there was little bread. They also told us that there had been many trainloads such as ours, but the previous ones had been mostly composed of men.

We had quite a lot of bread in our wagon so we threw them some loaves through the window. They thankfully picked up the loaves and quickly moved off, particularly when the soldiers began to brutally drive them away. Women brought us hot milk and eggs at some of the stops. They would not accept money but gladly accepted the bread we offered them.

Although we had so violently been torn away from our homes and deprived of elementary conveniences we were quiet and tranquil. We related various events and recalled the history of 1863 when our grandfathers rose against the Russians and were later sent to Siberia. The young folk showed much courage. They looked out of the window or through the cracks

23

in the walls with interest. I had an atlas among my things so that we knew exactly where we were during the journey.

We crossed great rivers and passed through many a station, through Voronezh among others. I looked with interest at the station where Anna Karenina threw herself in front of the train in Tolstoy's novel. It was here that we crossed the Don. We crossed the Volga at Kuybyshev. Our youngsters sang their scout and other patriotic songs on the way, and made a point of doing so when we were stopped at a station. They began to find the journey novel and interesting.

We asked the guards from time to time what our destination was. They answered, 'There where your husbands are waiting for you.' In hopeful anticipation nearly all the women had brought clothing and linen for their husbands, brothers and fathers. A railwayman told us that we were bound for Alga. We did not know where this place was and could not find it on the maps.

One day, while our train was held up in some big station, another one drew up on the next track. It was crammed full of men, and we could see their faces, unshaven and pallid, looking through the barred windows at us. We very soon found out they were Poles, and the inmates of both trains raised a great shout of indignation and protest. The station was crowded with Russians who realised now what had happened. The police hurried up and had the men's train shunted off to another track. In spite of this, we continued our protests for long after.

Our train proceeded through the wide stretches of the Soviet Union and made a very long stay at Orenburg-Czkalov, the last station before Asia. We waited with interest to see in which direction our train would go, for this was an important junction.

We finally reached the Urals and entered Asia from the south-east. The landscape was now the limitless steppe of Kazakhstan, a greyish rusty plain, covered with sparse vegetation and without a single tree in sight. Here and there we saw sand dunes and traces of snow on the ground. Spherical bushes of steppe *buzhan*, like filigree, floated past, driven by the wind. The children enjoyed watching the leaps and bounds of the flying plants. We passed large stretches of tulips in full bloom, sharply contrasting with the rest of the steppe these oases of colour broke the monotony of our surroundings. I looked at my companions in misfortune and saw that nearly all of them were smiling with pleasure. Later we saw some small creatures which looked like hamsters standing up as they quietly looked at the train passing them.

Thirteen days after we had set out, the train stopped at a station. We saw some people through the cracks and asked what place it was. 'Alga,' came the reply. We had at last reached our destination.

We waited long for the inevitable formalities to be completed but the doors were at length opened and we were ordered to alight with our things. We threw out our belongings before painfully climbing down ourselves.

I will never forget the sight before my eyes. The crowd of people, troubled and exhausted, barely able to stand, waited with children and various forms of baggage. Torn away from the ancient civilisation of the West, we were now dumped here, in another world, upon the primitive, wild steppe of Kazakhstan.

Women with children in their arms looked around in bewilderment and dismay. Some expected to find their husbands waiting for them and were sadly disappointed. Although we were such a multitude we were strangely quiet. Only a child would cry or wail from time to time. Each of us stood by our baggage and waited. Some mothers sat down after a time and cuddled their little ones, tired out by the long journey and its primitive conditions. My heart bled for all these poor people, and for my nation. Finally, I sat down on one of my bundles and, with my arms around my children, waited in silence with them.

A crowd of Kazakhs, kept some distance away by the guards, stood looking at us with curiosity. Dark skinned and black haired they had round faces and oriental eyelids. The men had enormous hats of fox fur and the elderly ones wore long quilted gabardines . . . and they all looked most menacing. The women, with their long black hair in plaits, smiled to us and looked most friendly. They wore long white skirts from under which their trousers peeped out. Most of them wore small, round embroidered caps. Children scampered among them and a number of very lean dogs prowled about. On the whole, these people looked healthy and well. Their houses were small, made of clay, with a flat roof and white-washed walls.

At long last, the NKVD guards drove up in lorries and began to throw our baggage onto them whilst others, shouting and pushing, placed us in rows. They then surrounded us and we were marched off at a sharp pace towards the Kazakh settlement. We entered an unfinished school building where we found all our things thrown higgledy-piggledy upon the floor. We were told to rest there and await further orders.

We sorted out our bundles and settled down as best we could. We were really all very tired and dirty. We had not been able to wash properly during the thirteen days of our journey. So we at once started a great and general washing. The local population followed us about everywhere and gazed at us just as we used to look at the animals in a zoo. Some of the bolder women and younger element passed bottles of milk to us, or a piece of strange looking cheese, indicating these were for the children. We were greatly touched by their kindness, the more so that the guards constantly chased them away. Night fell, the guards surrounded the building and we were able at length to fall asleep in relative comfort.

The guards were not so strict on the next day. The local people again appeared and were allowed to come nearer us. They brought hot milk and, fingering our clothes, smacked their lips in admiration and said to each other with profound conviction, a word that sounded like *jadraxy*, which we later learned found meant 'pretty' or 'nice'.

We stayed at Alga for three days during which we were not allowed to leave the school courtyard. In the meantime NKVD officers and representatives of the neighbouring collective farms examined us and sorted us into groups. Lorries drove up and took the new arrivals off to these farms. Many of us did not know what these kolkhoz* farms were, whilst when the local people were asked about them, they simply answered *jaman*, i.e. not good, bad. Finally, on the fourth day a lorry came up, an NKVD officer counted off 28 persons, we threw our things on to the lorry and got in ourselves.

The lorry drove off across the steppe and it was far from comfortable, since we had been crammed as tight as sardines. An armed soldier sat beside the driver. Some miles later we passed through a very dilapidated village the population of which came out to look at us with curiosity. The road was level and hard as asphalt in places but elsewhere it was covered with potholes full of melted snow and water.

The driver was drunk and drove at a high speed, disregarding any potential dangers. We begged him to be careful and slow down when approaching the potholes because someone might be jerked off the lorry, just as some of our things had been thrown off, but he laughed and the only answer he made was, 'Nothing to worry about. The devil won't take you.'

At length, Mrs S. (mother of three children) was jerked off as the lorry bumped across such a hole. Though she was picked up wet through and covered with mud, she luckily suffered no

---

* *Kolkhoz* or collective farms (as opposed to state farms *sovkhoz*) were nominally run as a workers cooperative with remuneration paid in kind based on number of days worked. In practice management and decisions were imposed by provincial authorities. Collective farming started slowly and peacefully after the October Revolution of 1917, but was rapidly expanded by the forced collectivization campaign from 1928.

harm. She only had to change her clothes and the driver thereafter drove more carefully.

The journey lasted several hours. The steppe was as flat as a table, with an enormous horizon, whilst the sky was cloudless with a bright, golden sun blazing down upon the vast scene. The air was clear and visibility was perfect. We could see no trees or signs of human habitation. On the other hand, we often passed abandoned settlements in ruins with their black chimney stacks reaching upwards, with bushes flourishing around them and colourful tulips in blossom. These ruins looked very strange to us. We learned later that they were all that was left of the burnt out *auyls* (villages) of the Kazakhs that had been destroyed during the collectivisation campaign of 1929–30.

The majority of the Kazakhs energetically refused to form collective farms and the authorities therefore did this by force. Part of the population was killed during the fighting. Part was deported to Siberia, while the rest left their homes and took refuge in the towns where they adapted to urban life.

It was evening before the lorry stopped some three hundred metres from a little Kazakh auyl. The soldier told us to throw down our things. We protested and asked that the lorry drive up closer, but in vain. The driver and the soldier threw down our things and drove off somewhere.

I well remember that evening. It was now after sunset and the whole steppe was bathed in a metallic violet shimmer which heightened the peace and quiet around us. We stood there helplessly on the steppe, a group of women and children with only two men among us, our things strewn around on the ground. Here and there a woman or a child would begin to sob, and even I felt my throat constrict. I gained control of myself, looked at my children and said, 'Just now we must not cry. Before it gets quite dark we must carry all our things to that place over there and find somewhere to sleep under cover.'

Everybody jerked out of the shocked despair which had

overcome us for a moment and we all started to transport our belongings to the buildings. The older children helped us with enthusiasm, but we women mostly dragged our bundles along the ground. They were too heavy to carry,

In such a way we finally arrived in the settlement of Tok-Man-Say Collective Farm and were greeted by a whole crowd of 'menacing' Kazakhs. They could not speak Russian, so they indicated by sign language where we were to install ourselves. A few of us were placed in a small schoolroom whilst I and some others took over an empty granary. It was dark inside and there was no light. The youngsters got some straw which they spread on the clay floor, and so we lay down to sleep.

CHAPTER 3
Life on the collective farms

I wakened next morning early because it was really very cold on the floor of the granary. Covering the children a little better I quietly went out to see a magnificent sight. The sun had just risen and its golden rays were lighting up the hoar frost on the steppe, which glimmered and shone in the morning light. As the sun rose higher, the apparently mailed surface showed patches here and there, more and more of these appeared, and they were growing larger and larger until the mail disappeared and the steppe took on its normal hues in daylight. I was profoundly moved by this scene and, as the shining armour disappeared like a mirage, I thought to myself, 'that's how my former life has disappeared, and today a new chapter of wandering has begun.

There was no time to ponder matters or to recall the past. It was necessary to quickly adapt myself to these strange new conditions and think of preparing the first meal for the children. There was a big hole in the ground near the granary and the local people advised us to do our cooking there. The young folk at once dashed off and rummaged about for scrap iron (there was a lot of it lying about) and straw, dug up some clay, and we started to make a fireplace. Within a few hours, we had an excellent fireplace and soon after were having hot soup made from the ingredients we had brought from Poland. We found it most appetising.

There was a small stream some twenty or thirty metres away from our 'kitchen' so we had water for washing ourselves and our cooking pots. From that day it was a regular chore to collect *kizyak*, the local fuel deposited by the cattle on the ground and dried by the sun. Sometimes, the natives supplemented it with the branches of the *karaganika* bush and with steppe grass. The *kizyak* has a high calorific value, keeps its heat long and is excellent fuel particularly if produced by calves.

The local people often visited us together with their children and dogs. At first they only smiled in a friendly way and we did the same, but our stock of words increased day by day and gestures were a great help with the result that we could soon understand each other quite well. We also soon realised that there was no hope of getting help to secure food. The natives lived very poorly and could offer us nothing but milk and, from time to time, some butter or cheese.

Some days after our arrival, while we were still lying tucked up for sleep though it was morning, the door opened and a big man stood on the threshold. He could not enter as the whole floor was covered with sleeping bodies. At night there was not a spare foot of floor space whilst in the daytime we rolled up the blankets and stacked them against the walls. The newcomer was the local NKVD police chief of Alga. He looked around at us all and we sat up and looked at him. Finally, he spoke.

'Good morning. How are you getting on?' Someone answered, 'As you see'. There was silence for a while as he examined us all carefully before addressing us.

'Well, this is how it is, for the time being we have no accommodation for you, and we brought you here so that you'd build yourselves houses and live here. You know that you're an unnecessary element which should really be destroyed but the Soviet authorities are humane and have brought you here so that you can repair your mistakes and give proof of constructive work for everybody's good, not as you have done in the past when you lived in a bourgeois country and drank the blood of the working people.

'Forget your past life. Build huts for yourselves. The women should marry, while we'll teach the children in our schools built upon the real teachings of Communism and not upon such false principles as in the rotten west. Don't think you'll ever return to your country.' Here he stretched out his arm and tapped his palm, and added, 'Unless hair begins to grow here.'

This speech struck us as being so funny that we burst out laughing. He fell into a fury, set his cap firmly on his head and stalked away. We were so certain then that our national tragedy was only temporary, that the world would not permit it to last. It would react strongly against the violence done to millions of women and children snatched out of the heart of Europe and thrown on to the vast plains of Kazakhstan to do forced labour under the most primitive conditions.

Not long after our arrival someone repeated a rumour of unknown provenance to the effect that England and America proposed we accept asylum from them. It was, however, believed and helped us to endure under the hard conditions awaiting us.

Thus we did not take the police chief's harsh words to heart and busied ourselves with breakfast. After his departure, we were called to the office where the gardener, a Russian, informed us we were to work in his fields from the next day. He would reward us on the basis of *trudo*-days, which meant work days, wages being in kind, payable after the crops had been collected. For the time being we would get one litre of milk and 100 or 200 grams of grain for each person at work. If we missed our work, punishment would be certain.

We held counsel as to what should be done. There were thirty-five persons in our group but of these only two were adult men. All of us had worked only in town and knew nothing of agricultural work, but, it couldn't be helped. We told ourselves that what others could do, we could too. We would work and see what we'd do later.

So off we went to work on the next day. We were given

spades (one per three persons, because there were not enough to go round) and we began to dig *arykas*. These are irrigation ditches of various dimensions, necessary for the cultivation of the soil where rainfall is low. Some of the young people and one of the men went onto the steppe to set traps for hamsters, of which there were great numbers and which did much damage to the crops.

The food stocks brought by us from Poland melted away very quickly as all we got from the collective farm was a little milk and barley grain from time to time. Famine stared us in the face. It was up to us to find some way of securing more food so we would pack our knapsacks with clothing or linen and set off to a larger settlement or hamlet, sometimes tens of kilometres away, where we could barter for food.

We would set off in small groups. Sometimes a lorry driver would give us a lift to one of these centres or to the main construction sites for the new railway, and usually he would refuse to accept anything in payment. Having arrived at a suitable point we would barter our things for bread, fats, or grain. Money then had little value of exchange. Loaded down with foodstuffs we would return to our children, marching from thirty to forty kilometres a day in many cases. We often met acquaintances settled in other collective farms intent on the same errand.

I remember from these days in Tok-man-say an incident, after which we had a good laugh. One of the women from our group had been so foreseeing that she had taken a porcelain chamber pot with her. (I have to add that in these conditions it was not only a comfort but also a necessity – we had young children and our 'toilet' was outside in hard frost and wind – moreover there was no possibility to buy this kind of utensil. I remember my happiness when one day I received parcels: a potty from my mum and an enamelled bowl from my friend.)

The mentioned chamber pot stood always in our vestibule. When calling the Kazakh women we looked at it with great interest and admiration. The owner of this marvel Mrs G. was even offered a good price for it, but because in the Kazakh's country this thing was priceless she had to refuse. Sometime later our potty disappeared and we could not find it anywhere. After a few weeks Mrs G. went with her daughter to the neighbouring settlement to change some of her things for food. In one hut she managed to negotiate some butter. Much to her amazement the butter was brought in her potty!

One day I again left Tok-Man-Say at dawn to get some bread for the children from a very distant settlement. Actually we were not allowed to leave without permission, but often I ignored this regulation and left unnoticed. I walked all day and met not a single living soul. Finally, I realised I had lost my way. Dusk was falling and I became very worried at the thought of spending the night on the steppe. I looked round carefully and to my intense joy saw a smudge of smoke in the distance. At once I marched towards the smoke. Visibility on the steppe is very good and objects seem to be closer than they really are.

It was a long march and night had fallen before I saw a camp fire. Some dogs scented me and at once dashed up, barking and sniffing around. I could hear a babble of talk in the darkness and the neighing of horses. I went on and saw that an enormous cauldron was hanging over the fire and letting out clouds of steam. Kazakh women, in their white skirts, were busy stirring the contents with large wooden spades. Their menfolk sat near the fire, dressed in their native attire and wearing their big hats covered with fox pelts. This head-dress made them look very fierce. Children and dogs wandered about. Everybody looked at me fixedly as I approached.

'*Salem aleykum*,' I greeted them in their own language. They smiled and answered my greeting, making gestures to indicate that I should sit down near the fire. I was tired out, so I dropped my knapsack and sat down with a sigh of relief where the women were. I told them, in a medley of Russian and their own language, whence I had come and that I had lost my way. They asked me whether I was hungry, but I answered that I was really more thirsty than hungry. The women at once brought me some curds and whey which I drank as I looked around.

It turned out that I had arrived at some family festival and that the whole auyl had been invited to the feast. A little later, the cauldron was taken off the fire and, still steaming, was placed in the middle of the group of men. The traditional dish of the Kazakhs was soon prepared, *beshparmak*, a fat ram cut into large pieces, with long home-made macaroni. The eyes of the men were fixed on the cauldron while all this was being done.

One of the Kazakhs, the master of the household, pulled out a large bone covered with meat, bit out a tremendous hunk and passed the joint on to his neighbour. This man did the same and so the piece of meat circulated round the group of men. Then each of them put his hand into the cauldron and took out a fair sized piece of meat. They then ladled out macaroni into beautifully coloured wooden bowls and ate it with their fingers. When they had taken the edge off their appetite, the women brought earthenware pitchers of *kumys* (mare's milk) which they drank until the cauldron was quite empty. They then patted their tummies and clicked their tongues to express their appreciation. A lively conversation was then started with much gesticulation of the hands.

In the meantime, the youths of the group had mounted their horses and were galloping about the steppe. They now rode up and reined in just in front of the fire. The dogs bustled around the group of people and gnawed away at the bones which had been thrown to them. Two large camp fires lit up the scene with its colourful group of feasting Kazakhs, while the background was provided by a pitch-black night sky, peaceful and quiet, and lit up by the marvellous summer constellations.

I sat among the women, eating from a bowl handed to me and observing the scene without saying a single word. It was late before the feast came to an end and the revellers scattered on the way back to their homes. Because I did not want to sleep inside I was provided with some sheep-skins to lie on and slept soundly near the fire now burning out. When I awoke in the morning I looked around for the auyl and found it was not far away at all.

The auyl was one of the many situated in a solitary position in the steppe, far away from any highway. The little houses had flat roofs and were made of bricks (grey clay with straw and *kizyak*, called *saman*). The houses were divided into two parts, one for the human inhabitants and the other for the animals. The entrance to the former was through the animals' quarters and the living accommodation consisted usually of a small kitchen (used only in the winter) and a square room. Along the walls of this room there is a large dais made of boards, covered with felt and various home-woven woollens. Rolled up rugs are laid against the walls. Cushions lay here and there.

There is always a large samovar* on the dais, and under this structure a number of clay pipes are fitted to supply heat in winter from the kitchen stove. The whole family sleeps on this dais at night and sits on it with crossed legs as they drink tea which they call *chay*. The all-pervading smell in the living room was, however, that of milk. Bugs infested the place during the whole year with flies reinforcing them strongly during the summer.

Every hut has a courtyard surrounded by a clay wall and with a fireplace in the middle for cooking. Here and there I saw old pitchers made of bronze and richly decorated in the oriental style and there were some clay ones, beautifully shaped. Bits of harness lay about, studded with silver or other

* Often very ornate, a traditional samovar is a solid fuel water heater, like an urn, used for making tea.

metal. This was a luxury handed down from more prosperous times, I was told.

The Kazakhs lived very modestly in their auyls. They cannot eat mutton every day as they used to and they do not use yeast for breadmaking on the whole. They grind flour in a two-stone quern and make very tasty barley cakes from it. The second item of their staple diet is a huge variety of dairy products, the favourite being a dry cheese made by boiling a large quantity of milk in a cauldron until a dense mass formed at the bottom. This was then spread on boards and left to dry on the roof of the house. They also widely use wheat groats, a sort of millet, and rice. They drink *kumys* and *ayran* (similar in taste to yoghurt) but the beverage they prize most is tea, often drunk seasoned with salt and butter. I was told that if they do not drink tea for a long time they suffer from headaches and fits of shivering (though, of course, there is malaria in some districts).

Their principal occupation is sheep breeding, supplemented by the raising of cattle, horses and Bactrian camels. Their form of nomad life is swiftly changing into a settled one, with the result that agriculture and market gardens are developing as a means to livelihood. The soil is very fertile and there are large crops during years when the rainfall is abundant. When there is a bumper grain crop, they hide much of it from the prying eyes of the authorities, keeping it as a reserve for the lean years which follow. I noticed large areas covered with a light white moss, the taste of which was distinctly salty, and learned that the soil here was not suitable for agriculture. Some of the wells yield slightly salty water which acts as a laxative. The summer climate of Kazakhstan is dry and hot. In winter there are frequent snowstorms and sharp frosts.

The sky is often clear and cloudless so the days are usually very sunny, and visibility is remarkably great. There is a constant wind which dies down in the evening, but there are frequent sand storms and in the summer very hot winds from the south last three or four weeks. It is then a great relief to take refuge in the cool and pleasant huts. It will be, I believe, no exaggeration to affirm that the air in Kazakhstan strengthened us and gave us the energy necessary to endure this very difficult period. I know many cases where the climate not only brought about cures of nasal catarrhs, diseases of the throat and lungs such as tuberculosis, but even of chronic stomach complaints.

The people of Kazakhstan are most hospitable, courteous and polite, but if they observe that someone is cunning and trying to exploit them, they withdraw all their confidence in them and treat them with enmity. It is an insult to reject their hospitality. Both men and women dress well, not grudging money for this purpose. As the women walk about the *auyl*, they always have a clump of wool under their arms and spin yarn from a distaff. They are talkative and lively, caring for their children, always smiling and apparently satisfied with life. Most families are small because infant mortality is high.

It was rumoured shortly after our arrival that many pretty foreign women had come to the auyl and every Sunday we had pilgrimages of eligible bachelors. They would come on foot, horseback, by oxcarts or lorries. They came from towns, *auyls* and other work points – Russians, Kazakhs, Tartars, they would look curiously at us and do their best to endear themselves to us. Dressed in their best clothes they would bring beer, vodka, accordions, and sing their traditional songs and ask for ours. They were proper and courteous, proposed matrimony and told about their earnings, qualifications and opportunities in living outside a kolkhoz etc. They did not take offence on being refused and would still give some little attentions with less interest.

I was astonished by one detail of their appearance – many wore galoshes instead of shoes. Initially I thought that it was their tradition to make advances in galoshes, but one of them when asked about it answered honestly: 'We have enough

money, but there are no shoes on sale here. We are happy if
from time to time galoshes are thrown on the market and we
still have to queue for them. It happens sometimes that a
factory releases only one size and for one foot, after a while we
queue again to get another one to match.'

In Tok-Man-Say there was a 14 year old girl named Danusia.
Her lovely fair curls reached her shoulders and her deep black
eyes looked anxiously and instantly at her mother. The visiting
Kazakhs watched her every movement. They talked to each
other enthusiastically before mounting their horses and riding
off. We could not understand what this meant, but Yanka,
mother of Danusia, decided to be careful and not to leave her
daughter for a moment.

One Sunday we all sat on the bank of our nearby river
talking and watching our children's play when suddenly a
group of Kazakhs rode up. They joined us sitting on the
ground in a semicircle, took out their bags of *machorka*
and smoked in silence. After a while the chat about this
and that began. We felt they had come for some reason. At
last the old one said to Yanka in poor Russian: 'We have come
to speak to you. You have goods and we have a purchaser – the
old chief, Ambayev, is interested in marrying your pretty girl.
He can give you a sheep, money, butter, cheese and linen.'

Yanka hugged her daughter close, pale and red in turns they
finally both burst into tears and ran back to our accommodation. The Kazakhs, smiling and nodding, actually could not
comprehend why they had run away. We had to explain that,
in our tradition, girls of Danusia's age did not get married.
Afterwards Yanka kept an even closer eye on her daughter.

Although in later years here I met a great number of
educated and intelligent men and women, life in Kazakhstan
was, on the whole, still very primitive. Life is strictly governed
by family law. The women obeyed the orders of the men.
The main religion is Moslem and, although the Communists

combated it earnestly, the nation maintained its religious traditions. It is a country of great possibilities in the moral and the material sense, and in the hearts as in the soil of this nation there are great natural treasures.

Life for us under such conditions could not last long. We knew that our work in Tok-Man-Say collective farm would yield us nothing. The farm was badly run and neglected. So we made efforts to get transferred to a larger collective farm and, after trudging several hundred kilometres in all, there and back, we finally secured permission from the Alga NKVD to transfer to another collective farm.

The Maxim Gorky collective farm was a much larger village than Tok-Man-Say and its population consisted of Ukrainians, Russians and Kazakhs. It was mainly a dairy farm but also bred pigs and camels. There was plenty to do in the fields besides hay making as there was a large area of vegetables. Some of the huts had been left empty by workers who had gone to the towns for a better living. We cleaned up and repaired these dwellings and moved in.

Efforts were made immediately after our arrival to have us join the collective farm's permanent staff. None of us agreed, but we had to work nonetheless. The younger folk worked on the steppe, running tractors, harvesters and mowers whilst the rest helped the collective farmers by cultivating the vegetable plot. Though in theory a collective farm should give a living to those working on it, we found these farmers in great want. If not for their personal smallholdings, they told us they would die of hunger.

The basis of their livelihood was the raising of vegetables in the vicinity of their homestead, potatoes and other vegetables being their chief foodstuffs. They also usually had one or two cows, some pigs, two or three sheep and some hens, but they were so heavily taxed for this individual production that, after paying the tax collectors in kind, there was barely enough left to last them until the next crop. Thus, though they badly needed clothes and underwear whilst we needed food, no barter transactions could be effected.

As a matter of fact, the collective farm was deep in debt and mismanaged. Those who ran it were frequently changed either because of incompetence or because they had been sentenced to a prison term for defalcations. The unit for the payment of wages was the 'work day'. Wages were paid mostly in kind and that after the crops had been brought in. However, every collective farm was bound to deliver a fixed amount of produce, irrespective of what had actually been produced, or how good or bad the harvest had been to the authorities. The remainder was then divided up amongst the workers on the basis of the total number of work days to their credit.

Together with my son, who worked as a tractor driver's mate, we amassed 240 work days on this farm. This worked out at 20kg of wheat, 20kg of potatoes, 25kg of other vegetables. All this was to suffice for the three of us until the new crops were brought in. I later received a notification, when I was back in Aktyubinsk, that I had been paid 2kg kilograms of wheat too much.

Well before the crops were harvested and my 'wages' calculated, it became evident to me that we could not survive the coming winter at the collective farm. I had to find some way of leaving it and finding another livelihood. It was a great help that we received food parcels from Poland from members of our family not deported by the Russians. Various illicit organisations also managed to send us parcels of this kind, but the Russian occupation made it more and more difficult. The number of post offices in Poland accepting parcels addressed to the Soviet Union was severely restricted, and so on.

After long thought regarding the advisability of settling in a town I set out at sunrise for Aktyubinsk with my knapsack filled with various things. It was well after dusk when I reached the town, and I was very tired. I knocked at the door of a small house and asked if I could stay there for the night. They were good people and agreed immediately.

I went out next morning well rested and looked around for some opportunity of finding work and getting more food. It proved much easier to barter my things for food than it had been on the collective farm and, as I wandered about the market place, I noticed much unprocessed wool was being offered, good quality, sheep's, camels' and goats'. The people I saw, however, were mostly dressed in cotton garments very much the worse for wear. Struck by this observation, I began to question them about their living conditions, about the chances of finding work and what types of manufacture were being conducted.

I soon made up my mind as to the situation and, plucking up my courage, went to see the local chief of light industry on the next day. His deputy received me and heard out my plan for developing a new branch of textile production in the town, the production of hand-knit sweaters, gloves, socks, caps, scarves, etc, from locally grown wool. I showed him a few samples made by me that I had intended to barter for food. He liked them very much and said the idea was most interesting. The matter would be presented to the Light Industries Commission by him and I could drop in again two weeks later to learn the result.

I left my samples with him and asked whether there would be any difficulty in getting a transfer from the collective farm to the town in this connection. He replied that there would be no trouble once the decision had been made.

Overjoyed with this promising beginning, and with my knapsack full of bread and fat, I returned to my children the next day. The manager of the collective farm was furious that I had left without his permission. He was personally responsible that we would not escape and had been very worried. I saw his point of view but, after all, I had returned to the farm. Two weeks later I went to the Aktyubinsk office for light industries and was received this time by the chief himself. He informed me that the Commission's decision was favourable and that we could start organisation at once. We discussed some technical matters and I asked him to arrange for our official transfer to Aktyubinsk. He immediately telephoned to the NKVD police who told me to report to them in person.

I did so and was closely examined regarding my own person and family. The chief listened to my plans with gratifying interest and told me that he had nothing against my leaving the collective farm, provided the regional chief agreed. So I took the train to Alga and was interviewed by the chief of police. He refused his consent for a long time but he finally agreed when I told him he knew very well that my children and I would not survive at the farm where starvation and freezing to death (in the absence of fuel) awaited us. He at once issued an order to the manager of the collective farm whereby I was permitted to leave it without hindrance on his part.

This small scrap of paper was the greatest prize I had ever won in my life.

The thought that I would soon be leaving the collective farm gave me so much hope and energy that, regardless of the approaching night, I set off at once across the steppe to reach my children on foot. I arrived at daybreak and told them the glad news. My little daughter set a fire and made breakfast for me, my son brought some water from the river so that I could wash, and they took off my boots so that I could soak my tired feet with relief. I slept the whole day.

It was nearly evening before I had rested and recovered my strength. I went to the manager of the farm and showed him the order of the Alga chief of police. To my intense surprise, he tore it up into shreds the moment he read the paper. He shouted, 'I'm the chief here, and I won't let you go'. When his fury simmered down, I started scolding him but after a time an idea struck me and I calmed down. I said to him regretfully,

'So you don't want to have a drink with me – half a litre of vodka, to celebrate our departure!'

These words acted like a charm. He smiled and we began to discuss my departure quietly and very much to the point. I clinched the matter by agreeing to pay 150 roubles for transport by horse and cart, and leave vodka as a token of esteem for the chief personalities of the Maxim Gorky Collective Farms.

I stopped working and instead busied myself with preparing for our departure. A few days later the horse and cart turned up, in the shape of a cart to which two camels had been harnessed. Everybody helped me to load my belongings. I had acquired some furniture by this time, a table, two stools, a packing case (my son later made a bed out of it, wood is very valuable in Kazakhstan), three hens in a cage and, of course, my daughter's kitten. Finally, we sat on top of our things and, with merry cries of farewell and good will from all and sundry and my promise that I would try to help them to move to the town as well, we took our leave of collective farm life, as I thought, for good.

We rode very slowly. The camels were senile and had to rest often. A chill wind blew across the steppe heralding the coming end of autumn. The steppe was taking on a grey monotonous tone, broken here and there by clumps of leafless bushes. Filigree *buzan*, spread by the wind, jumped about comically in the air. Hour after hour passed as we drove deeper and deeper towards the horizon. Tossing and jerking on the high cart, we slowly sailed across the steppe ocean as if in a tiny craft on its way into the unknown. It was quite dark when we entered a small village where we spent the night.

It was in the evening, two days later, that we arrived in Aktyubinsk and put up in the home of an acquaintance who let us sleep in a corner. She was a Russian, very kind-hearted and decent, whose husband had abandoned her and was in hiding somewhere in the Union. As she had five children the room now housed nine persons all told. In spite of this overcrowding we lived there for several weeks in the utmost harmony.

CHAPTER 4

Aktyubinsk and work for General Anders

The province of Aktyubinsk is so large that one or two small western European countries could fit into it. The city of the same name was inhabited by a mixed population of Kazakhs, Russians and Tartars, and a medley of other nationalities compulsorily settled there. Aktyubinsk was one of the towns where politically doubtful elements were placed. Most of these exiles were fairly well educated and came from the major towns and capitals of the Soviet Union. They could not always find work in their specialities and had to report to the local secret police every fortnight.

There were many Ukrainians, Turcomens, Georgians, Koreans, and even Communist Jews from Palestine who came with great enthusiasm in 1937-38 to visit Moscow and after some time were deported to Aktyubinsk with even greater 'enthusiasm'. One of them worked as a gardener in the park and he often told me of the beauty of Palestine as we chatted, sitting on a bench.

The town was obviously developing quickly year by year. There were many new buildings, mostly government offices, and blocks of workers' dwellings. The streets were of asphalt, parks were laid out and trees planted. Huge industrial works were constructed in the suburbs with a large isolation camp for those political prisoners with a speciality useful in heavy industry. The town was an extensive one and the central section looked quite European, but all around this the population lived in huts similar to those of Kazakh auyls.

I left the home of my acquaintance after some time and began to make sweaters from the knitting wool I had brought from Poland. Bartering the finished product for food enabled us to carry on quite well. More and more Poles were leaving the collective farms and arranging their lives in Aktyubinsk, with relative success, under much better conditions than on the farms. The women worked as seamstresses, in kitchens, as lift attendants and so on. The men could only find physical work, regardless of their professions, and laboured on road construction, railway building, etc.

It was towards the beginning of February before the organisation of the local textile industry made it possible for me to start making sweaters on a larger scale. I assembled a few Polish women, whom I had managed to bring here from the kolkhoz, and we began to knit. Our products were very well received and were in great demand, but we received only a pittance for all our hard work. The terms of payment were not respected by the Soviet officials and we were bitterly exploited by them with the constant threat of being sent back to the collective farms if we did not work enough. We had to work long hours of overtime and find supplementary means of earning a living if we were to survive.

In fact, most of the town population had come from collective farms in search of better living conditions. Apart from working in the various enterprises, each of them had his little house, garden and a small plot of land from which much less was taken in taxes than on the collective farms. These smallholdings provided a firm basis for their livelihood. They were independent of the market to some extent and could sell their surplus production of food. As I learned later, the population of the majority of towns in the Soviet Union managed to survive in this manner.

As already stated, most of the educated classes had been deported from larger towns in Russia. Friendly relations were established with nearly all of them, and they trusted us more than people of their own nationality. It was therefore quite easy to sub-let a room from them. I observed their life with great interest, the more so that it differed so much from what I had known in Europe.

I admired the Russian women in particular and the gallant way in which they bore the difficulties of life for so many years. I talked with them in their homes and standing in queues for many hours at a stretch. Nearly all of them had outside jobs, in offices, factories or even as manual labourers carrying sacks of grain in the elevators, on building and railway construction, etc. Then, after a hard day's work, they would take up their household duties, stand in queues for bread and other foodstuffs, and only too often return with nothing after many hours of waiting.

At home, they began their second daily job. The children had been without their parents all day long. The younger ones had to be brought from crèches, the older ones returned from school and, after lessons, spent most of their time on the streets or queuing for food. The mothers had to cook for the whole family (no canned foods available), wash clothes and linen, do some sewing and repair work, and so until late at night throughout the year.

On Sundays, the authorities considered a change of occupation to be the best rest and everybody had to go and do some social work called *udarniki*, helping on the construction of government buildings, factories and roads. I often saw women being rounded up on a Sunday in the markets, put on to lorries and taken away to work as 'volunteers' on a collective farm for some hours. Some of the women escaped the round up and hid until the press gang had gone. In summer the women were forced on Sundays, often for several days on end, to help harvest crops or dig potatoes.

Thus it was that the women looked neglected and tired. The men, for their part, were in little better shape. They would drop in to eat something at home and then immediately hurry out to attend compulsory meetings, political courses, etc. The result was that family life was disjointed and irregular. Divorces were common. There were shortages of all kinds all the time. Crime and armed robbery flourished in Aktyubinsk. Young hooligans would form gangs which attacked passersby at night, stole their victims' clothes and often killed them.

There were few cultural recreations at that time. The cinemas served a purely propaganda purpose, the films mostly depicting 'the joyous and flourishing life' on a collective farm or on a factory construction scheme. Few people willingly looked at these films, but the theatres and concert halls presented quite good programmes and were deservedly popular. One had the feeling that at least here there was greater freedom of expression.

All this does not mean to say that there were no moments of joy and triumph, in the strictly relative sense. Everybody carried about a bag made of strong threads which could be easily rolled up and kept in the pocket. These bags were called *avos*, meaning 'just in case something turns up'. What greater joy was there than unexpectedly to be able to buy an item of clothing or underwear, a piece of cloth or a pair of boots for the children, for the husband or for oneself? Or the triumph of securing two or three servings of sugar, fat or flour by dint of hurrying to the end of the queue and waiting again? I myself personally experienced this pleasure and must say I prized it very highly when I thought of my children.

Life in Aktyubinsk differed greatly from life in the west not only for these reasons. There was also the continual fear of being arrested by the secret police. I did not meet a single family which did not have at least one member, near or distant, in prison or a penal camp. I was told this as a matter of course, almost with indifference, just as the Soviet five-year plans follow each other ceaselessly without any change for the better in the personal life of the people.

Winter and spring passed quickly. My son went to school whilst my ten year old daughter helped me gallantly, willingly, with the cooking and queuing for food. Somehow, as with the other Poles, we made both ends meet and lived without extreme privation.

The Russo-German War broke out on 22nd June 1941 and, strangely enough, took nobody by surprise. Actually, the population had been expecting it from day to day. Everybody knew that the Russo-German alliance would end with the partners fighting each other. The Soviet citizens were discreetly overjoyed and expressed their hopes to us in the strictest confidence. They counted at first on the Germans and, later, the Americans. We Poles were certain that the war would basically change our status and that the Germans would ultimately be defeated.

The Russian police vehicles known as Black Crows had scurried about the town some days before war broke out loading up with freshly arrested people and taking them off to the prisons. On the third day of the Russo-German war (24/06/41), it was a Tuesday, by the way, carts drove up to all the houses where Poles lived and the secret police ordered us to take our things and leave the town. I hurriedly packed our things and clambered into the little cart with the children and the cat as we again set off into the unknown. Two Polish women and a four year old child were added to our number before we left Aktyubinsk.

It took us four days and nights travel by this horse and cart transport to arrive in some collective farm, so isolated and distant that (as the inhabitants described it) 'the Devil says goodnight there'. It was certainly very far from the nearest railway line or highway.

There were only seven huts there inhabited by Russians who looked as if they lived in the greatest misery and want. Their chief crop was hay, and they immediately invited us to help getting it in. Unfortunately, we could not eat hay whilst they promised to pay us for our work after the crop was harvested. So I again began wandering about the locality in search of food and news.

The workers on the other collective farms made no secret of their joy that the Germans were so swiftly advancing into the heart of Russia. They would certainly liberate them! They often said, however, that they would prefer the Americans to liberate them from the 'accursed collective farms'. In general, I was surprised to find America so popular among the population, everything American was the best, according to them.

Luckily, my wanderings did not last long. We learned from the newspapers in August that the Polish Government in London had concluded an agreement with the Soviet Government and that an amnesty had been declared for Polish prisoners and deportees. Our conditions of life were to change in the sense that thenceforth we were to be treated as 'guests' in the Soviet Union.

I at once took energetic steps to get back to town. It took us three days journey on foot, hitch-hiking on carts and lorries to reach Aktyubinsk. Mile long queues of Poles were forming everywhere and still more came into the town from the various collective farms. I rented a flat and we began life again under new conditions.

Shortly after my return to Aktyubinsk, groups of Poles released from Soviet prisons and concentration camps, began to arrive. They were half starved, in rags and without means of existence. They needed immediate help. There were rumours that somewhere in the Soviet Union a Polish army was being organised but I had no news about the arrival of representatives of the Polish government in London. We were far distant from Moscow and from reliable sources of information. In spite of this, it was obviously necessary to act and, in company with a few other Poles, I organised the first makeshift relief action for the released prisoners.

I went to the local authorities and asked where the Polish army was being formed in the Soviet Union so that I could direct able-bodied ex-prisoners there. But the only answer I received was that they did not know. In view of this, referring to the stipulations of the Soviet-Polish agreement (the terms of which I knew nothing), I asked that they provide means of subsistence for the released prisoners until their position became fully clarified. I stressed that these people were starving, exhausted and homeless besides being temporarily unfit for any physical work.

The authorities were rather taken aback by my demands and gave me some vouchers for meals at a reduced price while allotting a bread ration for the future soldiers of the Polish Army. I likewise secured accommodation where I set up a reception centre for new arrivals. This initial relief work was badly hindered by lack of funds but even the little we could do meant very much for these homeless and starving people.

One day I learnt that a rallying point for former prisoners of war had been organised in Totskoye. I looked at a map immediately and to my contentment found that Totskoye was not far away from Orenburg-Chkalov.

I sold one of my dresses and with the permission of the authorities bought a ticket. A journey in those days was quite onerous – I managed to climb and slip on to an upper shelf. After three days I got off on Totskoye station where I could not believe my eyes! The station was full of Polish uniforms – although worn out, but on the faces of their wearers joy and enthusiasm were visible.

I approached a group of officers and after a short greeting I told them for what reason I had come. General Tokarzewski told me to take the next train and get off on the next station – Buzuluk. 'There is the main headquarters of General Anders. You will have to see him tonight as tomorrow morning he is flying to Moscow for a conference with Stalin'.

I took the next train. It was dark when I got off the train and the station was not illuminated. The town was still a few kilometres away and no transport was available, apart from my feet. I cannot remember how I reached the town. I know I joined some people walking in the darkness. They expected air raids.

Somebody showed me a half illuminated building, which was the headquarters. It was 11.45pm and I was exhausted. I asked to be reported to the General, but a sergeant in charge replied: 'The General has already gone to his hotel'. I asked for a guide and after a short walk we arrived. Thankfully General Anders had not gone to sleep yet. When one of his assistants asked who was to be reported I answered: 'A woman from Kazakhstan', and was welcomed immediately.*

Shortly afterwards I established contacts personally with the Polish Embassy in Kuybyshev and with the Polish military authorities in Buzuluk. This army† was ultimately to fight against the Germans since Poland was one of the Allies, joined by the Soviet Union after Germany had attacked it in 1941.

I received official documents from the Embassy and from the Polish military authorities in Russia whereby I was nominated relief officer for Polish citizens in the Aktyubinsk region. I also received the first money grant and the joyful news that we would shortly receive help in kind from England and America.

On my return to Aktyubinsk, I organised a permanent relief

* Urszula says nothing of this meeting. Her son, my father, said that she was one of the first to brief General Anders, newly released from prison, on the harsh conditions endured by the thousands of Polish women and children forced to work on farms and in construction in Kazakhstan.
† Anders Army moved to Tashkent, Uzbekistan over the winter of 1941/42 and then on to Persia (Iran). About 41,000 combatants and 74,000 civilians left the USSR with limited resources and many obstacles created by the Soviet authorities. On reaching Palestine solders were posted to different duties with the 2nd Polish Corps fighting the Germans northwards through Italy and distinguishing themselves at Monte Cassino. Wladyslaw Anders was prominent in the Polish Government in Exile in London, where he died in 1970, and was buried amongst his fallen solders at Monte Cassino.

What Urszula was too modest to mention is that she had been awarded the rank of Colonel to give her authority when dealing with the Soviet authorities.

station for ex-prisoners and for deported families. This was a period of very intensive work and effort. Very often, when the secret police released prisoners, they would purposely not inform them where the Polish army had its recruiting points. Thousands of ex-prisoners, without any means of subsistence, spent weeks wandering across the enormous spaces of the Soviet Union without knowing where the Polish army was stationed. If they travelled by train or boat they would alight at major towns or river ports where they could earn a little money . . . sufficient for a small stock of food and for another stage of their journey. Many of them died of hunger, exhaustion, from the cold and from disease before they could reach their destination.

When we finally organised a system of information centres at the main railway stations, we succeeded in directing this mass of bewildered and helpless people to the proper point. Those ex-prisoners capable of military service were sent to the recruiting stations of the Polish army. Others, incapable of such service, were given monetary grants and paid jobs found for them, after their strength had been restored by adequate food.

Much confusion was caused and many difficulties arose owing to great masses of deported Poles and their families trekking from the far north without any organisation and regardless of the enormous distances which had to be covered in the most primitive conditions. It was as if some blind instinct bade them to press southwards, to warmer regions and closer to the frontiers of Iran, so that they would not miss an opportunity of escaping from the Soviet Union. Whole families travelled thus, with babes in arms and small children under appalling conditions of under-nourishment and cold. We would often extract nothing but corpses from the wagons.

The Polish Ambassador Kot and General Anders did all they could to help these Poles, but encountered hindrance after hindrance set up by the Soviet authorities. These promised much but gave little. In fact, apart from a meagre supply of bread we received nothing else. The money loaned to us was next to nothing compared with the high market prices. It was not until Anglo-American relief supplies came in that it became possible to afford proper relief to these very unhappy people.

The news which I brought from the Embassy that England and America were sending relief shipments for the deported Poles created an enormous impression not only on the Poles, but also on the Soviet people. The local population refused to believe that the Soviet government would permit other countries to supply relief to anybody upon its territory. They said they remembered the period when the United States sought to bring help during the hard times of famine, that Russia categorically refused this aid, stating that her inhabitants had more than enough of everything.

They were therefore most surprised when the first wagon load of American gift parcels reached Aktyubinsk railway station. Crowds of Soviet citizens stood around and gazed with enormous interest at the things we were unloading. The authorities set aside a store house where we deposited the gifts and distributed them. We had to arrange a fair division to embrace the groups of Poles in the various regions and worked at great speed as we wanted the Poles scattered in the kol-khozes to receive their gifts before Christmas.

It was at this time that I heard many of the Poles could not leave their homes and go out to work simply because they had no footwear. Again, some of the regions were hundreds of miles distant from Aktyubinsk and in winter time could be reached only by sleighs. It often required several weeks of journeying in such difficult conditions for people to secure what had been allotted to them. Finally, with food supplies now assured, we established orphanages and homes for the aged, set up a mobile kitchen and met all trains bringing in ex-prisoners so that these poor people could get some hot soup and bread directly they arrived at the station.

The groups that reached Aktyubinsk were given money and a bundle of clothes, after which they were sent to the baths where, after careful disinfection, they left their lice and rags. They would be so glad to regain a civilised look again that they hurried back to our office to express their thanks and to show us how they looked in normal life. I remember how, time after time, they found notes written by British or American students, and others, who collected and packed these gift parcels. Letters sending them fraternal greetings, encouragement and hope for the future. These expressions of humanity and goodwill moved us tremendously and were particularly gratefully received by those who had well nigh lost all hope.

I may mention that the frost in Aktyubinsk was really intense that year . . . 40–50 degrees of frost was nothing unusual. I would like all those who donated clothing and other gifts for these poor people to know that not only did they warm us up, but that these kind words expressed in the short messages found in the pockets of the clothes gave encouragement and hope. I would often see tears of emotion in people's eyes. They wept and were not ashamed, for they cried for joy that there are human hearts which so spontaneously and humanely strove to relieve the tragedy of another country and nation, people who had passed through such a debasement of human dignity in Soviet prisons and labour camps.

They restored trust in human Christian love and enabled these shattered people to bear their future trials with fortitude and unshakeable enthusiasm.

CHAPTER 5
My arrest

It was snowing and raining as I made my way back home after a visit to acquaintances in the suburbs with Mme. N. on Sunday, 10th May, 1942. It was heavy going through the numerous puddles and deep mud, but we finally reached the bridge over the railway track, crossed it and started to go down. My heart jumped a beat when I saw a car waiting at the foot of the stairs with an officer of the NKVD, one with whom I had already had official business.

He immediately came up and most politely asked if I would mind going with him to the NKVD office where his chief was anxious to discuss something important. I was not surprised, as the NKVD chief had often held meetings with me to regulate the affairs of the Polish citizens I was looking after. I handed my briefcase to my friend and asked her to leave it at my home. I got into the car and glanced back to see that some civilian had taken the briefcase away from her and had now got into the car beside the driver. We moved off, not stopping until we had passed the main entrance of the NKVD building. We drove through a side entrance and the car drew up in the courtyard.

I was now sure some trickery was under way. I got out of the car and the officer led me to his room, asked me to sit down and, after pulling some papers out of the drawer of his desk, informed me that I was being arrested for espionage on the strength of Paragraph 6, and that the Polish Embassy had already been informed about this. The chief of the NKVD entered a moment later and the officer now barked at me, 'Prisoner, stand up'.

Having a clear conscience, I accepted all this with complete equanimity. I was sure it was all some misunderstanding which would soon be cleared up. My personal data was noted down and a woman in uniform led me to another room where she made a careful search of my person. All this took quite some time and it was about 11 o'clock before the NKVD officer led me to his car and we rode off to my home. My little daughter was waiting for me, very quiet, so without paying any attention to the search being conducted in my belongings, I hugged her and sat on the sofa. She was crying quietly and clung close to me as we waited. As I had been forbidden to speak to her in our own language, I said nothing. The secret police agents behaved correctly. They put aside only whatever written material they found, even my children's school exercise books. It was, on the whole, very quiet in the room.

The old Granny, whose rooms these were, sat in the kitchen and from time to time sighed deeply and intoned, 'God have mercy on us'. My daughter was a great favourite of hers and she was very much upset by my predicament. The search lasted for three hours, after which I was told to dress and go with the secret police. I should mention that during the search my friends had prepared a little bag containing the essential articles for a prisoner in jail. This is the normal last service for one about to be arrested in the Soviet Union. I took leave of old Granny and asked her to look after my daughter for a time. Making a great sign of the Cross, she replied, 'Go in peace'.

I hugged my daughter and, as I did so, saw my wedding ring on my finger. I took it off and slipped it onto one of her little fingers. Only then did she break into loud sobs and clung desperately to me with her little hands crying out, 'I won't let you go . . . I won't let you go, Mummy'.

Petrified with pain and shock, I could not utter a single word as I felt my heart constrict with dull pain . . . a strong heart that did not break, nor split that stony outward calm. The guards urged me to hurry, and I carefully pried away her hands, kissed her again and went out. The child ran after me calling, 'Mummy, Mummy'. At the gateway I turned and looked back at her once again.

For fourteen years thereafter I could still hear my daughter's voice by dint of memory, and I believe it will always remain there.

I was incarcerated in a cell for one. The walls and floor were of cement, and there was no furniture. I dropped my bag and rug on the floor and sat down. My mind was a complete blank. I was still in a state of petrified calmness and, strangely enough, it seemed a familiar one, as if I had already experienced such a state before. I sat motionless until morning when the warden opened the door to lead me to the toilet. Little by little consciousness returned and again, at the thought of my little girl, I felt a stab of pain in my heart.

Day passed after day without the outside world showing any interest in me. Some stinking soup was brought to me three times a day. It had fish eyes in it and I immediately poured it into the bucket in the corner. I ate nothing but bread and drank water. Every evening three guards and the prison commandant entered the cell, sounded out the walls and tried the window bars. It was a narrow cell and normally lit by a dirty grey light, except at noon when a bright and merry ray of sun entered through the window, traversed the wall in care-free fashion and soon disappeared.

I sat in my corner every day waiting for it to appear. It was my only entertainment here and also a short ease of tension, caused by concerns for my children.

Some days later I heard a quiet knocking. I approached one of the walls and noticed a crack in the plaster covering the bricked up place where a stove had once been built in. I carefully widened the crack and found that it was quite deep. It seemed to me that I could hear a whisper, so I put my ear to the crack and listened. The woman in the next cell was whispering to me. The crack must have stretched through the whole thickness of the wall.

I moved my cot to the spot and sat there for hours as I listened to the whispered talk of a woman who had been sentenced to death. Obviously, we wished to keep our communication secret so every time a warder passed our doors we interrupted our conversation.

The prisoner in the death cell was a young Georgian doctor, arrested while in charge of a train load of children being evacuated from the Caucasus to Uzbekistan. Some of the children had died of food poisoning on the way and she was accused of wilfully causing their death. Sentenced to the supreme penalty, she was now awaiting execution. She spoke as if in a confessional.

'How good it is that I have someone to whom I can show all that burdens down my soul,' she exclaimed. 'It may be that they'll lead me out very soon . . . to shoot me. There's nothing I can do about it, and I must scream in a whisper . . . I must speak of all that troubles me. Why was I condemned to death? For I'm innocent . . . innocent . . . I'd only just begun to live . . . I was working with all my heart and soul . . . I loved my work as I do my mother. I was always sad with the mothers when they brought their sick children to me, and I was glad when I handed them back cured and well. Then, during the evacuation, my colleagues intrigued against me because I was a witness against them. I had too energetically demanded that the children get their full food ration during the journey.

The others stole the food, sold it . . . and wanted me to be their accomplice, but I refused. So I was brought to this place . . . the judges wouldn't believe me . . . they believed the others, fully . . . you see, the others and the judges were Party members . . . while I've never belonged to the Party . . . politics never interested me . . . my Party was composed of sick children and their relief . . . Politics never interested me. I want to live . . . to live.'

On another day she said to me, 'If you get free, tell my mother and the whole family that you met me here, accused of such a shameful thing. They'll never believe it! They'll never believe I could do such a horrible thing.'

She spoke constantly, almost without stop. I felt she did not want to remain alone with her thoughts. She told me her whole life story, from childhood, her joys and sorrows, how she loved her mother. How glad she had been that, with her profession, she could have assured her mother of a comfortable old age.

She could not sleep at nights . . . I could hear her walking up and down . . . and when morning came and I got up, she tapped at the wall and asked me to speak with her. I was only too glad to help her in any way I could, to relieve her of suffering. True, I was worrying about my children. On this side of the prison wall, a mother's heart, and on the other side the heart of a child going to her death. She wasn't my child, but the suffering of a child must be felt by all mothers and I asked myself why should there be all this suffering?

I was only one of the millions of ordinary women in the Soviet Union who so often asked this question.

It must have been on the fourth day when she said goodnight to me and added that she felt much better. Her talks with me had helped her tremendously and she felt more at peace with the world. I told her, 'You'll see that you'll feel still better tomorrow'. She must have fallen asleep soon after for she did not walk about the cell as usual. On the other hand, it was long before I fell asleep. I was thinking of this poor young woman, of the hard life and conditions in the Soviet Union. It must have been nearly morning when I began to doze off, only to hear the heavy tread of a squad of guards in the corridor. A door was opened and then closed . . . and I finally fell asleep.

I waited long for the usual tapping from the neighbouring cell and, finally, signalled myself. Nobody answered. The young woman doctor had a difficult Georgian name and I completely forgot it during the many years of compulsory isolation from the outside world which followed this episode. Perhaps someone of her family will read these words and thus learn of her fate.

The door was swung open and I was ordered to go out with my belongings. I was led to a serving hatch where some bread, sugar and dried fish were handed me. I was still ignorant of prison procedure and wondered what this all meant. Not for long, I was led out on to the courtyard and for a moment I stood there blinded by the full daylight. A car was waiting. I was put into it, and very soon got out at the railway station with an officer and two agents of the NKVD to escort me. The Moscow-Tashkent train entered the station just as we arrived.

We all got into one of the carriages but found there was hardly standing room in it. The carriage was crammed with Red Army officers and officers' families being evacuated from Moscow to the south. With an NKVD officer on either side, I stood waiting until the conductor, summoned by the NKVD, expelled four Red Army officers from a compartment for our benefit. The officers were furious and there was a sharp exchange of words, but they had to submit.

A young NKVD woman agent came along and we all entered the empty compartment. This woman's duty was to accompany me whenever I went to the toilet . . . nothing more. I thought to myself, so much expense and trouble all because of one very ordinary woman who wanted to help her country-men in a perfectly legal and humane enterprise.

I was warned, before the train moved off, that I was not allowed to leave the compartment (unless it was to visit the toilet) and that I should speak to no-one. After two days, I rebelled and demanded that I be allowed to stretch my legs. They refused at first, but when I threatened to scream, they agreed with ill grace. Thereafter, once or twice a day, I was allowed to walk up and down the platform at the longer stops, under the close escort of the two agents.

The Long Bridge

The route we were following was the same as that taken four months earlier when I was escorting a wagon load of Anglo-American gifts to Aktyubinsk. Only that I was now a prisoner and did not know my destination. Eventually we approached the Sea of Aral. The region was sandy, sparsely populated and with but feeble vegetation. All in all, the land looked as if the sea had just withdrawn from it.

The journey was unpleasant in other respects. A widespread epidemic of spotted typhus had broken out in this part of Soviet Asia. Not only the local inhabitants suffered from that disease, but also the enormous masses of Soviet citizens evacuated from the areas affected by war, as also the masses of Poles released from prisons and concentration camps in the far north.

Tens of thousands were killed off by this terrible epidemic and I learned of cases where whole families were wiped out. It would often happen that people travelling for weeks on end, under terrible sanitary conditions, succumbed to the disease on the way. The sanitary authorities would then simply dump their bodies at the next stop. There were many places without hospitals and, where there was one, it was usually hopelessly overcrowded.

The sufferers were left in the railway station, or in the station courtyard or allotments, and there they lay on the ground, untended, with high fevers or unconscious. From time to time, some merciful soul would hand them a drink of water. It often proved impossible to identify the dead. At rare intervals, a lorry would drive up and cart the corpses to the local cemetery. The largest heap of corpses I saw in the grounds of a station was at Arys . . . an awful sight. The Soviet authorities did what they could to combat the epidemic but were handicapped by the shortage of medicines, medical personnel and accommodation.

As we journeyed from Arys towards Alma-Ata the landscape altered with more vegetation and a settled population. It became hot and the arrival of spring was evident everywhere. When we passed Chimkent, mountain chains appeared on the distant horizon.

A funny incident occurred on the fourth day of the journey. The NKVD agents escorting me ran out of tobacco, and could not replenish their supply at the stations we stopped at. Their addiction to smoking was so great that, after a short discussion, they decided to invite one of the Red Army officers into the compartment for a game of chess, arguing that he would certainly treat them to cigarettes.

The invitation was gladly accepted. An officer came in, treated them to cigarettes and sat down to play chess. After a game or two he began to pay more attention to me than to the chess and engaged me in conversation. The agents were worried by this change of situation and constantly either urged him to go on playing or tried to distract his attention by plying him with questions. He handed them cigarettes, answered very laconically and seemed to have lost all interest in playing. He learned from me that I had lived near Lwow and this greatly increased his friendly interest in my person.

It appeared that, until the Soviet-German war broke out, he had been stationed in Lwow and had had a fine time there. He liked the city, the womenfolk and the beer. He told me how street traders used to swindle Red Army men at first when selling watches, fountain pens, petrol lighters and other appliances hard to get in Russia. He roared with laughter at some of his experiences. He certainly had a keen sense of humour, and had the knack of describing events wittily and colourfully.

As I listened to him with interest, I examined the faces of my 'guardians' as they betrayed ever greater disquiet. Quite ignorant of the fact that I was a prisoner and that these were NKVD men, the officer began to express his opinions with greater and greater frankness and praised life in the west with more and more enthusiasm. I began to fear for him but did not know how to warn him. When he asked me where I was going I told him, 'To Alma-Ata', but this did not suffice. He was very curious and asked me where I expected to stay so that he could visit me. Looking at my guardian angels I said calmly, 'I don't know how long I'll be staying there but it will be in the NKVD building'.

He was taken aback, and there was silence for a moment. One of the agents broke it by saying, 'Well, it's time to get ready'.

They stood up and began to pull down their suitcases from the rack, although it was still a day and half to Alma Ata. The officer got up and with a few words of farewell went out. I went on looking at the landscape. On the next day, the enormous Tian-Shan mountain chains began to rear higher and higher, and the glaciers upon them could be clearly seen. The train reached Alma-Ata before evening and there we alighted.

CHAPTER 6
Alma-Ata

One of the police agents alighted and returned for us when all the passengers had left the train. I took my things and, still closely escorted, went out through a side door to the station courtyard. We went up to a lorry which looked like a great dark box covered with iron plate. The sight was not a pleasant one and a slight shiver went through me. I recalled that the Soviet people call this type of vehicle the Black Crow.

The moment I entered the door was slammed and I found myself in absolute darkness. I could not move about because the lorry was crammed full of people. The air was hardly breathable and I could hear the others gasping. The Black Crow moved off and I felt I would have fallen if the press had not been so great. When the lorry stopped in the prison courtyard I was pulled out half unconscious and soaked with sweat. Breathing deeply I slowly returned to normal.

The warders led me to a large room where my 'guardian angel' was already waiting in the company of a very tall man. The latter looked at me sharply and, taking the papers handed in by the agent, rang the bell. A warder entered and he said to him, 'Take her away'.

Before I reached my cell, I was taken to the bathroom where I found to my great indignation that all the personnel were men. My protests were unavailing, for this is part of the system purposefully applied in the secret police prisons and concentration camps. In this case, it was a prison fully administered by the secret police and its inmates were mostly political prisoners.

After four days in my cell, I was led one morning to an interrogator. He greeted me as an old acquaintance and asked whether I recognised him. I looked at his face more closely and then saw he was the tall man who had taken me from my escort.

He was most polite during the first few weeks, asked me about this and that, mentioned as an aside that they already knew everything very well, that I was a Fascist and worked for Hitler and that if I spoke the truth my situation might very well change for the better. He changed his tactics after a fortnight or so, becoming less polite. I learned from him that London had provided me with directives for conducting economic espionage in the Soviet Union. He assured me that I had been sending information and reports to London through the Polish Embassy. He constantly exhorted me to speak the truth and to sign whatever he had written in his protocol.

I very willingly carried out the first part of his request but signed not a single statement containing his imaginary charges. The investigation continued day after day. Two guards would take me by the arms and rush me through the corridors at the double, very frequently, so that I arrived quite breathless before the inquisitors. As the days passed I became more and more hungry and sleepier and sleepier. The sessions would last from sixteen to twenty hours and I would often eat my dinner together with my supper only to be called out for further investigation and to return to my cell at dawn.

During one of these meetings, sometime after midnight, the senior inquisitor came in, looked through the protocols, shook his head and told me, 'This will end badly for you'. He then ordered me to get up and follow him. As I went out behind him the guard fell into position at the rear and so we marched for a very long time, along various long corridors, up and down winding staircases, until doors were opened before us and I entered a large, well lit room with luxurious carpets covering the floor. There was a large, handsome looking desk at which there sat a tall, stout man. Seven senior officers, lavishly decorated with medals, sat around the room. The presiding figure was, it appeared, a minister of the Kazakhstan Soviet Republic.

I was asked to sit down and a preliminary questioning began, followed by a sharp cross examination. I had been seen in General Anders' headquarters . . . in such and such section, on this or that day . . . and so on. Why did I visit the Second Department? What did I say there? Where and from whom did I get a message? Which of the Polish officers instructed me in my espionage work? And so on, interminably, and all sheer imagination. They then again assured me that they knew all and mentioned the names of Polish officers who had given me orders. All I had to do was to confess and sign and I would be released the very next day. I denied every charge quietly but with determination. For that matter, they knew as well as I did that there was not a word of truth in their accusations.

It was dawn when the hearing ended and I was led back to my cell. My whole being wanted sleep and nothing else but sleep but, as soon as I dozed off, the guard would bang on the door with his rifle butt and shout, 'Sleeping not allowed'. Suddenly awakened I could feel my heart thumping violently and my whole body trembling. At six o'clock, after the usual reveille all prisoners were directed to the wash room.

The water here must have had some special qualities. It was piped from Issyk Kul, high in the Tian-Shan mountains. Icy and refreshing, it somehow acted marvellously upon me. I firmly believe it kept my strength up and fortified my waning health. After washing in it my sleepiness vanished and I felt much stronger. I even felt less hungry after drinking some of it.

The inquisition became much sharper after this event and I had patiently to bear further pressure of various kinds, insults and foul language, not allowed to sleep at all, constant threats that I would be beaten up if I continued to refuse to sign the confessions.

More and more often, I heard the terrible screams of men and women being beaten and tortured in other cells. My inquisitors would then say, 'Do you hear? That's what you'll get tomorrow if you don't confess and sign!' Every day as I went to be examined, I morally prepared myself for a beating.

One day, the inquisitor came up to me and swung back his arm, saying, 'I'll smash you in the face'. I answered him quietly, 'It's no great thing to hit a weak, defenceless woman. I'll certainly not hit back but even so, it'll come back to you.' He cursed me as vulgarly as he could and went off.

The interrogation went on for weeks on end. Often the inquisitor would make notes for hours on end, from time to time asking the same question, after which the inevitable insulting words would follow my reply. I watched him closely as he wrote and, to pass the time, used my finger nail to scratch my initials in several places on the wall.

One night the inquisitor went with me and the guard on another 'visit', stating that he had had enough of me and that I'd be finished off soon. Again we walked through long corridors until we came to a door. A whispered talk and they opened the door. I was pushed into a small room, dimly lit, with a fully armed soldier standing in the middle, his gun aimed straight at me. Apart from a small table and a large cupboard, I could see nothing else in the room. Suddenly the cupboard opened and the soldier waved me into it with his gun. Strangely enough I felt no fear but walked into the cupboard quite calmly. The door shut and for a second or two I stood there in pitch darkness before, just as suddenly, finding myself in a well furnished study with beautiful carpets on the floor and lighted electric lamps on the walls.

My inquisitor was already in this room.

A man stood at the desk dressed in a suit of excellent cut (quite in West European style), but when I looked at his face a shiver of fear passed through me. He seemed like a man who had escaped from the gallows. I had never before seen a face with such criminality engraved on it. He was exquisitely polite, offered me a cigarette from a handsome silver case, and when I refused (as a non smoker) he lit up a cigarette, and in general behaved as if I had come on a friendly visit. He asked me how I liked Alma-Ata and whether I had ever before seen such enormous ice-clad peaks. He mentioned that the climate was splendid for those with sound hearts but murderous for people whose hearts were weak. Finally, he asked me how I was getting on and how I was being treated.

In line with his friendly tone, I asked him in an equally friendly way why they did not release me so that I could enjoy that splendid climate and get a closer look at the Tian-Shan range. I also asked, by the way, why they were trying to force me to sign untrue statements and used such foul language at the questioning. After hearing me out quietly he opened the file lying on his desk. He read through the protocols of my case in silence, finally shut the file and said, 'From what I've read, it's obvious that the investigator has been too delicate with you!' After which he called me a whore and various other quite inappropriate names, none of them complimentary and all distasteful. It seemed to me that my inquisitor could have learned a thing or two from him in the domain of foul language. There is probably no other country in the world where this disgusting habit has developed such a rich vocabulary as in Russia.

When he finished his performance, he ordered that the investigation be intensified and I went out of the room as I came in, through the cupboard. I later found out that this dignitary was the chief of secret police for all Kazakhstan.

Shortly afterwards, I was again to 'visit' the Kazakhstan minister I had seen before. He had, actually, dropped into my inquisitor's room twice during the investigation. The entrance to his study likewise led through a cupboard. I wondered why they had this mania for hiding behind cupboards and could find no reasonable explanation.

The minister greeted me like an old friend. Glancing at the group of senior officers already in the room he asked about my health with the utmost solicitude and inquired whether I should like to be released from prison. He remarked, with compassion, that I wasn't looking so well as during my last visit and added that it was really all my own fault. If only I would confess to all and sign a document testifying to this. He shook his head in bewilderment that I couldn't realise this. I had only to sign a statement that such and such officers on General Anders' staff gave me orders to spy and I would immediately be sent to China by aeroplane. The frontier, after all, was only 7km away. He implored me to forego the pride that was so pathologically developed amongst us Poles. In any case, neither the Polish Embassy nor the Army Head Quarters showed any further interest in my person.

I answered that while the thought of going to China was most attractive, I would not sign such a document. This annoyed him and he began to express the most adverse opinions about Polish officers in general, quite insulting he was about them. He spoke of the abject poverty rampant in Poland, and mocked the Poles for having been so quickly defeated by the German and Russian armies in 1939. I heard out all this, red with fury and repressed indignation.

Clutching the arms of my chair tightly, I replied that they had probably not arrested me merely to make me listen to insults directed against my country and her officers. I assured him I was not qualified to judge why Poland had been so quickly over-run by the invading armies. That was a matter best left to the judgement of history. I noticed that the Russian officers sitting near the walls were listening attentively and in silence. I also had the impression that an expression of distaste would flicker across their faces from time to time and that they rather sympathised with me.

The session ended with the minister losing all control. Purple with rage he struck the desk with his fist, called in the guard and shouted, 'Take away this proud Pole – show her a looking glass. She'll talk on the other side of her face then. I'll make her pay for this.'

The investigation of my case had lasted four months when I noticed some initials had been scratched in the wall of my inquisitor's room just beside my own initials. Rather surprised, I made them out to be those of our chaplain in Aktyubinsk. I stealthily scratched a line under his initials, and now understood why the inquisitor had for some days spent less time upon me. I noticed a fresh scratch on the wall on the next day.

One day, the inquisitor politely asked me what I used for writing on when I wanted to write something and I guessed he had discovered our means of communication. I answered boldly, 'If the need arises I write on the wall'. He answered, 'Yes I've noticed that. I saw your initials on the wall so I scratched a set of initials beside them myself.' I cannot imagine why he said this since he knew as well as I did that this was untrue. We both knew that poor Father Kapusta had been arrested. The outcome was that the investigator shouted a little, threatened me with a punishment cell and that was all.

The course of this strange investigation was now amended. Its object was not only to accuse me of economic espionage but also, under paragraph 10, of criticising the Soviet authorities and expressing dissatisfaction with them. He claimed that Father Kapusta had testified in this spirit. I disbelieved this, and demanded a meeting with the priest. This was soon arranged.

I was brought into the inquisitor's room and found our chaplain already seated in my usual place. I was told to sit down at the other end of the room and neither to look at nor speak to Father Kapusta. There were two other people in the room, a junior 'investigator' and a woman who spoke Polish. In spite of the prohibition, I glanced at Father Kapusta from time to time. He was unshaven and looked ill and I could see he was very depressed. I pretended to be in better shape than I really felt so as to encourage our poor chaplain.

The questioning began and the good priest answered all the questions supposed to incriminate me with negative answers. Whatever I was accused of he took upon himself and, with this, the so-called investigation of my case approached its end. I was transferred to a general cell and thereafter summoned for further questioning at night only at ever longer intervals.

The cell I entered was light and clean. It contained about forty beds separated from one another by a small space and not all the beds were occupied. After several months in solitary confinement, I was now to meet imprisoned women for the first time. They all looked at me with curiosity, just as I looked at them. I hesitated a moment and put my things on a bed next to that of a woman who was kindly inviting me to settle down there.

The women came up to me, asked from which cell I had come and how long I had been in prison. I was told all the customs current in the cell. The prisoners were mostly charged with political offences and their cases were under investigation. The population of the cell changed continually with some women transferred to other cells while others were transported to penal camps.

Some of the women sat for hours motionless and lost in their thoughts. Others sobbed quietly, or sewed using needles made from the prongs of combs or fish bones, but the majority simply chatted with each other. It seemed that most of them had been unjustly arrested owing to the denunciations of neighbours, acquaintances or friends. It was those who had left their children without anybody to care for them who were the most depressed.

Most of the women were Russians, but there were also Uzbekians, Kirghizes, Kazakhs, Germans, Latvians and others. Here and there among the prisoners were women who had agreed, during the investigation of their case, to act as stool pigeons, to report what the other women were saying and doing in the cell. Somehow we were immediately warned and the stool pigeon identified. Not one of us believed other than that everything would somehow be cleared up and that we would return home. I was taken at night from time to time during the investigation into my case so it was only during the day that I could sleep more or less regularly and recover my strength.

The woman who had invited me to the bed beside her was named Helena. She was a pretty woman, a dramatic actress from Riga, whose father was a Pole and mother a Russian, and she spoke Polish only with difficulty. She had been arrested in Riga, shortly after its seizure by the Red Army, on the strength of a lying denunciation, and been awaiting preliminary investigation and trial for the last two years. Her health was beginning to suffer and she had lung trouble, was often feverish and had haemorrhages.

An old woman was pushed into the cell one day. Her face looked like a net of a dry leaf, wisps of grey hair protruded from her woollen cap and her too-big shoes were visible below her long skirt. She stood at the doorway holding her possessions in a basket and looking round helplessly. I went up to her, took her things and showed her to a free bed next to mine. She threw her cap and scarf on it, her hair scattered in all directions. She said: 'They were so pressing that I had no time to comb my hair'. She could not find a comb in her basket. So I took mine and soon two fine plaits encircled her head.

Anastasia Petrovna was one of the first few women allowed to study at universities under the Tsars and had duly graduated with a degree. She had a gift of the gab and often women gathered around her to listen to her stories.

The first time she was taken to Alma Ata was in 1908, when she was charged with being a revolutionary. But this town was then called Verniy and while working as a geologist she experienced a severe earthquake and a flood in 1910. The Issyk

Kul lake, high up in Tian-Shan Mountains, burst its banks during the earthquake and flooded most of the town, covering it with boulders and stones. Many people perished but, when the waters fell, the townsfolk returned. All of them worked hard to drain the water and break up the enormous rocks with dynamite. After this the whole town had to be rebuilt. She told me that Alma Ata is a beautiful town, located 900m above sea level and close to the highest peak in the mountains, which used to be called Tian Shan but is now called Stalin Peak, and is over 7000 metres above sea level. The mountain ranges here are young and there are frequent earthquakes as a result. There were, by the way, two slight earthquakes while I was in this prison.

When her period of exile ended she returned to Central Russia and lived through the 1918 revolution. Thereafter she concentrated on her speciality and kept away from political matters. Maybe this had been the reason that she was swept up during the Great Purge of 1937 and exiled to the same place as in 1908, the only difference being that it had been re-named, was now called Alma-Ata and had a meteorological station where she had worked up to the time of her arrest. She could not imagine why she had been arrested, and did not even try to guess. She said she was so old that every day of survival was a gift from God anyhow. If not resting on her bed, she would walk about the cell reciting beautiful poems by Pushkin, Lermontov, and others. Other prisoners would listen to her in silence. She was not called for interrogations at all and after three weeks an officer in charge took her with her belongings. After her leaving, both Helena and I felt really useless. During those three weeks I had combed Anastasia's hair, poured water for her hand-washing and brought her meals. Those acts had given me the feeling of, and the satisfaction of, being needed.

I found the life of inaction very tiring. I was walking up and down the cell in rather a helpless fashion one day when I noticed the besom standing in a corner of the room. It was made of stiff twigs so I pulled two straight ones out and smoothed them with a piece of glass which I had borrowed from one of the prisoners, unravelled some old sweaters and began to teach the women to knit. Everybody livened up wonderfully and the besom simply dissolved as a result.

The warders at first kept on taking away our 'knitting needles', but we filed a solemn protest with the governor of the prison, we could harm nobody with these twigs. He ordered that they be returned to us. We also began to make sewing needles from fish bones and the teeth of my American comb. Half of it was sacrificed for this purpose. We secured thread by unravelling the upper part of our stockings and could hence now repair our clothes. The warder would watch us through the Judas but left us to our own devices.

In between his observations I would often climb to the window and look through the bars while I wandered freely in my thoughts among the sunlit ice covered peaks of Tian Shan. The air was so clear that they seemed quite close, close enough to be touched . . . and, how I wanted to get out from behind those iron bars.

One day, a young Gypsy woman was brought to our cell. It appeared that she had gone mad when her baby had been taken away from her while she was still suckling it. She would sit on her bed, all day long, with her arms cradled as if rocking her lost child. She would sing a lullaby, always the same one, monotonously at first and then louder and louder until she was shrieking. She would stop for a moment before beginning again, and repeat time after time. Sometimes she got off her bed, clambered to the window and, clutching the bars, cursed all the commandants and guards of the secret police, after which she jumped down, ran to the table and threw the clay bowls and mugs at us with the desperate fury of madness.

We collected the earthenware which had survived and hid it in our beds, but she would pull the various items out. From time to time she smeared her face and hair with excrement, and then sat down in the middle of the cell to sing her lost baby to sleep. The warders came in and dragged her away to the bathroom but after a few days she would come back, only to start all over again. Life in the cell was really very difficult with her. We had to watch her all the time, taking it in turns at night. One day, she fell into a fit of raving madness, upturned all the beds, and threw all she could at us. We began to shout for help and made such an uproar it was heard throughout the whole prison. The governor came within a few minutes with double guards and she now directed her mad fury at them, throwing everything moveable until they finally put her into a straitjacket and took her away.

We heaved a sigh of relief, thinking she would not return to our cell but, within an hour, she was brought back on a stretcher fast asleep. We protested, demanding that she be transferred to another cell, but in vain. We decided to go on hunger strike to clinch our protest, refusing to accept our bread ration for breakfast, supper and dinner. The prison authorities tried to persuade us by shouting and uttering blood curdling threats. Most of the inmates of the cell gave in on the next day under the influence of these threats and of hunger.

The governor called us in one by one to find out who had suggested the hunger strike, two soldiers taking each delinquent by the arm and running her down the corridor to the governor's room. For some reason or other he suspected Helena of being the ringleader. When I appeared before him, out of breath, he at once began to shower me with a flood of foul abuse. Shaking with fury he asked who had told me to refuse food. I answered that it was merely the disordered state of our nerves which had forced us to do so after the attacks of that mad woman. He replied, with even greater fury, that when anybody's nerves got the better of them they ought to take a dose of laxative and clear their bowels, although his language was couched in rather more vulgar terms.

His advice seemed so funny to me that I burst out laughing and rather thoughtlessly told him he must have forgotten to apply this means before receiving me. He seized his blotting rocker and threw it at my head. I ducked and it missed me. He called the soldiers and ordered them to get me back to the cell without any nonsense. They held my arms tight and we ran off through the corridor at top speed. The sole of one of my shoes came loose and I tripped, but they still ran on, dragging me with them until I found myself sitting on the floor of my cell, not quite certain whether to laugh or to cry. My shoulder joints certainly ached badly.

Helena was taken out of the cell last of all, and she never returned. I was very worried about her for a stay in the punishment cell would certainly be most harmful to her health, already badly impaired.

Three days later I was called into the corridor and told to take my things with me. With four guards surrounding me, I walked to another building where a long queue of prisoners stood at the door of the 'left luggage' store. As I waited the queue became longer and longer.

Most of the prisoners were men between the ages of twenty and fifty. They all looked very haggard, with earthy complexions. Their clothes were creased and crumpled. Some had tattered military greatcoats. Their clothes bore not a single button and, as they had no belts, each of the prisoners held up his trousers with one hand. I found out that the prisoners were given back their personal property here and a supply of food theoretically sufficient for the journey to a concentration camp. The routes taken by the prisoners to the place of their incarceration are known as 'stages' in the Soviet Union.

I joined a group of women, who stood on one side waiting their turn. I found the women's clothes were in better shape than the men's. They all looked at me inquisitively and at once guessed I was from another country. They asked me where I came from. A pretty, young girl with dark curly hair came up and asked whether I had met her sister, Lila, in my cell. As it happened, I had, and she had told me that her sister Galina was also in the same prison. So introduced, Galina and I stayed together during the whole journey.

I noticed Father Kapusta among the group of men and immediately went up to him. He was as overjoyed as I and quickly told me what had happened with my daughter and about his arrest.

He told me that my daughter had behaved most gallantly after my arrest. She went to the secret police headquarters every day and demanded to be allowed to visit me. She often brought food parcels and these would be accepted by the prison authorities for delivery, even when I was no longer in Aktyubinsk.

The Polish Embassy found out about my daughter two months later and sent her to Iran together with a party of other children. My son was already in Iran where he was attending the Polish Army cadet school. I cannot describe how glad I was to hear that both my children were safely out of the Soviet Union.

This knowledge was of infinite use to me in later times, when I was going through a very difficult period in my life. It appeared that the good priest was arrested at the beginning of August just as the Polish Army under General Anders was leaving the Soviet Union on its way to Iran. In fact, Father Kapusta was already on board ship in Kazakhstan when he was summoned to the secret police headquarters ostensibly to settle some final formalities. Quite unsuspecting, he went there and was arrested. The ship left with all his things while he was sent to Alma-Ata where he was questioned in connection with my case.

It was already very late when we were led out of the prison. Heavily escorted by armed soldiers we trudged through the streets of Alma-Ata. These were illuminated, and here and there were lighted windows in the houses. Passers-by looked at us with curiosity and hastened on. I walked beside Galina who looked around at the streets and squares of her native town with profound emotion and, once, burst into tears as she pointed to her home, with lit up windows, in the middle of a garden.

We joined an even larger group of prisoners from other prisons in and around Alma-Ata when we reached the station, soon finding out that most were criminals. All of us were ordered to sit down on the ground between the tracks and we were warned that anyone changing his or her position would be shot.

There we sat, well over a thousand of us at least, enfeebled by long lack of exercise and fresh air and quite tired out. It was a cold night and many of the prisoners were in light summer clothes and felt the cold very bitterly as they sat on the bare earth. We squeezed together more tightly and tried to warm ourselves up a little as we waited through the night. Finally a special train with barred windows appeared. We entered the wagons, some of which were reserved specially for us women, and found ourselves packed as tightly as herrings in a barrel. Apart from the benches there were wide shelves at either end. So, we set off for Karabas by a very roundabout route, via Semipalatinsk, Novosibirsk, Omsk, and Petropavlovsk.

The route followed by prisoners on their way from one prison to another or from one concentration camp to another in the Soviet Union is called an *etap*, a stage. These routes are often thousands of miles long and it can be safely said that, used as they are by millions of political prisoners in that country, they constitute the most shameful feature of present day humanity.

Incarcerated in trains with barred windows or in sealed cattle wagons, unbelievably over-crowded, the prisoners spent whole weeks, even months at a time, under well-nigh incredible conditions of squalor and heartless treatment. Unwashed, deprived of normal sleep and exercise, we were half starved and parched with thirst. All that each prisoner received per day was a spoonful of sugar, a pound of black bread and a piece of dried, over-salted fish, the latter increasing the suffering caused by thirst enormously.

We all felt the lack of water to such an extent that it seemed every cell in our bodies cried out for water, but all we received was a small mugful once in two days. It often happened that prisoners would suffer diarrhoea on the way. We were admitted to the toilet twice a day only, otherwise physiological needs had to be satisfied within the compartment. The lack of fresh air, the lice and bugs, the heavy fumes of the lowest grade of tobacco (*machorka*, it is called), the general nervous atmosphere – all these combined to make these over-crowded little cages an inferno beside which Dante's Hell could well have seemed like paradise.

To make matters worse, the political prisoners were mixed up with the criminal prisoners, hardened habitual offenders of the worst and most savage type. Wherever they out-numbered the political prisoners they did just as they pleased with them. They were not only stronger and more ruthless, but were privileged by the authorities.

Political prisoners invariably received the worst treatment. If some non-criminal prisoner wore passable clothes, these would be torn off them, his boots or shoes likewise, and some rags thrown him in exchange. Sometimes such a prisoner received nothing at all in exchange. He would then have to endure the journey clad in nothing but his shirt and pants.

From time to time, our group would alight at some large station where there were transit points for prisoners. Here we would be segregated for delivery to various prisons or camps and sent there with a new group two or three days later. The regulations at these points were much less strict than in prison. The cells were kept open during the day. We could go out into the courtyard and fetch our own food, which was more abundant and of better quality.

Though each transit point had its baths and de-lousing centres, we could never rid ourselves of lice during the whole journey. Things were invariably very lively in these transit points, with much noise and shouting, crowds of prisoners arriving and departing and a constant background of juicy curses and a goodly crop of real and of untrue news from the outside world.

As can be imagined, such a journey soon enfeebled the prisoners and they arrived at their final destination extremely exhausted. Once after travelling a whole week, we alighted at a large transit point. We were told to march off to the prison some miles away outside the town and off we trudged through the howling wind and sleet, up to our knees in mud. We were very tired and wet through when we at length reached the prison, a hoary and damp edifice. The guards treated us with furious shouts and curses as they drove us off to the baths like a herd of animals.

We washed but had to put on our wet clothes and only then were admitted to the general cell. It was more crowded than anything else we had seen and the stench was overpowering. Not only were the bunks crammed with prisoners but every inch of floor space was occupied by women and bundles. I still do not know how we managed to push in and occupy a place near the door and the latrine bucket.

Beside our cell there was one specially reserved for nursing mothers arrested with their babes in their arms. Although I had seen so many terrible things in the Soviet Union I was deeply shocked to hear, within these damp walls, amidst this stench made still fouler by vile curses and epithets, the pure and innocent crying of infants. I visited the 'mothers' cell' the next day and stood astounded at the threshold. I looked and could not believe. It contained some forty women who sat on their pallets in the murk of the cell, breast feeding their little ones. A profound sadness overcame me, and a still deeper shame.

A lorry drove into the prison courtyard on the next day and

deposited a squad of fully armed soldiers and some hospital nurses in their white smocks. Quite a panic broke out amongst the women in the prison. The rumour at once spread that some kind of special injection was to be tried out on us.

The group of mothers, who had been standing just outside their cell, turned pale and swiftly ran to their babies. Some of the soldiers surrounded the prison block while the rest entered with the nurse and went to the 'mothers cell'. Frightful screams were heard immediately after. The soldiers were tearing the babies away from their mothers. The poor women raved in despair. Some fought the guards, broke up the furniture and began to belabour the warders and soldiers. Others hugged their children and screamed frantically. The cries of frightened children added to the horror.

At length the babies were taken away and some of the mothers tied up in straitjackets. In the neighbouring cell we shivered with anger and felt as one with the poor mothers in their pain and sorrow. Not one of us slept throughout that night, if only because the bereaved mothers were still screaming, even howling like heartbroken animals. The secret police came the next day and split them up, sending each mother to a different destination.

Galina and I were heartily glad when we left this hell two days later for another hell, although the way became harder day by day, worse and worse . . . and still worse. One afternoon, to our great joy, we stopped at a small station. It was the transit centre in the Karaganda prison camp, the Karabas theme in many a ballad sung by the criminals of the bandit type.

CHAPTER 7
Karabas

We left the train as the sun was beaming its last rays over a number of long, low huts with wooden watch-towers at regular intervals. Beyond the watch-towers we could see a range of hills covered with eroded cliffs and stones bearing traces of snow. The sun set soon after at the place where heaven and earth meet, and the scattered rays from behind the horizon bathed the whole district, together with us, in a reddish-yellow dusk which made the scene still more melancholy and severe.

Looking at this landscape and at the crowds of emaciated prisoners standing alongside the train with their bundles and bags, I suddenly felt I had seen all this before. As I racked my memory it all came back. This was the scene which I had dreamt during the first days of my stay in the prison at Alma-Ata, and I noted how I had dreamt every detail of what I now saw in reality.

We were formed up in ranks. The leading authorities of Karabas came up with guards and first aid men bearing stretchers. The last named went up to the wagons and bore off the corpses and those unable to walk. This was the normal procedure at every transit centre. We were then counted and receipted for, after which we were taken to the baths.

These were in a large hall, where we found quite a number of women already undressed, so we took off our clothes and tied them up in bundles so that they could be disinfected and de-loused. We had to hand everything in, even our towels. This worried me because my fur coat had been invaluable through both days and nights and I had so far managed to preserve it from disinfection. The hot air of the disinfection plant often caused clothing to rot away and fall apart. It often seemed that this destructive process was conducted purposely, to lower the morale and well-being of the prisoners, and to bring them down to the lowest common denominator of rags as soon as possible.

It was very stuffy in the bath hall, and very crowded. The acrid smell of long-unwashed bodies, exhaustion caused by the journey and under-nourishment caused many women to faint. We prisoners gave first aid ourselves, and then nursing sisters would come and dose out some drops to revive the sufferers. Some of the newcomers were assigned to the local hospital after they had finished their ablutions.

As we stood there, naked and crowded together, the doors opened and a number of men walked in. They were warmly dressed in new jerkins, high felt boots and large fur caps, and looked solid and well fed. These were various commandants, from the various prison camps, and they examined us with lewd looks. The prostitutes engaged them in conversation and both sides made various proposals to each other without being too choosy about the sort of language they used. I did not know what all of this meant until much later I got to know that they were choosing new 'goods' for their camps.

We political prisoners bunched together in a corner and passed sarcastic remarks about the behaviour of the others. After a long wait two men came into the hall. They wore the smocks worn by the medical personnel and behaved discreetly and politely. This was the 'sanitary inspector' and his assistant. The inspector was aged about fifty and he began to read out our names. He divided the women into groups whilst his assistant led each one to another hall where he allotted the water ration.

When the inspector read my name and I replied, he at once

broke off and walked up to me. He then asked me in Polish whether I was the wife of forestry engineer Muskus. I was very surprised and, of course, told him I was. He then told me that he had met my husband before the war when both of them had been expert witnesses in some agrarian and forestry court cases. There I stood in front of him, quite naked, confused and very ashamed. All I had was a small handkerchief, and I did not know where to keep it or what to cover with it, the upper part or the lower part. He noticed my confusion and said, 'Just think to yourself that I'm a doctor. You'll have much worse things to bear in a prison camp. I want to help you and after the baths are over I'll wait for you at the door'.

I whispered, 'My fur . . .' 'Right,' he answered, 'I'll see that it avoids disinfection.'

After the bath, sure enough, he was waiting for me at the door. He whispered something to the duty attendant and led me to a small house located by the bath building. When I entered I was dazzled by the sight of a splendidly laid table. A large bowl of potatoes, bread and margarine and tea made a totally unexpected banquet. I was more than hungry and my appetite would have made me eat everything, but I knew that after some months of under-nourishment my stomach would not bear a heavy meal so I ate slowly and cautiously.

He told me how he had met my husband and all about himself. He was a Polish Jew, and the owner of a country estate near Stanislawow in Poland. He was arrested immediately after the Red Army invaded the country in 1939 and incarcerated in a prison camp without any trial, and only after some time was informed that he had been sentenced to ten years hard labour in a NKVD prison camp. In spite of the 'amnesty' for Polish citizens issued in 1941 he was not released.

Lawlessly kept a prisoner, he had managed to get transferred from hard labour some months before my arrival to the post of 'sanitary inspector' with the duty of keeping the transit point clean. He had established some contacts with the local authorities and felt that his life was now relatively bearable.

After giving me much valuable information and advice regarding life in this camp, he promised he would try to arrange for me, Galina and the Reverend Father to stay as long as possible and recover our strength. None of the transient prisoners were forced to work here, whilst really hard labour awaited us in the concentration camp. He also said he would do his best to have all three of us allotted to the same penal settlement when the time came for us to go.

I looked at all the food on the table and thought how nice it would be if I took a little for Galina, but I could be searched on entering the barrack and then not only I but also the gentle 'sanitary inspector' would get into serious trouble. So I bade leave of him, very much fortified by the meal and by his kindness and humanity. It was rather a comedown when one of the guards at the control point to the prisoners' huts looked at me with disdain and loudly exclaimed, 'Just look at her! Barely into the camp and she's already found herself a lover!'

I entered the hut and found it frightfully dirty and overcrowded, the usual thing at the transit points. Galina had prepared a place for me on the ground by her side and now listened with keen interest to my report on this unexpected encounter.

Some of the women were sent off in the morning to their penal settlements, and we occupied their places on the bunks, but it was real torture to sleep on them. Thousands and thousands of bugs crawled from their crannies when the light went out and feasted on our blood.

I began to study the conditions of life in Karabas and two weeks passed as I continued to observe this strange way of life.

Karabas was really like a large slave centre. Thousands of captives passed through it every day, prisoners from the far north, frightfully exhausted by hard labour in the mines or forests of Siberia, and now discarded as no longer capable of sustained physical effort, arrived crammed in cattle trucks. Many died on the way or were dying when they reached Karabas. Work in the Karaganda penal camps was mostly agricultural. The convicts had to develop virgin land for the cultivation of crops or the raising of livestock.

Some of the prisoners managed to recover their strength while engaged on this type of work. They would then be sent back to the mines. The commandants of camps in the vicinity came here to select convicts. They first chose those with special qualifications. The others would be lined up and the commandants then walked along the ranks picking up the strongest and healthiest to whom a doctor would immediately allot a labour category. No commandant wanted to take the weak or those advanced in years. These were called *barhor* . . . rubbish. The Karabas commandant, did not want the *barhor* left on his hands. Prolonged bargaining, bickering, even impassioned disputes were necessary before an acceptable arrangement could be made.

The selected prisoners were then taken to a special encampment where they were well fed, given fresh clothing and, most important, footwear. Winter was just setting in, and no convoy commandant would accept the responsibility for delivering poorly clad prisoners who might freeze to death on the way and thus impair his reputation for efficiency. Considerations of humanity played no part here at all. *Valenki*, felt boots, were necessary but in very short supply, and some prisoners got only large galoshes and rags to wrap round their feet. Such were the elements of the bargaining among the camp commandants.

Among the prisoners there was also lively trading, but of a different nature. They bargained from morning to night. Money and gold had no value. The chief unit of exchange was the *pika* (one ration of bread weighing about 500 grams) but tobacco ran a close second. Almost all our modest needs could be satisfied by such barter: needles, thread, buttons, a piece of string, half a safety razor blade, a small knife, an empty tin can, a broken spoon and such typical luxuries. We could then mend our clothes or improve them, even transform light clothing into winter wear. I made a very advantageous exchange once. My silk blouse and three *pika* for a length of colourful home-spun wool matting from which I made something like a skiing suit. It was a great convenience to wear trousers instead of a skirt and this suit served me well for four years.

Every transaction was carried out to the letter. The goods and the price in bread or tobacco were always delivered faithfully. One's bread ration was absolutely inviolate, protected by an unwritten law respected by all, even, with very few exceptions, by the dishonest and lawless. Anyone caught stealing a bread ration was beaten to death, and even his best friend would not try to defend him.

The prisoners were clad fantastically, mostly in the tattered remnants of clothing of many hues, from Asian to European . . . the latter somehow appearing most ridiculous in our circumstances. Prisoners with many years penal servitude behind them were issued with a quilted jacket and trousers, invariably dirty, creased and torn.

There was a babel of languages in Karabas. Every language spoken in the Soviet Union and the neighbouring countries was represented, as well as many a language from other parts of the world. There was a colourful mosaic of nationalities, women of so many countries, proud Georgians, quick-witted Greeks, Jewesses, Azerbaijanis and Chechens thirsting for revenge, thick-set Turkmen, smart Uzbekians, Lezgins, Afghans, kind-hearted Kazakhs, talkative Tartars and taciturn Yakuts, quiet, modest Chinese and Japanese women, and lovely Korean girls, fair-haired Estonians, Finns, Latvians and most distrustful Lithuanians, industrious German and Ukrainian women, courteous Austrians, Bulgarians, gallant Hungarians and courageous Poles, three Americans, one French woman and a Swede. There were also thousands and thousands of sincerely good Russian women.

The convicts could at once easily be distinguished as belonging to two distinct categories. Some were quiet, badly dressed and as if terrified by all around them. These were the political prisoners. Others were sure of themselves, ready to laugh and shout, to dance and sing. These were the 'bandits', the worst habitual criminals in the Soviet Union. I had never before encountered them in such enormous numbers.

They constituted a strange, quite different world. They seized the best places in the barracks, elbowed their way to the food vats (queues meant nothing to them), wore better clothes, spoke their thieves' cant, sang their own songs and respected their own code of conduct. They obeyed no outside orders and did as they pleased. The camp authorities often feared them and turned a blind eye.

It was immediately evident that they felt quite at home in a penal camp and that they fended very well for themselves. They would often exclaim with satisfaction, 'Now we're really at home!' Just as we political prisoners tried to keep together, occupying bunks next to each other, so did the criminal element. Full of vitality, they were also the most temperamental. Immediately after some furious quarrel, the participants would sit down at a common bowl as if the best of friends, merry-making and ready to share their last crust of bread with each other.

The range of age was enormous: from eleven year olds to sexagenarians. Some were pretty while others were as ugly as sin, but all were vulgar, quite shameless and invariably foulmouthed, with a predilection for sexual epithets. Endowed with a sense of humour, most of them were cunning and quick to size up every situation. Their crimes were larceny, murder, armed robberies, and many of them were prostitutes.

This criminal world was ruled by one or two experienced habitual criminals, famed for their exploits in banditry and whose orders were implicitly obeyed. They stole nothing themselves while in the camp, but all the loot of the minor thieves was at their absolute disposal, to be handed over to whomsoever they saw fit. Carefully made up and immaculately dressed, they sat on their bunks as they chain-smoked or played the guitar and sang to the sycophantic delight of their retinue.

They never fetched their own food. One of the younger criminals served them in this, and always brought them double rations. Contacts between this criminal world and the camp authorities were maintained solely through these ringleaders. Where this criminal element constituted a majority of the prisoners in a given barrack or hut, the warders never entered alone. Two or three of them would come in together with drawn revolvers. Even so, many a guard was beaten up by them.

When dissatisfied for some reason or other they would lie in ambush on the upper bunks near the door and swoop down on a guard. A rug would be thrown over his head, his revolver would be taken away and the women would give him a sound thrashing. They cared not that punishment would follow with transfers to severe isolation zones or camps. The salient point had been gained, mainly, that they enforced their predominance over the whole penal settlement and made it clear that the camp authorities should not show too much zeal if they wished to avoid the need to make humiliating reports and lose prestige.

The penal zone was divided by several barbed wire fences into two parts, one for men and one for women. These barriers did not hinder visits from either side, it being understood that the criminal element was the only active one in this domain. Whatever was stolen in one zone was immediately smuggled through to the other and prostitution was practiced at all times of the day and night.

Whenever the strains of a concertina or mandolin came from the men's zone, the women criminals would very soon slip through the fences, and then dancing, shouts, and songs would begin. They danced with great *elan*, to the rhythm of song, hand-clapping or musical instruments. The folk dances of every nationality in the Soviet Union were those usually performed though they always adapted these to the customs of their underground world, but they also had their special bandit dances, solo or duo. These dramatised their life, occupations and hazards, all that was low, vulgar and earthbound.

From time to time some of the younger ones would beg older criminals of either sex to execute a dance so that traditional forms might be preserved. They would dance with such power of expression that the onlooker would watch with bated breath, personally experiencing it all: the laying of plans, stealing up to the victim, the attack, robbery and murder, escape, the thieves' den, their joy and drunken orgies. As I stood at the fence and watched these dances, I felt frightened and sullied.

While at Karabas, the arrival of an enormous contingent of Chechen prisoners made the greatest impression. I asked one of them why so many had been brought to the penal camp. She told me that the whole Chechen nation apart from the elderly had been deported from their country in the Caucasus, having been collectively accused of greeting the Germans with enthusiasm and attempted collaboration.

The men were either executed at once or sent to penal camps. The women and children were to be sent as 'free exiles' to Kazakhstan. Five thousand of them were entrained at Grozny and transported under frightful conditions of hunger and cold. Small wonder that they arrived in very bad shape. Many corpses were carried out of the wagons and still more were taken straight to hospital as dangerously ill. Only 2000 of them had managed to reach Karabas. We were all very depressed by the fate of these newcomers. I met one of them some years later and he told me that only a hundred and fifty of his companions were still alive.

The Chechen women were very good looking with black hair and large blue eyes. They all wore their colourful national attire. The men were all slim and well dressed. Both men and women bore themselves with pride and were quick to take offence. They kept together, hated the Russians and made no secret of this. The camp authorities treated them with the utmost brutality, and in many cases killed them on the spot for even the slightest infringement of orders.

The bunkhouse became more and more crowded. Though groups of women left every day for the penal camps, their place was immediately taken by new arrivals. Nearly all the women had been sentenced on the basis of some 'political' charge and, being arrested for the first time in their lives, were terrified by the conditions into which they had been plunged.

They were on the whole perfectly loyal Soviet citizens who had been too busy with their work to engage in any political activities, and they came from every social and intellectual level. The enormous majority were guilty of having uttered some thoughtless remark 'harmful' to the state. Such remarks as, 'I didn't get any bread today and the children will be hungry', or 'When will all these queues end?' and so on.

Some had been arrested because they had been abroad, nearly always having been ordered to do so by the authorities, or because they had a relative in America or somewhere else abroad and had received a letter from a foreign country. They would be kept for some weeks in the local prison and then, without any trial, sent off in groups to the penal camps where their sentence (issued in their absence), of from eight to ten years hard labour, would be read to them.

As long as they were in prison, it never occurred to them that they could be sentenced for nothing or a mere nothing. They would be sure it was all a misunderstanding which would soon be cleared up and they could then return home. Unfortunately, once they got to the transit point on their way to a penal camp, they had passed the point of no return and there could be no appeal. Every one of them had to face ten years of separation from their dearest ones, ten years of hard labour, under-nourishment and brutal treatment.

They were in despair at the thought that their children had been left without anyone to care for them whilst their husbands, brothers, fathers and sons were either also arrested or shedding their blood in defence of the country. They often complained that, instead of providing their men with moral support and bringing up their children, they had to labour in the penal camps and work for nothing. Nearly all of them ceased to menstruate as a result of their shocking experiences.

For a long time after their arrest they would talk and think of their homes constantly. 'They've still the flavour of home', the veteran prisoners would say of them.

Engaged in all these conversations, we found the day passed quickly. We all, without exception, had passed through tremendous shocks and experiences. Disquiet, separation and sadness, longing for our children and homes, fear for their fate and the terrors of yet unknown penal camps filled our hearts.

I listened to the narratives of the Soviet women with pity and with interest. It was now three years since I had been torn away from normal life and plunged into this abyss of the unknown. I kept myself under better control now and tried to comfort my fellow sufferers with heartening words, but every sigh pressed down upon me heavily and every tear scalded my heart. I could actually feel the pain within me, the pain of all the imprisoned mothers and wives.

What of it that the women came and went? The emotions experienced remained the same and sadness permeated my whole being ever more deeply. I could not weep and I felt that tears could not wash this away. I sought something else to overcome this sadness, to bring in at least a little light amidst the gloom.

Galina, too, became sadder and sadder. She was suffering greatly for she had left at home her ten year old foster daughter, whom she loved as if she were her own child. Her husband had stayed at home but could not help her. Lying side by side in our bunks one evening, she told me the story of her arrest.

Her husband was a senior official in Kazakhstan. She had graduated from a course of economic studies and worked in an office and she was a most loyal citizen of the Soviet Union, but a malicious neighbour wrote a denunciation (in which she was falsely accused) to the NKVD.

The agents of the secret police made a search of her belongings and found a Japanese dressing gown amongst them. This sufficed for the NKVD to arrest Galina and her sister Lila, and to accuse them of espionage in favour of China. As a matter of fact, she had bought the dressing gown some years before, quite legally, but it was obviously difficult for her to indicate who the seller had been.

Like Galina, I could not make out the connection between a Japanese garment and spying for China. Alma-Ata is of course only seven miles or so from Tian Shan as the crow flies, but Japan is much farther away. It was all very confusing, but that is how the Soviet secret police works.

Galina had lived happily with her husband but during questioning by the NKVD she was shown a statement signed by him which read, 'As you are an enemy of the people, I renounce you and on this basis have been granted a divorce'. This was a great blow for her, but she did not blame him. Instead she insisted that this was the only way for him to retain his post.

Finally our rest house stay came to an end. Galina and I were summoned and told to leave the zone with our belongings. We were then put into the group of prisoners posted to another camp without any explanation. My friend sent me a piece of bread for the journey and thus kept his promise. I noticed Fr. Kapusta, my friend, amidst the men in the same group which consisted of over two hundred men and about thirty women, both political and criminal prisoners.

Formalities concluded, guards marched up with their weapons aimed at us, and the commandant read out the order, including the warning that anyone leaving the lines of the convoy and trying to escape would be immediately shot. The order to march was given, we moved off and soon colourful and unquiet Karabas disappeared from sight. The ranks of the prisoners soon fell into disorder. Everyone marched as he or she wanted and chose his own company. We were careful only not to stumble out beyond the lines of the convoy. A line of sleighs drawn by oxen followed us, bearing our bundles and supplies for the penal settlement that was to be our destination. That is how I went amidst the motley crowd towards the unknown life of a NKVD forced labour camp, absolutely unaware of my fate for the next 14 years.

Such convoys of prisoners routed through transit points and camps consist of a mixed batch drawn from various prisons and penal camps. The prisoners therefore do not know one another as a general rule, but whether the journey is on foot or by rail, a bond of common feeling and liking quickly appears. There is then a tendency for pairs or even small groups to keep together in companionship.

I was walking with Galina, Father Kapusta, and a professor of Economics from Kiev University when a young Russian joined us. After a brief talk we trusted each other and held together as a group. The professor was 60 years old and sentenced for ten years of labour camp, because he had prepared "without enthusiasm" some statistics, which in this country were specially fabricated, and the young man wrote poetry 'without the spirit of the Communism Age'. He could rest assured he had 10 years of hard work ahead of him as well.

Telling our stories and commenting on fresh news about an amnesty (we, new prisoners, had no idea that the authorities skewed news regularly) we entered deeper into the steppe area. Although it was the second half of December the onset of winter was exceptionally mild. The steppe was covered with a slight layer of snow through which patches of dark earth could still be seen.

I had rested at Karabas and thanks to an additional ration of bread, which my acquaintance had passed to me from time to time, I felt much stronger, walked briskly and even happily. After a month with limited opportunities to move I could enjoy the open space in front of me with hope in my heart. My investigation had been ended with no evidence found of my guilt. Due to international agreements, Polish authorities may have begun to intervene in my case and Father Kapusta's.

I shared my thoughts with my new friends. They listened to me patiently and said: 'You do not know our authorities and that is why you still have so much enthusiasm. They do not respect their own law, and you expect them to consider other countries'? They promise, but they do not keep their word – their strategy is based on falsehood. Don't you know the NKVD phrase: the way to us is wide, but from us really narrow.' The priest also did not share my optimism, walking in sadness and low spirits. Galina was totally terrified.

Around 2pm our leader gave the signal for a break. We sat down on the snow and took bags off our shoulders. Smokers smoked and non-smokers ate their bread and dried fish with appetite. In the distance we could make out certain shapes, which later turned out to be watchtowers above a camp.

We continued after a while, but now we walked much slower than before. Galina's legs became swollen and she was permitted to sit on carts from time to time. In the evening all talk ceased and everyone walked absorbed in his own thoughts.

Orion was high as we came to the outskirts of a settlement. They expected us. One of the warders led us to an old shed. Soon they set up a field kitchen and we were given hot water with some groat traces and locked in straight after 'the meal'. We lay down on straw side by side, fatigued, in intense cold – but for the first time in a few months there were no bugs.

On the second day the weather changed. Around noon severe wind started to bite our faces and hands. We took out all our clothes from the bags and helped each other to cover up. Father Kapusta had nothing apart from a light officer's uniform, not even a hat. I gave him my blanket. My pyjamas' trousers served as a wrap for my head and a blouse was given to the young poet. Galina took out a kerchief to cover the professor's head. In silence we moved as shadows. That day we did not eat anything apart from 500 grams of bread and some snow.

At last tired, hungry and in darkness we reached the barbed wires of a bunkhouse. Listening to foul cursing for being late we were urged inside. The bunkhouse was narrow and long. Bunks, made from bare planks, stood on both sides. On the very end, several women were sleeping with a little oil lamp lit. They got up quickly when they heard us and invited us closer. They were intimidated and helpless – they could not say anything about this camp, because they had been brought there two days before. Amongst them a few bandit molls appeared and happily jumped down from their beds to greet their comrades.

In the next minutes local authorities showed up to count us and to see what sort of 'goods' had been sent to them. Our demands for hot food were refused with the words: 'You will not die before morning, tonight you have not been allotted rations of food and fuel.'

The oil lamp darkened, the bunks were damp and cold – we lay down with all our clothes on but, despite exhaustion, none of us fell asleep that night.

CHAPTER 8
Shakhan

A gong stroke: The bunkhouse was still dark. The door opened and a sharp voice assailed our ears: 'Get up, bitches!'

We got up, gradually recognising the shapes of the bunkhouse and its contents. In the corner there was a barrel of water. Each of us who had a bowl took some outside and tried to wash her face and hands – and later passed the bowl to those who did not have their own.

It was dawn. We lined up in a rank outside. Warders began the assembly rituals – counting and calling out names. We had to answer by our first name and the name of our father. Soon a breakfast of sorts would be given out. When I looked around I saw that our bunkhouse was in a closed zone with warders and watchdogs around the wired fences. On one side of the bunkhouse there was female accommodation and on the opposite male, and a kitchen.

A gong stroke: thirty women received seven bowls. There were no spoons at all – so we had to wait for others to finish their portion of stinky soup made from old fish and a few groats. I became convinced what a good deal I had done by starving for three days in order to buy a bowl and a spoon.

A gong stroke: the *urbe* (a trusted prisoner allotting other prisoners work) with warders came into the bunkhouse shouting, 'Everybody out!' Outside our zone there was a kind of 'work market', where prisoners were distributed to particular jobs. There were not a lot of us women and, apart from criminals, it was our first time in a labour camp. The *Urbe* lined us up to one side and, cursing, moved on to a large group of men encircled by warders with dogs. Most of the men were emaciated and badly dressed. They were mainly from the Kazakh nations.

Soon a commandant and a chief came and started a roll call. Those with bare feet or half naked were sent back to bunk-houses, those dressed only a bit better were divided between brigades and sent to the steppe to work. Then the whole entourage of officials (about 14 people) approached our group. The chief looked closely at every face and standing in front of me asked: 'Who are you?' maybe because I was dressed a bit differently from the others.

I replied: 'I am Polish.' A moment later he said, 'A Polish lady', and his entourage burst out laughing.

Some women, who had been here longer than us went to work and we, having arrived only the night before, returned to our zone.

A gong stroke: In the bunkhouse it was cold, in the morning we had not got bread. Galina sat on her bunk and cried, I put on all the clothes that I had and walked to and fro. Bandit molls were sitting on the upper beds, smoking, talking lively, and hunting lice. I asked them why one of the women, Zoyka had gone to work when she had not had to. They answered joyfully: 'Do not you know, Auntie? She wanted to see her boyfriend. She came here from Karabas to see him.'

I could not understand anything, but had an impression that the bandit molls felt as confident here as in their own homes. The hours went past slowly for me.

A gong stroke: Dinnertime. The bunkhouses were opened and brigades working near the camp returned to the settlement. Those who had their own bowls queued first and received a bowl of soup and a spoon of fatless groats.

Shakhan proper was a collection of about twenty dilapidated, rickety clay huts, with 'windows' stuffed with rags or straw, an eyesore against the white expanse of snow.

Our bunk house stood apart from this hamlet and was

surrounded by double lines of barbed wire fence patrolled by guards with dogs. This was one of the punishment types of penal settlements since it housed the worst types of habitual criminals and, of course, political prisoners condemned to forced hard labour under a strict guard.

As far as the eye could see the snow clad, flat expanse reached away to the horizon and was absolutely empty and lifeless amidst a sinister silence. The monotony was disturbed only twice a day when we prisoners, dressed in our rags, trudged out as labour detachments to work and then back again at night. The detachments often worked five to ten miles from the camp and sleighs would drive up to the prisoners at noon to provide what was euphemistically called dinner.

While we women were strictly isolated from the men when in camp, men and women worked together outside and could speak to one another. Our task was to break the frozen earth with crow-bars and then dig deep ditches. We were also required to erect fantastic columns and walls of snow, which stood with an icy calm waiting for spring to come. They would then melt gradually and produce a more prolonged supply of water for the fields, instead of suddenly flooding them for a short time. Atmospheric precipitation in Kazakhstan is very small in summer and it is for this reason that such means of storing the snow are used.

We went to work when the stars were just beginning to fade and returned to our bunk houses when the winter constellations were already travelling across the heavens. It was hard work and the long marches to and from the work places were exhausting, while the food ration was so inadequate that we soon lost our strength and energy. The sleighs which brought our midday meals often returned with the corpses of prisoners. Although I was not strong enough to wield the crow-bars with any effect I had to do something in order not to freeze to death.

Winter in Kazakhstan is nearly always sunny (unless there is a blizzard), but the sun is frozen too. The temperature variations are very small, and frosts remain constant for weeks on end, fluctuating between minus 35 degrees and minus 50 degrees Celsius, but the most unpleasant weather was when there were dry, icy winds. Many of the prisoners then had their hands, feet and faces frost bitten, sometimes very badly.

While at work we all awaited noon with great impatience. As soon as one of us saw the dark spot of the sleigh in the snow-clad distance, the glad cry of 'Dinner!' would be heard and would be passed on from group to group far into the distance. We would then immediately drop tools and get our bowls (actually cans or other utensils) and spoons from our bags, and put them under our jackets so as to warm them a little with our bodies. The bread ration had, of course, been kept next to our skins since morning, to prevent it freezing hard.

Animated, rubbing our hands and flapping our arms, jigging about on our feet, we kept our eyes on the approaching dinner sleigh and when it arrived swarmed around it, in detachments, waiting for the hot serving. There were two large vats well insulated with straw upon each sleigh which everyone stared at with hungry eyes, closely watching the food being handed out. Steam rose from the vats and we could smell the aroma of the soup, most often a fishy one, as we queued. We ate standing or sitting on the snow, holding the black bread in one dirty hand and washing down each mouthful with a drink of soup. For a while, the bowl would pleasantly warm our hands while the watery soup warmed our insides.

The groats (the second course) differed little from the soup and in any case all we got was two little spoonfuls which were devoured with incredible speed. The final stage was carefully to chase and catch every piece of groat sticking to the side of the bowl until the bowl was really empty.

The sleigh would depart and, as we watched it recede with regret, one or other of us would remark, 'There it goes, just as I had worked up an appetite'. We would then return to our work and longingly wait for the command, 'Home!'

When we returned to the camp in the evenings, hungry and tired out, I could not help remarking on the marvellous sunsets. The clarity of the air in this land gives rise to extra-ordinary hues spreading across the sky and earth. One then has the impression of being in some charmed countryside. Looking at the splendid play of colours, I absorbed this sole beauty which morning and evening uplifted my heart and brought me added strength.

The work-weary day shuts its gates,
And snows have covered the sunny orb
The evening northern lights appear beyond the worlds
And limn their hues around
The rose encarnadine by the last ray
Seen by the sun beyond the snow
A belt of honey topaz reveals
And decks the mountain in emeralds
Turquoise looks down curiously
And sends down his beloved smile to the snows,
And then begins their many hued dance. . . .

When, sudden, strange guests come down
From the sky close knit in white and frosty garb,
Their feet dip in the blood red rose . . .
These crosses and pillars of the north
When frosts are great do daily
Stand in dignity, and calmly look
As the dawn trembles and caresses . . .
The white breath of heaven and earth
Night now proclaims her power ever more,
And the stars more boldly lead their worlds
The strange celestial guests fade away
And the setting orb is lost to sight.
Alone you stay, trudging slowly in the ranks
And feel your soul is praying to the Lord.

The more inhuman treatment of the prisoners in this penal camp was when we were being allotted work in the morning. It would often happen that the exhausted, weak and ragged prisoners were driven out of the bunk houses by guards flogging them with the heavy *nagaikas* (a short, thick whip) and by vicious guard dogs. On more than one occasion the woman doctor, who was always present in the mornings, would intervene in an attempt to get some sick or enfeebled prisoner left in the bunk house, but the commandant would pretend not to believe that such prisoners were ill and incapable of work unless they actually lay in bed unconscious and with a high temperature.

As already stated, dead prisoners and badly frost-bitten ones were often brought back to camp by the sleighs. Although many of the prisoners had not yet been formally sentenced as guilty of some offence they were all forced to work in such conditions.

As can be gathered, we were close to starving in that camp. Kept behind barbed wire it was difficult to steal some food from the granaries and store houses.

We noticed some grains of wheat scattered on the snow on our way to work one day. The men started to scrape them up, but the guards noticed and let loose their dogs on us all. The fierce animals began to tear and bite us, shouts and screams made the confusion greater and it took the guards a long time to call off and leash them. The wheat, of course, was trampled into the snow. Those who had managed to pick some up and hide it in their pockets now chewed it with enormous satisfaction as they went on their way. This incident will show, however, how even a few grains of wheat were prized as a valuable addition to our starvation rations.

Day after day of such hard work and severe under-nourishment quickly undermined our strength and health and the death rate amongst the prisoners soared. Most of the prisoners were Caucasians and, unaccustomed to such extreme cold, died like flies. Several corpses would be carried out of the bunk houses every morning. The bodies would be stacked up in a shed near the smithy and kept there until the earth thawed sufficiently to make it possible to dig a common grave. The gaps in our ranks were very quickly filled by batches of new arrivals.

Though the women's bunk house was planned to hold a hundred prisoners, there were as many as 180 of us usually and many had to sleep under the bunks on the clay floor. The hygienic conditions were terrible. We had no baths for two months on end and, when we complained to the commandant he invariably replied that he had no fuel and that we would all die off soon, anyhow.

The lice had optimum conditions for multiplying themselves and there were no rest days at all. The bunk houses were not lit when darkness fell, whilst the conditions of work and the intense frosts ruled out undressing oneself in order to get rid of the vermin. To make matters still worse, we all suffered from the intense itching caused by scabies.

Returning from work, every woman longed for the blessing of night to soothe our sadness and relieve our fatigue, but after scabies began to afflict us, the nights became torture and we longed for the morning so that we could go out to work. For, although our bodies were warmed as long as we lay in our bunks the itching became quite unbearable and we all scratched until the blood ran. There was no remedy in the sick bay to kill off the parasites and compresses of urine gave only temporary relief.

It happened that I had remained in the bunk house one day on the doctor's recommendation, having a high fever, when a Medical Commission arrived. I was very glad for it seemed certain that they would inspect our bunk house which would enable me to complain about our conditions. I waited long and still they did not come. The commandant showed them only those bunk houses and buildings which were outside our zone.

Then I saw the Commission were getting into their sleighs to set off. I dashed to the guard and told him to let me out of the zone as I had a personal matter to present to the commandant. He let me go and I ran up to the sleighs. Without any preamble, I told them of the terrible conditions in which we lived and proved it by tearing open my blouse and showing my body covered with the fistulas of scabies and the bites of lice, and my body criss-crossed with scratches.

The commandant turned red with fury, but the Commission immediately went to inspect our bunk house. Here the other invalids backed me up and demanded baths and medicines. Within a few days, we had ointments and disinfectants. The former rid us of the scabies and the latter helped to reduce the incidence of lice and bed bugs. Moreover, some fuel was found and we had a bath.

The commandant, however, decided to hit back at us in rather a mean way. He issued an order that when the women went to the baths we were to be completely depilated and that this was to be done by the man who issued us the water. He was a coarse and vulgar type. We protested and demanded that one of our number, a hair dresser by profession, clip and shave off our body hair, but the only reply was that we would be severely punished if we insisted.

The women, very much ashamed, submitted to the ordeal but when my turn came and Vanka turned to me with his razor I snatched up a heavy wooden bucket and said to him, 'If you touch me, I'll smash your head with this bucket!'

He started shouting at me and threatened to call the guard, whereupon the other women, encouraged by my attitude, seized the pails of hot water and began to surround him. This scared him thoroughly and he swiftly backed out of the place. From that time he never even ventured to glance at me in the bathroom. Nevertheless, he reported me to the commandant who called me in on the next day and sentenced me to three days in the punishment cell, where I got only 100 grams of bread daily and one helping of soup.

I was greatly moved when, on the second day Sgurn, one of the prostitutes, stole up to the cell and threw a heap of small pieces of bread through the grated window. My companions in the bunkhouse had each of them cut off a small piece of bread from their ration and sent it to me.

Some time later, a new *urbe* was appointed by the commandant. He was a young habitual criminal from Khabarovsk who, apart from his general depravity, was a sadist. Undoubtedly he wished to toady favour with the commandant by being as cruel as possible to the other prisoners. When he stormed about our bunkhouses there was something devilish in his hatred. He brutally threw out the weak and ragged prisoners in order to force them to go to work, making free use of the stick he carried. Many people lost their lives through him. The prisoners hated him, but also feared him.

My strength was steadily ebbing and, supported by the decision of the medical examiners that I was incapable of heavy work, I went up to the *urbe* and said, 'I'm not going out of the zone to work anymore'.

Perhaps I took him by surprise because he flared up in a fury and pushed me away with so much force that I fell down. I got up and, in the absence of something more suitable, used my long fingernails upon him. He was better nourished than I and much stronger, with the outcome that he forced me out of the bunk-house where the guards helped him to push me into the ranks of waiting prisoners. Before I could recover we were surrounded by guards and dogs and driven off to work again.

I was still quivering with indignation and did absolutely no work. All I did was think up ways and means of reporting the *urbe* to some superior authority. I could not reconcile myself to the thought that such brutality and inhumanity towards the prisoners could pass with impunity, that the recommendations of the medical authorities could be so flagrantly disregarded. It was 41C below freezing point, yet all I had on my head was a little beret and light summer shoes. I had to keep on rubbing my feet all the time to prevent them getting frost bitten. All my companions advised me not to file a complaint against the culprit. They said that the *urbe* would merely revenge himself more bitterly, but I remained firm in my intention to make official complaint.

It so happened that the Chief Commandant of the penal camps in the district came to inspect ours for the first time on the very same day this happened. When he visited our labour sector he approached our group and I related the whole incident with the *urbe*. He called his secretary, made a note of my name and asked whether there had been any witnesses. The other women testified in unison to the truth of my allegations. As we were making up our bunks to go to sleep that evening the commandant entered and, to everybody's surprise, announced that the *urbe* had been sentenced to three days in the punishment cell for his misconduct.

This turn of affairs greatly encouraged the prisoners and they sent more and more complaints against the trusty to the authorities with the result that he was finally removed and relegated to the same conditions of life as the other prisoners.

We grew more and more hungry, and outside it became even colder. It had been a late winter but it now began to make up for its tardiness. The thermometer fell to 40C below freezing point on the Celsius scale, and very often my plaits and blanket would freeze to the wall during the night. These conditions did not, however, hinder the authorities from sending ever new batches of prisoners to liven up our life in the huts.

Tania used to live in Moscow, Anait was from Yerevan, Kiviyaki from Finland and Elizabeth used to live in Leningrad (now Petersburg) and others from different parts of the Soviet Union. Our hut became more and more multi-lingual as time went on. Tania had only recently graduated from a school of dramatic art. She was a fresh, unspoilt girl, pretty because of her youth. Her approach to me was as to an elder sister, and she told me in simple words how it had happened that she was now a prisoner.

One day, she went with some of her girl friends to enjoy a little dancing in a restaurant where she met a young man with whom she had two dances. It turned out later that he was an official of the United States Embassy and this sufficed for her to be arrested a few days later and sentenced to five years penal servitude. Tania now resembled nothing so much as a dilapidated scarecrow. She had bartered all the things she had taken with her to get food during the journey to the penal camp and now her jacket and trousers were studded with scraps of wadding sticking through the holes and tears. On her foot she wore galoshes made from rubber car tyres kept in place by swathes of rags.

She was still very young and always hungry so, immediately after her arrival, she did her best to get out of the zone to find some work which would earn her more than the normal food rations. She thought work on the dairy farm would be best for this purpose. True, she was very much afraid of cows and had in fact seen them only in films, but hunger bolsters courage and she volunteered one day for work as a butter making specialist.

She explained that though she had attended dramatic arts school she had also attended a dairy course and had, during the summer holidays, acquired practical experience by working on one of the best farms in the Ukraine. The commandant heard her out and then asked what percentage of fat the Ukrainian cows had yielded in their milk. Without hesitation, she answered that it was 80 per cent. Everybody in the office burst out laughing, so she thought the figure was far too low and added, that, of course, she should have said 180 per cent. The laughter this time was simply Homeric, and poor Tania was ordered back to her hut with scant ceremony.

She was very disappointed, and told us all about it. We explained to her that cows' milk never has more than 7 per cent of fat. She found it hard to get over her disappointment and finally, with dour resignation, continued to dig potatoes in the frozen soil. She used to lie by my side at nights, and before falling asleep she would relate all that she had felt during the day with dramatic verve, almost as if she were on stage.

Many of the labour brigade leaders and other men found themselves mistresses as they had opportunities of getting extra food, and Tania kept on receiving offers of bread and potatoes for a price. She repelled these advances with indignation, even rude words, and continued on her hungry way. They would then allot the heaviest work to her in attempts to break her resistance, but in vain. She had never loved a man for she distrusted men and even was disgusted by them. She concentrated all her love on her mother for whom she longed greatly. She always said, 'Good night, mummy' before falling asleep and, as she expressed it, kissed her mother's face and hands in her thoughts. When she awoke, the first thing she would say was 'Good morning, mummy, don't worry about me. I'll manage'.

She would sometimes succeed in getting out of the penal zone in the evening and drink a little milk at the milk-maids', or bring back a frost-bitten carrot . . . a distinct delicacy for us, one that somehow reminded one of the flavour of an orange. These additions to her diet helped little. She began to swell from under-nourishment, her teeth became rickety and her body covered with sores. One day the medical orderly took her to the little hospital attached to the settlement and so, for a long time, I lost contact with her.

We met again four years later in another penal settlement. She looked well but was still dressed in scarecrow fashion. Tania now worked in the vegetable plots and in the store houses in winter. She told me that letters from home came very frequently, and food parcels from time to time. It was this extra food which had put her on her legs. The letters were always written by her sister at their mother's dictation. It appeared that the mother had gone blind after Tania's arrest. Tania read to me all the letters she received and her answers. The letters were gems of poetic feeling in their expressive longing and enormous love, both a mother's and a daughter's love.

Tania lived only for these letters from her mother and these gave her strength to endure to the end of her sentence. There were only a few months left. She counted the days and joyously calculated how their number decreased. Her love for her mother seemed to have grown, and her hatred for men increased at the same time. She walked proudly about the settlement and repelled every male advance with scorn. The settlement doctor was a young Georgian who pursued her with his love and proposals and, though she suffered much unpleasantness as a result, she firmly resisted.

A month before her release, Tania received a parcel of clothes and a letter. Overjoyed, she ran up to me to share her news. She started reading, but after a few words turned pale and fainted. We tried to revive her and someone ran for the doctor. A heart attack was the diagnosis, and an injection was made. Tania revived for a moment but immediately fainted again and remained unconscious for a long time. She lay in a high fever for three days, constantly calling upon her mother and sister in her delirium. I read the letter:–

'Our dear little sister,

Very soon now we will able to hug you to our hearts. Forgive us, dearest, that for the last five years we have been deceiving you by giving you joy, but it had to be so for your own good. Today, the truth we give you will bring pain, and we must reveal a secret. When mother learned that you had been sentenced to five years, she had heart failure and died. We invented her blindness so that you could endure those five years with courage and hope.'

Tania was released a month later and we embraced for the last time. As I blessed her on her way, she left the settlement, looking like a withered flower.

Kiviyaki was a school teacher in Finland. In 1940 when her district was annexed by the Russians after the Russo-Finnish war, the Finns there were arrested in great numbers and deported to the labour camps. Kiviyaki was a gallant and brave woman who, apart from her teaching, occupied herself with social and political work. She loved her country and sorrowed deeply that tragedy had overcome it. She endured all the insults cast upon her by the Russians in the camp and made no secret of her opposition to the Soviet government. She said what she thought and we all admired her intensity for this. All the Finnish women in the camp treated her with the greatest respect and helped her in every possible way, but her sojourn with us was short, the flame of her life was extinguished whilst she was still in her prime.

At that time, I would stay in the hut with the other women and weave mats. This privilege was accorded only to very weak prisoners unable to do heavy manual work or prisoners who had no footwear and warm things to put on.

One day Lila, a young and very resolute girl came into the hut with her belongings. She had been living in a bunkhouse outside the zone up to that time and had worked in the book-keeping office. She was always very well disposed towards us and willingly helped when we had some business in her department. Although she had already served five years of her sentence, she still looked fresh and untroubled.

As can be imagined, we welcomed her in our midst. She had completed her sentence some weeks before and was now joyfully awaiting the arrival of her release papers. Since she had done nothing meriting punishment, we could not make out why she had been put into the punishment hut instead of being given relative freedom.

Lila and I became close friends from her arrival. She was born in Odessa and when the Revolution broke out her father, a rich man, fled from Russia with his wife and children. They stayed in Germany for some years and then they all went to the United States, where he bought a farm in South Carolina and, together with his whole family, became an American citizen.

When Lila grew up she became an art student and after some time went with her mother to Germany. Thereafter she lived in Europe and America in turn, spending all her long vacations with her mother. While in Germany in 1936 she fell under the influence of Communist propaganda and decided to visit the paradise of the proletariat, her former homeland. Without notifying her father, she set off for Russia where she was received with great enthusiasm. She was charmed with everything they showed her and in her naive way assumed Soviet citizenship as soon as possible.

She could speak several languages and was immediately engaged as an interpreter, but when she got around without a guide, she discovered that life in the Union fell far short of the ideal propagated abroad and of what she had been shown on her arrival. She was arrested a year later and sentenced to five years penal servitude in a labour camp as an American spy. It so happened that her sentence ended in 1942, during the war, and all the political prisoners were retained in captivity 'until special orders came'. Thus it was that Lila was beginning a new term of imprisonment without being informed on what grounds.

She became a brigadier leading a women's work gang and would go out with the bandit molls to work. She was by this time a veteran inmate and knew all the tricks to apply so that the prisoners could get the maximum bread ration. In general she took good care of her subordinates.

One day she fell out with the molls and they crowded around her threatening to kill her and a fight started. Lila defended herself boldly. It is the camp custom that nobody helps until the situation becomes too menacing. So we sat on our bunks and looked on. Lila fought alone against six of the molls but, to everybody's surprise, she threw all of them, one by one, to the ground with lightning like movements. We began to cheer her so as to encourage her, for the molls looked dumbfounded and stared at Lila. It appeared that Lila was not only in good physical shape, but also knew something of fencing and judo. This impressed the molls so much that they immediately accepted her authority and blindly, even with profound affection, obeyed all her orders.

Sometime later, together with Elizabeth and Anait, I was transferred to a hut outside the zone, and my contact with Lila was broken off, to my regret and to hers.

CHAPTER 9
Winter on the Steppe

On my first Christmas Eve in camp the frost was intense. In the quiet of the evening one could hear the snow crunching underfoot as the guards marched around our penal zone. The air was so clear that one could see the whole wilderness covered with snow. It was like some magic dance, like the stars which spoke with the snow. All the winter constellations led their worlds to the heavens when white Sirius appeared in the east. When Orion magnificently and slowly arose from his bed I rose with him.

Mary the milkmaid had promised she would try to give me a few frost-bitten little carrots for Christmas Eve, but that I would have to come to the base camp myself. I pondered all day long how I might get out of the penal zones until, when evening came, I tied up my arm with a rag. Groaning loudly I went up to the guard complaining that I had dislocated it and must go to the sick bay immediately. He must have been a good-hearted boy, because, asking no questions, he let me go. When I reached the sick bay hut, I turned and cautiously proceeded towards the base where Mary was waiting for me. She pulled me behind the door swiftly, and pushed the carrots under my fur. A little later she brought me some milk which I drank greedily.

I was returning to the zone, very well satisfied with myself and pressing the carrots with my elbow, when the commandant suddenly appeared before me. 'Where are you hurrying from so late, girl?' he asked.

I lost my head and could only babble in a confused way. 'Let's go to the office and clear matters up there,' he said.

Naturally they searched me and found a carrot. I was asked, 'Who gave you this carrot?'

I answered, 'It was lying on the ground, so I picked it up.'

'Right,' he replied, 'as you won't tell me who gave it to you, you'll go to the punishment cell straight away' and, sure enough, that was where I found myself a few minutes later, for the first time.

The punishment cell was really a cellar dug in the ground. When the ground was too frostbound to make it possible to dig graves, the corpses of dead prisoners were kept there until it became warmer.

I clambered down the ladder into the hole, and the opening was then covered with planks, and I was left alone in the dark. I did not like it at all. There was a mound of earth in the middle, and I sat down upon it. I tried not to wonder whether there were any corpses in the cell with me, and I still had fresh in my mind's eye that starry night and its influence on my soul. I began to recall the Christmas Eves of my life year by year back to my childhood.

The last two Christmas Eves had been with my children in Aktyubinsk, in exile. The last Christmas Eve in Poland had been with my husband in 1939. We had sat at table, silent and sad, for our country was under Soviet occupation. I worked back to 1924. Through the years every Christmas had been a family and joyous festival, when I was a happy wife and mother. Then I recalled when I was a schoolgirl and would come home with my brothers and sisters for the Christmas holidays. How glad we were to be home and how lively home was!

I dwelt in memory a little longer on the Christmas of 1918. Ukrainians were fighting Poles and some partisan group of the former had crept up to my home town. Christmas Eve then was to the accompaniment of machine gun fire and bursting shrapnel. That evening my mother prepared baskets of holiday fare and I, with my sisters, took them to the outposts of Polish soldiers who, in some cases, were as young as 15 years.

In the year the war broke out, 1914, we had left everything to escape before the Russian army. We had stayed for 3 years in Austria, every Christmas Eve in another town – our family not so numerous and not the same as before.

Then my childhood memories flooded in. I remembered that large snowflakes were falling and we children kept on going out in front of the homestead to gaze up at the sky, anxious to see the first star to appear so that we could rush indoors and bring the joyful news to Mother. For, according to Polish tradition, the Christmas festivity begins when the first star appears on Christmas Eve and all should then take their places at table.

Ours was a large family: father, mother, five girls and four boys. One chair and one place at table was always left unoccupied . . . to symbolise the memory of my mother's brother who had died young. I could again feel the warmth of our home, its very flavour, the enormous table dressed in its holiday best, bearing all the typical dishes sanctioned by tradition for that festival. I recalled every single dish and dwelt long and lovingly on each memory. There had to be twelve dishes, perhaps I dwelt on this aspect because I was hungry now. All I had was a crust of bread, which I was keeping for Christmas Eve, now due in a few hours.

I remembered how waiting for Christmas Eve had always seemed so long when I was a child. I would look at my mother time after time with impatience, waiting for her to open the door so that we could enter, look at the illuminated Christmas tree and then dash up to it for our presents, allegedly laid there by a little angel.

I must have dozed off at that stage, because I awoke with a start and felt chilled through. I got up in the darkness and began to swing my arms about in order to get warmed. That night was really a very long one, but my Christmas present was waiting for me in the bunkhouse, yesterday's ration of bread saved up for this day. I was still fortunately unaware of another present, a ten year sentence from the Soviet Union.

At long last the 'door' was opened and the guard shouted down merrily, 'Well, didn't you freeze through and through? All right, get out.' So I climbed up the ladder with difficulty for I was stiff with cold, and went to my hut in the punishment zone. I found the odorous air of the hut and its stuffiness quite pleasant in the relative sense, and the clean, hot water I drank seemed like the nectar of the gods.

I saw Fr. Kapusta only when I was going out to work. He was dressed in rags and looked very exhausted. The other prisoners thought very highly of him, impressed as they were by his invariably Christian approach to his companions in misfortune. He always accepted a greater burden than his shoulders could bear.

It was on the second day after our arrival in that penal settlement that our priest was beaten up by the duty guard during a roll call because he had tried to hand my rug back to me. When I learned of this I was so indignant that I demanded the commandant hear me out. I was received at once and boldly related that I had lent the priest my rug and that when he had tried to return it to me the next day, asking the duty guard for permission, the outcome was that the latter beat him up and was still maltreating him.

I asked whether it was Soviet law or in the regulations of the camp that prisoners could be so brutally treated and stressed that Fr. Kapusta had not been sentenced, that he was a senior officer and chaplain of allied troops, and could be released any moment now. It was only a passing misunderstanding that he was in the camp anyhow, I exclaimed to clinch the matter. Unaccustomed to such a speech from a prisoner the commandant was rather taken by surprise and promised he would investigate the matter. In any case my rug was returned to me that evening and the guards left my priest in peace.

Four weeks later, a sleigh drove up to the sector where Fr. Kapusta was working and took him to camp. He was given a bath, clean linen was issued to him with new wadded outdoor clothing and he was sent to Karabas. I was not allowed to say goodbye to him, and it was only in the strictest confidence that someone in the office told me that a special order of release had come from Moscow. On the morning of the next day I looked at the ranks of ragged men shivering in the cold and was happy that Fr. Kapusta was no longer amongst them.

Every day I observed the prisoners who inhabited one particular hut from a distance. We could not establish contact with each other because any of their group who even approached one of us could be deprived of the privileges allotted to those who lived outside the punishment zone.

They had their own brigadiers when they went to work and were allowed freedom of movement in the rest of the penal camp. They had already spent from six to seven years here and were called 'the wives' by everybody. Their husbands and also some of 'the wives' had occupied responsible positions in the civil and army life of the Soviet Union, but, during the purge of 1936/37 which Stalin had instigated, their husbands had been arrested, after which came the turn of 'the wives', even of their older children.

A special item in the penal code had been established for the wives and children. All members of the family of a convicted prisoner were, for the most part, sentenced to eight to ten years penal servitude. The husbands were sentenced to longer terms and were not allowed to write to their families. At first, the wives were likewise not allowed to write to their families but, by dint of years of insistent effort, they were at length allowed to communicate with their children.

They had been sent, immediately after their arrest, to the enormous isolation camps in Segera and Tymiaki, where there were special workshops for women prisoners where conditions were reasonably endurable. They were evacuated from there when the war broke out and distributed to various parts of

Karaganda. They were brutally treated in these camps and had to do the hardest work, but in course of time and as the camp grew larger, the authorities used them as office workers since they had the necessary qualifications.

They were educated women and mostly university graduates. They worked with resignation and stubbornly, as if feeling that it was their own fault that they had met with such a fate. They assured me that before their arrest they had no idea of the 'second life' within their own country. As they put it, they used to sit behind green tables and believed in Soviet justice. It was only here that their eyes were at length opened to the duplicity of the system.

Nearly all in this settlement worked in the granary, carrying heavy sacks, shifting the grain from one heap to another, etc. Their clothing consisted of the usual wadded rags, dirty and dusty, for they had no facilities for washing. When it snowed they would rub their hands and faces with the snow and wait longingly for the next bath, which was due every two or three weeks, but sometimes only received once a month. It was so hard to secure a comb that many of them shaved their heads in order, as they remarked, not to provide a reservation for the lice.

In general their appearance was very far from that of a woman. When I was transferred to their hut they greeted me politely but with distrust, but we soon broke the ice and lived in friendship. I listened to their narratives with great interest while they listened to the narrative of a woman from the west with astonishment and enormous interest. Most of them were sure that in Europe and in America there was extreme poverty, exploitation of workers, eternal unemployment and lack of any social insurance. Those who had been abroad before now remained silent. They went out to work every day, except one who had sunk into apathy and depression and lay hopelessly on her bunk.

Tonia was a daughter of general and had been conscripted

into the Red Army. Her husband was a colonel and both had been deployed in the Far East. She was arrested not long after her husband and father's arrests. She told us that life in the Far East was much better. She had been comfortably off.

Tonia could not get used to physical work and stayed in the hut, receiving only 300 grams of bread a day. When I first made her acquaintance she looked like a ragged, dilapidated porcelain doll, and her long unwashed blond hair was in disorder. Her blue eyes, framed with long dark lashes, looked helplessly and dully at some distant point. She had lost all hope and any physical and spiritual strength she may have had was gradually slipping away. Already she was dead in life although, true, she livened up a little when I became an inmate of the hut. She liked to look at me, to touch my things. She smelled my fur coat which still retained some of the perfume I had put on it and would say, 'How you still smell of another life! I'll never return there, what do you think?' Shortly afterwards, she was transferred to a settlement for sick and disabled prisoners.

In the heavens, the spring constellations moved ever more boldly, but Earth still slept soundly under the heavy coat of snow and nothing indicated that spring was already asserting her rights in the sky.

Another Medical Commission turned up at the penal settlement and began to sort us out, that is to say, to change our allotted health categories. Immediately afterwards, there was a rumour that some of us would be sent away. The commandant was anxious to get rid of the *barahlo,* the 'garbage' as they called those unable to work, and recidivists, just sending them to another commandant. Thus, we were not taken by surprise when the commandant came in to the bunk house one day and read out a list of prisoners due to be sent away.

I was glad to hear my name called out and at once began to pack my few belongings. I took my leave of my companions and went out with the others to the assembly area. The men selected for transfer were already waiting there with their little bags of belongings. They were all terribly emaciated and in frightful rags. It was customary that prisoners transferred to another settlement were deprived of any decent clothing they had and issued the worst in stock.

We were searched and we threw our bags into the sleighs but the more experienced among us held on to their belongings. The medical officer arranged that a few persons, the weakest, were put on the sleighs. All this took place amidst the noise raised by the shouts and curses of the commandants until at long last the guard read out the final order and we were off. We were stiff after the long wait in the cold, but we marched off at a smart pace in order to get warm.

We prisoners were glad to get out of this settlement, the more so that it was rumoured there was no punishment zone in the new settlement and that the commandant there was a humane man. It was a very frosty morning although sunny. The snow crunched cleanly under our feet and the white waste around us sparkled in the sun's rays. The whole scene looked like a field sprinkled with diamonds. The tiny crystals of snow quivered and shone with ever changing hues.

Among our number there were the young habitual criminals and those who refused to go out to work, whom one commandant was now passing on to the next.

Immediately our column left the settlement the bandit molls joined forces with their lovers and marched with them. Soon after, some of them went up to the sleighs, pushed off the weak prisoners and took their places. We protested against this but the guards paid no attention. Our onward march was slowed down in order to allow the weaker prisoners to keep up with us whilst the molls pilfered the bags we had thrown on the sleighs.

I had no idea how far it was to the nearest penal settlement but knew we should have been able to reach it before nightfall, but hour by hour the sun became ever warmer and the snow more and more damp. The rags and felt boots on our feet became soaked through and it became more and more difficult to march onwards. Finally, about two o'clock, we heard the long awaited order, 'Sit down!' We threw down our bags and sat down on the snow with relief, pulled out pieces of bread and dried fish and began to eat. The smokers screwed up some tobacco in strips of newspaper.

During the pause we argued with the guard commandant about the weaker prisoners, urging that if he put them on the sleighs the column could march faster. I am glad to say that we finally convinced him this would be a good thing and we proceeded on our journey.

The rest did us good but the snow got deeper and deeper, not trampled down, and our feet sank deep into it with every step. The increased effort made us perspire to such an extent that our clothes were soon steaming in the sun. Having eaten the dried salted fish we all became very thirsty and stooped from time to time to gather up some snow. This only increased our thirst and our fatigue.

The column of prisoners stretched the longer and marched ever more slowly. People stopped chatting. The stronger held up the weaker and our eyes hurt more as the sunlight reflected from the snow became more glaring. The weaker prisoners often sank to the ground with exhaustion. The guards would then shout at them and set their dogs on the poor people to force them on.

I felt ill that day and my back ached worse and worse as we went on. So I ran on to the head of the column, lay down to rest until the last prisoner came along, and then hurried on to the head and repeated the procedure. While I relieved my pain by lying down, the running to the head of the column made me more tired than before, and I soon became thoroughly exhausted. So I went up to the guard commandant and asked his permission to ride on a sleigh for a time, but he looked at my cheeks, rosy with exertion and heat, and refused to believe I was at the end of my strength. There was nothing to do but grit my teeth and carry on, nearly unconscious from the pain.

The sun was setting and we were still far from our destination. After such a sunny day we felt the frost all the more. Our clothing, wet through with perspiration, and the soaked rags on our feet began to freeze. We were not allowed to stop and rest, even for a moment. We knew that we must reach the settlement before night fell, but we could feel ourselves getting weaker and could only drag our feet along. When we fell to the ground the guards would use rifle butts and dogs to force us up and on.

I thought bitterly to myself how, only a short time ago, I was in such good physical condition that I often walked 50-90 kilometres during twenty-four hours to bring the children something to eat and now it was so difficult to march even these few kilometres. How quickly people lose their strength in a Russian penal settlement.

Finally, some of the prisoners could go on no longer. They fell to the ground and neither blows nor rifle butts could force them to arise. 'Kill us,' they moaned, 'We can't go on.' The guards did not know what to do. They took counsel and finally said, 'Those who can carry on, get on your way,' they said, 'and we'll leave the others here. They can freeze to death.'

I was at the end of my tether with exhaustion and pain. All I wanted was to lie down on the snow and close my eyes for a moment. I was about to do so when some powerful current passed through me and I heard my little daughter's voice, crying out, 'Mummy! Mummy!' Strangely enough, at the same time I felt my strength returning with a surge and I rejoined the marching column, looking back at those left lying.

The snowy plain quivered in the silvery light of the full moon, its pale disc calm and indifferent to our fate. I tried not to think of those poor people, although in fact, even to think at all was a great effort. I went on like an automaton worked by the magic of my daughter's voice.

For some kilometres I even felt quite strong but after a time my strength again began to ebb and I dragged more and more to the rear. As if in a dream I could hear the guards urging me on, and then two tall, young bandit molls, Marusia and Nina, took me under the arms and helped me on, although they were very tired too. 'Chin up, Auntie,' they called, 'it's not so far now.'

I do not know how long I trudged nor how I found myself lying on straw in a barn. When I awoke greyish daylight was seeping through the cracks in the walls and I could see, here and there, the outlines of heaps of rags on the ground around me. I felt cold and my feet were icy but slowly came to myself and found that my backache had gone. I thought of those who had remained on the steppe and I shivered.

Carefully, so as not to awaken those around me, I found my bundle and got a pair of woollen socks from it. I took the wet rags from my feet and wrung them out and rubbed my feet hard. Putting the socks on I felt pleasantly warm although very thirsty, especially for something hot. It became lighter in the barn and the reveille gong sounded out. The other people awoke, rubbed their stiff limbs and put their clothes into some kind of order. Finally, the door was unlocked and the guard told us to go out for breakfast.

It was quite light outside and the prisoners were already beginning to go about with their cans. When I asked one of them what this place was called I was told, 'Death Point'.

I had heard of the place before, but to this day do not know its real name for all the prisoners, no matter where, invariably called it so. It was an assembly point for prisoners from the surrounding penal settlements, prisoners completely exhausted by pellagra or other diseases who were sent here to end their days. Some lay in the local hospital, others in the bunkhouses, and those who still had some strength wove mats and baskets.

I thought it would be a good idea to visit Tania who had

been sent here two months earlier, so I entered one of the bunkhouses, but I could not go beyond the threshold, held up by the sickening smell of decaying human excrement. Here and there I could see the shapes of men, bones covered with skin, most of them lying without movement in their bunks. I greeted them and received only a grunt or a murmur in reply. Their eyes livened up for a moment but their faces remained stiffly indifferent. They reacted feebly to external stimuli and could not even control their own physiological needs. Though much better fed than elsewhere, the food they ate slipped undigested through their bodies and gave them no strength. Most of them were in the last stages of pellagra or scurvy, and nothing could help them now.

Still living, they were already dead.

I went out and opened the door of another building. Things were livelier here, women were sitting on their bunks and everyone was busy with something. When I asked for Tania, they told me she had 'released' herself three days before and she was now in the mortuary, waiting to be buried in the spring when the ground thawed.

After breakfast we lit a fire in front of the bunkhouse and dried our things, or rather our rags, and moved on at about noon. It was a better road this time, trodden hard. The sun was not so hot that the snow would melt under foot. Moreover, I felt much better and so, together with my companions, reached the new camp in quite good condition.

CHAPTER 10

Berazniki

We were expected in Berazniki, my second settlement, and supper and baths were awaiting us. When we entered the bunkhouse the women there were still awake and came up to us with curiosity to find out who we were and what news we had brought. The bunkhouse was clean and tidy, quite spacious, lit by several oil lamps, and the bunks were in tiers. The head woman of the bunkhouse showed us our places and we began to undress with enormous relief.

I was very tired after my two day journey and just as I began to undress, a handsome young man, wearing a new *telogreyka* (quilted jacket) and quilted trousers, came into the barrack. I stopped undressing and waited for him to go out, but he undressed and quickly slipped under the blanket in a bunk, put his arms round the young girl lying there and began to relate something most vivaciously. There was a free bunk next to mine and I thought, panic-stricken, that it might be for some man.

There had been so many fantastic tales current in Karabas about life in the penal camps that it did not seem extraordinary for men and women to be quartered together here. A woman opposite asked me why I didn't undress when there are men about here, and I pointed at the young man. She only laughed heartily and then, leaning towards me, said, 'Go on, undress. That's our Nadia', adding in a whisper, 'a hermaphrodite'.

During the ten years I spent in Soviet penal camps, I met quite a few bi-sexual people. I observed them closely, and found their characters were very much alike. Their ages were for the most part between twenty and thirty, and they reminded me of figures from the paintings of Caravaggio. Their faces showed various degrees of male or female predominance but their bodies were usually masculine with broad shoulders, little or no bust, and slim waists. They looked very youthful and their faces had a strange charm, as if they were inclined to be bashful, but their characters evinced a preponderance of male characteristics.

They were on the whole ambitious, brave, taciturn and impressionable. Slow to make friendships they always kept other people at arm's length but, once they endowed someone with their friendship, it was sincere and lasting. They were extremely jealous of their mates and faithful to them and no obstacle would stop them satisfying even the slightest caprice of their mistresses. The camp authorities treated them with tolerance and did nothing to break their unions with women, it being argued that such unions caused them to work better and never think of escaping. They were assigned to the women's barracks though their names were given in masculine form and they were officially inmates of the men's barracks.

Shura was the most notable among them. It so happened that we spent two years in the same settlement. I was her confidante and her mistress's too. Her intelligence was high, she was a graduate of a high school of economics, and she was really a handsome youth, subtle in her feelings yet with a strong, determined character. When I first met her, she was twenty-seven, serving a fifteen year sentence for forging bank notes. For the most part she worked in the camp office.

On the morning of the next day, all the women scattered to go to their various occupations, but we were granted three days' rest and I took the opportunity of inspecting this new penal settlement. Its external appearance differed markedly from that of Shakhan. The buildings were in better repair, the bunkhouses more capacious, well lit and clean. All the women prisoners sentenced for 'political' misdemeanours could move about freely and went out to work alone or in the company of their brigadier forewoman. On the other hand, only criminal prisoners among the men were allowed to move about without a guard, whilst the men political prisoners were kept under guard, together with dangerous bandits, in the penal bunkhouses.

At the periphery of the settlement were the other buildings and a large dairy farm with a separate bunkhouse for the milkmaids. Nearly all the milkmaids at the base camp were convicted criminals, not political prisoners. They looked well fed and healthy. For that matter work on a dairy farm was always highly valued as it afforded the best opportunities of recovering one's health and strength.

Apart from the milk there were the very nourishing, dark barley groats and potatoes for the cattle. Thus every worker on the dairy farm had an, unofficial, supplementary food ration over and above his or her normal ration. It was for this reason that the workers there were not allowed to contact us and we were categorically forbidden even to approach the base. Nevertheless, both sides found ways and means of helping each other. In short, the fodder set aside for the cattle helped to keep many human beings alive.

Most of the women prisoners were 'wives'. Some of them worked in the office whilst the rest had general duties. The stronger women worked in the storehouses, or at shovelling snow. The others made willow baskets. I was allotted to the sewing workshop, where I patched the dirty, wadded clothes of the prisoners.

The forewoman here was Zenia, a Kazakh, always quiet and calm, with a kind, smiling face. She willingly helped everyone and gave practical hints to the newcomers. She had been in the camp for the last six years. Her 'crime' was that she was the wife of an official in Alma-Ata arrested by the Russians. She had had no news from or about him, but her children were being brought up by relatives who often wrote to her and sent food parcels. She had great influence upon her younger compatriots, cared for them conscientiously and saw to it that they behaved properly towards the other prisoners. She did all this out of a great love for her native country.

To my left worked Lydia, frightfully emaciated and still exhausted after a serious operation she had recently undergone. The woman to my right was named Margarita.

Margarita was a modest, highly educated and intelligent woman who had devoted her life to the political side of social reform. We became great friends and I listened with the greatest interest to all she related about her own life and the history of Communist action in her country. Both she and her husband came from old gentry families in Russia, but both had, from their adolescent years, belonged to the extreme left wing of the freedom movement against the Tsarist regime.

She graduated from the *Berauzva,* the first university for women in Russia. After this, not wishing to remain in the capital, she settled in a distant province, actually not far from the old Kingdom of Poland, where she taught in a secondary school and at the same time conducted clandestine activities against the regime in conjunction with the Polish Socialist Party. Some years later friends arranged her husband's escape from Siberia and he reached Switzerland safely. It was there that he made the acquaintance of Lenin and was sent to the United States on a confidential mission by the Communist leader. He completed his studies in political and economic sciences in America where she managed, somehow, to join him.

She told me how, together with some other students, she visited Jack London's farm* on several occasions during the long vacation. The students noticed that the manager of the

* A successful author and passionate advocate of Socialism. In 1905 he had bought a ranch in California which he desperately wanted to be a successful example of best practice. It was an economic failure, partly due to his long absences and alcoholism.

farm over-exploited the labourers and even maltreated them. So the young people organised a strike and wrote a letter of complaint to Jack London. He immediately dropped everything and came to the farm where he personally set things right to the complete satisfaction of the students and the exploited workers.

The students gave him a tremendous ovation, whereupon he invited them all to table and they had a grand feast. Jack London, she told me, spent several days on the farm during which he personally discussed all kinds of things with the labourers and invariably showed great understanding for the working class movement. He drank a lot, Margarita told me, and often to excess.

Her husband often travelled to Europe in the execution of his Communist assignments, under assumed names. He was in Russia when the Revolution broke out in 1918. Margarita returned to Russia a year later in company with some other American Communists. Both she and her husband could now work openly for the Revolution and devoted their whole life to improving the lot of the masses. Full of enthusiasm and hope, both worked in the field of educational culture with great distinction and occupied important posts under the new regime.

Shortly after Lenin's death conditions began to change. Little by little, the old guard of his co-workers was appointed to posts in distant provinces, at the back of beyond, all for the good of the Party. After 1930, there were more and more arrests among them. Many simply disappeared without trace. Her husband was amongst those who disappeared, without open arrest, and she was arrested soon after. Sorrowful and sad, Margarita could see how the brave ideals of her youth were being ever more brutally distorted in practice.

The sewing workshop was extended but even so there was not enough room for all of us. Margarita and I were transferred to a small hut behind the bunkhouse where it was clean and very quiet. For the first time since my arrest I could spend days on end in virtual solitude and without seeing the guards and various 'commandants' who were constantly going to and fro. Both of us were pleased with this turn of events.

One afternoon a cat came through the open door and looked around the room cautiously. This was such an unusual sight for us that we stared at the animal for a long time without uttering a sound. It was a beautiful cat, fluffy silken fur, grey on the back and pure white on the under part and the tops of the legs, and great emerald eyes which regarded everything with curiosity

We flipped a little piece of bread in an effort to gain the creature's confidence, and in this we were successful. When work finished for the day we shut the cat up for the night as we feared the animal might stray towards the men's huts outside the zone and there meet with a miserable end, for they would certainly catch our cat and eat it. We told the other women about our newly acquired pet and they were delighted. They unanimously decided everything should be done to keep the cat at all costs.

One by one, they dropped into our room to have a look at it. Each left a piece of bread as a goodwill offering, stroked the cat's silky fur and went off with a smile. Finally, it was agreed that the cat spend the days in our work room, lying in the sunlight, whilst the evenings and nights would be spent in the bunkhouse with all the women petting and stroking the pleasant animal to everybody's content.

At the beginning of June I was taken to another camp for a few weeks. While I was absent Margarita remained alone in our work room and became ever more attached to our cat. She was therefore very sad when the animal disappeared. She and the other women were convinced that the men had killed and eaten it. But one morning towards the end of autumn, we entered the room and stood there astonished. Our cat lay full length on the ground surrounded by kittens. She greeted us with a purring sound and ran up to us, rubbing herself against our legs. The six kittens were quite wild. They hissed at us and would not let us approach them, finally hiding behind the stove, emerging only when there was nobody in the place.

It seemed that our cat had given birth to her kittens in a nearby wood. As long as the weather was warm she kept them there, fed them and taught them to catch field mice and other small animals, but when the nights became colder she brought her offspring to the warmth we could offer. All the women were delighted and decided that every help would be given to bring up the new family. Avina told the dairymaids and they promised to provide a little milk whenever possible.

The kittens became quite tame after a few days and no longer hid behind the stove when we came in. The other women would now not go to the bunkhouse after dinner, but would come to us and watch the kittens playing. The mother lay on the ground wherever there was a patch of sunlight and, extended at full length, played with her little ones. These attacked her from every side, tugged at her fur, bit her ears and waylaid her tail. She would slap them mildly one at a time or, sometimes, two or three at a time, before gathering them up and tenderly licking and petting them.

We women looked on with emotion, and recalled how we used to pet our children and then, with a sigh, we would go off. I was transferred to another settlement shortly afterwards, but before doing so, put the kittens into good hands except for the loveliest which I kept for myself, smuggling him out of the camp when I left.

One day Marianna was transferred to the sewing workshop. She had up to that time been in charge of camp inventory records, but she had done something wrong and was sent to work with us as a punishment. She was a young and pretty woman. She differed from the other 'wives' because she was careful always to be well groomed and did all possible to evade doing any heavy work.

Her hair was long, twisted into two plaits which reached her knees, and her beautiful dark eyes were always on the look-out for something to eat. By profession she was an actress and belonged to an aristocratic Armenian family. Her parents had perished during the Revolution when she was still a child and she had been brought up by relatives. As soon as she reached mature years she achieved independence and married a man much older than herself, a senior official in the Communist Party who worked in the Kremlin, but both were arrested in 1937.

Marianna was amusing, quick witted and full of caprices even in the penal camp. Very soon after my arrival, she came to me and, after a short exchange of banalities, said, 'I want to be friends with you, but I won't bear it if you show friendship to any other woman'.

I answered that I would willingly be her friend but saw no reason why I should not be friendly with other women. Marianna spent every free moment with me and did her best to interfere with my conversations with other women. She told me about her life before her arrest and after. She found hunger very hard to bear, and when she was hungry gave the impression of being nothing but a little animal thinking solely of where and what she could get to eat.

At such times she could speak of nothing else but of the various meals she had eaten when in the Kremlin. She loved eating, and this was the reason that, in every penal camp, she sought out a lover who had something to do with food supplies. In our camp, Vasia was her lover. He managed the bases and lived in illicit luxury, wallowing in such luxuries as groats, meat, potatoes, bread and milk, besides having his own private cabin.

Vasia was not an educated man but he was decent and kind hearted. His crime, by the way, was that he had killed somebody in some passionate affair. He loved Marianna dearly and in his way cared well for her, but she was so capricious that he often could bear it no longer and gave her a good beating, after which she calmed down for a time. She would come to me then, show her bruises, call him all manner of nasty names and solemnly affirm she would never go near him again.

Vasia would come along in the evening and invite her to his place for supper. Marianna would always tell him to go to hell and she would sulk for a time, but not for long. Before three days were out she would slip along to his quarters in order to get her fill of food and sex. When she had eaten well and was in a good humour, she would often give us a performance in the bunkhouse. She was a marvellous imitator of the voices and gestures of other people, even of children. We would then sit on our bunks while Marianna amused the whole audience with her faithful caricatures of the commandants, their wives and ourselves.

She and I worked together weaving mats for some time in an old barn at the end of the camp. The minimum standard production was set at a very high figure, and we received our full portion of bread only if this standard was met. Neither of us was able to do so until Marianna had the brilliant idea of adding mats made the previous day to the given day's output. In such wise we always had a larger bread ration, and Marianna's name was inscribed on the red notice board as a *Stakhanovitess* – an outstanding worker.

One day a hen came to visit us. Overjoyed by this unex-pected guest, we received her with great hospitality, throwing her some crumbs of bread. She ate the crumbs, looked around the barn and settled down quietly in a corner. Marianna and I waited impatiently until the hen cackled and hurried out of the barn with pride and loud clucks. I went up to the corner and saw an egg lying there. I had not seen an egg for the last two years so I took a good long look at this one. Marianna took two twigs, one longer than the other, and I had to choose one blindly. I pulled out the shorter one, so Marianna drank up the contents of the egg.

The hen came the next day with a friend. Both settled down in the corner and both of them laid an egg. Marianna and I were very pleased, and she slipped to Vasia's place to get some grain which could serve as bait for the hens. The hens came every day afterwards until the commandant's wife came in and asked whether the hens weren't coming there and losing their eggs in the barn. Marianna solemnly assured her that she had not even seen a hen in that part of the camp, but the commandant's wife did not look convinced, and the outcome was that the hens stopped coming after another two or three days. Marianna was much put out by this and made a strict investigation to find out what had happened. Her report was that the commandant had boiled hen for dinner one day and baked chicken on the next. That is how our egg idyll ended, and I never saw another hen or egg for the next nine years.

Marianna had another bout of capriciousness one day. She would not weave mats, kicked aside the willow branches and strode up and down the barn. She hoped that 'he' in the Kremlin would have to do such work. Finally, she announced she was hungry and ran off to Vasia. Somebody noticed this and told the commandant. As life in the settlement was rather monotonous the senior officials often set traps for loving couples and then had a good laugh at their expense.

The commandant had Vasia come to his office and ordered an inspection of buildings needing repair. Vasia locked the door of his cabin with Marianna inside, and together with the commandant's suite set off to inspect the buildings. The group went towards the building where Vasia had his cabin and went up to his quarters. The door was locked, of course. So the commandant said to Vasia, 'Let's have the key'. Vasia pretended to search for the key in his pockets but could not find it. 'I've lost it,' he reported to the commandant. So the commandant had the blacksmith come and force open the door.

The room was empty, but everybody crowded in and began to look for places that might need repair. They even looked under the bunk and then the commandant called out,

'Marianna, crawl out', which the unfortunate Marianna did, in great confusion and to the immense gratification of those present, except Vasia.

Marianna was at once sent off to the punishment cell and was soon after transferred to another penal settlement. Vasia took the separation very much to heart and sent whatever food he could get to her by various devious ways. When his term was nearly up he succeeded in getting transferred and they remained together until he was released.

Two years later I heard from some prisoners that Marianna had also been released and was going to Karaganda where Vasia had been sent.

In 1943 we all awaited the great national holiday of the Soviet Union, on the first of May, with longing. Rumour had it that we would be free from work for two whole days!

Special gangs carted out the winter accumulation of refuse and the last patches of snow from the penal settlement. Buildings were patched up and repaired and the bunkhouses were white-washed. When the great day arrived we were shut up in our bunkhouses with an increased guard. Even so, we rested with profound gratification, the more so that we received a better dinner that day.

Soon after 1st May I was summoned to the office and informed that two large parcels had arrived for me. The contents had been examined and would now be handed over to me. They had been sent by the Polish embassy in January and contained gifts of Anglo-American provenance. The food and articles of clothing were of the utmost value to me, but still more heartening was the thought that the embassy would certainly intervene on my behalf and that I would be released in the very near future. Alas, I did not know then that the Soviet government had in April broken off diplomatic relations with the Polish government In London.

My companions in misfortune, who had always been

sceptical regarding my hopes of being released, now began to hope for the best, too. They were nearly as overjoyed as I was. I was again summoned to the office a week or two later. We all thought it was to announce my release, and I stood before the commandant with joyful anticipation. He told me to sit down, pulled some papers out of a file and began to read, that on such and such a date, on the basis of a regulation of the 'special assembly', I was sentenced, under Paragraph No. 6, to ten years in the NKVD camps for civic upbringing and labour.

My hopes were still so high, in spite of all, that I received this notification very calmly. I thanked the commandant for the hospitality he had shown me for so long and told him that I would certainly not take advantage of it for too many years to come. I concluded with the assurance that, if not now, then the moment the war ended, my case would be cleared up and my person rehabilitated. The commandant smiled and replied, 'The gateway to us is very broad, but from us, it's very narrow'. With that he dismissed me.

My companions were probably no less disappointed than I was, and told me sadly, 'Now you'll have to stay to the very end, from one reveille and roll call to the next'.

CHAPTER 11
Inner peace

Summer was approaching and all the women, regardless of the state of their health and their capability for physical work, were suddenly transferred to general field duties. Those in the work shops were not exempted. Some of the women worked with the men on building works, whilst others helped in the weeding of corn fields, mowing hay and digging ditches.

Some of the fields were many miles distant from the camp. This meant an exhausting march followed by hours under the burning rays of the sun in a stooping position. Hunger and thirst made the work all the more exhausting. Our food became worse and the rations were cut. On one occasion we were given soup made of wild sorrel and all of us fell ill. Not a day passed without someone being transferred to the 'Death Point' camp for the disabled and seriously sick.

To make matters worse this was also the mosquito season in Kazakhstan. It lasted for six weeks and was real torture. The local mosquitoes are small creatures, not larger than the head of a pin, but their assaults upon our bodies were more painful than the effects of the glaring sun. Each of us would be surrounded by swarms of the insects, which would penetrate everywhere. They stung us mercilessly and their venom was very potent. We had to work without masks, so by the time evening came our faces and hands would be swollen and scored with bleeding scratches. The more susceptible women had violent fevers as a result. It was by no means rare for many of the women to lie unconscious on the ground suffering malaria while the ubiquitous mosquitoes kept on stinging them.

All the time, from a cloudless azure sky, the sun would pour its intense heat upon the land. There was absolutely no relief for there was not even a single tree to offer the solace of shadow from the burning rays. Our most frequent wish was that the sun would reach the horizon as soon as possible. It was more obliging in winter, but in summer it made us wait a very long time. I was reminded of an old Polish verse which my companions liked to hear me recite:–

> Dear little sun, fair eye of day,
> Thy ways are not our head man's
> You rise at your time
> But for him that is not enough
> He'd like you to rise at midnight
> And set at midnight, too.

When the long day ended we trudged back to camp, grateful that the evening cool soothed our weary bodies while we held up the more enfeebled amongst us and guided their stumbling steps towards that haven of rest and oblivion, the bunkhouse. Lusia was usually my side partner during these return marches.

Lusia was a very pretty, thirty two year old woman who was due, in the next few months, to finish her five year sentence. We slept next to each other for a time and she became as attached to me as to an elder sister. Her father had been a well known singer in St Petersburg, and her mother an actress. Both died of typhus during a severe epidemic soon after the Revolution. Somebody leased the family home immediately after her parents died and Lusia, then still a child, became homeless.

She could recall little of her childhood days, except that her home was a pleasant, warm place and very fine. She also remembered the times when she and a gang of other homeless orphans wandered hungry through the streets and alleys of that large city. Sometimes somebody would throw them a crust but most often they had to steal. She would often sleep out in the open, huddled up against a wall or under some bushes in the park. It was very late in the year and quite cold when a woman picked her up and took her home, washed her thoroughly, gave her decent clothes and fed her for some days before taking her to an orphanage.

She was sent to Georgia with other children and there she found her second mother-country. Hunger, chaos and cold were rampant in the orphanages in those times, so the children would break out in mass escapes and form gangs for the better plundering of food. They raided the fields and gardens for the most part, though in winter the markets and shops were their hunting grounds. They lived on raw fruit and vegetables and grain. In those days homeless children were common within the Soviet regime.

As long as Lusia was a small girl, the others would cut down her share of the loot, but when she grew up a little, she became the chief of a gang, and, she assured me, always saw to it that everyone got his or her fair share. For that matter, her conduct in the penal camp seemed to bear this out.

The authorities would, from time to time, round up these homeless orphans and send them back to the orphanages, and so life went on: orphanage, escape, orphanage, escape, and so on. Conditions in the orphanages at length improved and Lusia began to study. It appears that she showed a great talent in the organisation of performances for children, so great that the teachers helped her to secure special training in this field. She graduated from a school of dramatic art and then joined a touring company which performed plays in the summer resorts of the Caucasus.

It must be borne in mind that the theatrical world in the Soviet Union enjoys a privileged position. Actors and actresses are popular among the public, are well paid and to some extent have more freedom of expression than the mass of the population. Lusia told me that she earned very much and saved nothing, for she had to make up for the privations and sadness of her childhood.

She was not fated to enjoy this delightful life for long. She married a most dishonest man and divorced him shortly afterwards. As she was his source of income, he was furious and in revenge denounced her to the NKVD, affirming that his ex-wife had often expressed dissatisfaction with the laws of the land. This was enough for Lusia to be arrested immediately and then, as an act of grace, to be sentenced 'only' to five years penal servitude in a camp.

Lusia found life in the penal settlement very hard. She could not get into the swing of physical work. She had a delicate complexion, so sensitive that strong sunlight and mosquito bites often made her swell, whilst the skin of her fingers cracked until the blood oozed out. She went through frequent bouts of malaria when she would lie unconscious in the fields. These attacks of malaria affected her adversely. They not only weakened her heart greatly but also led to profound depression so that she often thought of suicide. It was then that I tried to show her the greatest solicitude, some words of comfort, so as to switch her thoughts to other matters.

I became very fond of her and admired her valiant and decent character. Despite the hardships of her childhood she was by no means immoral. She never lied, even to the authorities. All our companions admired her courage and resourcefulness. None of us was so clever in accruing extra food. She would, for instance, creep up to the barns at night and extract several pounds of cooked black barley groats from the boilers, thus reducing the bulls' ration but increasing our own, and that with very nourishing food. Sometimes she would filch some eggs from the farm, or milk some cows on the steppe during the night and bring back a pot of milk, always sharing her loot with us.

The bandit molls would have gone through fire for her, and often took part in these nocturnal forays under her leadership.

Such expeditions always yielded enough food for a few days. During the whole time that Lusia and I were together she was caught by the guards only once, when she was returning at night with a sack of barley. She was at once incarcerated in the punishment cell.

It was considered shameful by the guards to steal food from the fields or from the official store houses, but the constant hunger we felt made this unwritten law a dead letter. In the Soviet Union, this is well expressed by popular sayings, such as, 'they do not punish for theft but because you don't know how to steal'.

The very idea of theft became deformed by the double thinking of 'a bad thing lay there so I picked it up'.

Lusia was always dreaming of arranging a concert in the penal settlement, and thus gain some respite from hard labour. The camp regulations envisaged cultural educational work amongst the prisoners. There was even a special section for this in every camp, but in our settlement nothing was ever done along these lines. As a matter of fact none of the political prisoners longed particularly for such events, but many of the younger criminal elements gladly participated, the bandit molls especially. So Lusia used all her cunning and began to urge the commandant to permit a concert. She assured him that the molls would work better for it and give less trouble. Finally the commandant yielded to her importunate demands.

We again admired how resourcefully Lusia betook herself to organise the concert and I became her costumes assistant. She 'borrowed' a few sacks from the base store and we brought many coloured clays from the fields and a lot of steppe grass. We made exotic skirts from the sacks which we dyed with the clay, and broad brimmed hats from the grass.

No variety performance would be worthy of the name without a 'Charlie Chaplin', so an authentic copy of his attire was made. There was enough soot in the camp for his little moustache and beetling brows, whilst the tattered boots in general use were so decrepit that the real Charlie Chaplin had probably never even imagined anything like them.

I remember the concert well, for it was the first I had attended while in the penal camps. All the camp's oil lamps had been collected so as to light the hall effectively, or at least so-so. The molls chased all over the camp in search of cosmetics, a little face powder from the free workers, some beetroot to redden cheeks, lipstick. Finally the long awaited evening came.

The first rows were occupied by the senior officials with their wives and all their children (including babes in arms). Behind them sat the lesser officials, and so on down the scale to the back where the brotherhood of prisoners crowded together in their rags.

The programme had been carefully vetted by the relevant authorities The harmonica player, who was the most privileged among the prisoners, entered and the concert began. The choir rendered the inevitable 'There is no place in the world where man breathes so freely' and the bandit molls let themselves go in dances, and sang ballads. Various sketches were produced.

Lusia filled in the waits, dressed in her only theatrical dress (which she guarded like the apple of her eye) and sang in a velvety voice about the beauty of love, the longing of lovers, and so on. When she put on her exotic dress (the sack and clay one) and began to sing 'Kukurachi' all the children present began to cry and scream with terror. I don't know what frightened the children, the exotic dress or the song, or something else, but the combination of the song with the howling of the children made the whole adult audience roar with laughter. Lusia heroically held out to the end and, what is more, was nicknamed Kukurachi from that day and excused from all hard work.

I met Lusia again, in another settlement, during the last year of her sentence. She was released but permitted to settle only in

Karaganda. When the time came for her to leave, I tore off a piece of my rug and made a little cap out of it for her. She gave me a needle and an old pair of stockings which I could unravel and so secure some thread. Her parting gift was therefore a valuable one for which I was really grateful.

At length, the long awaited harvest time came. I was posted to the patching of sacks in the fields and worked near the combine harvester. I was no longer so hungry, as I chewed uncooked grains of wheat all the time. The youth who helped the harvester operator frequently lay unconscious in a hut while he recovered from a bout of malaria. I would then get on the machine and do his work. I would raise the arm and leave small heaps of straw behind. It was pleasant to watch the ripe wheat bow before the machine and give up its ears and haulm, to meet its destiny when the grain flowed into the sacks, not sullenly and unwillingly but, as it were, eagerly on its way to feed humanity.

Every one of the prisoners dreamt of plunging his hands into this ripe goldenness so that he could stuff as much as possible into his pockets. This was our life and our daily ritual. It can be stated that, as a general rule, prisoners who worked on farms recovered their strength during the summer because of the raw, ripe grain.

When the harvester was at work far from base camp we would spend the night in the open air on the steppe. The length of our day was measured not by the sun, but by Venus. When that planet was bright in the sky we began our work, and we ended it when she re-appeared. On one occasion we reached a spot whence we could see, far away on the horizon, the outlines of Temirtau, the new centre for the chemical industry.

During the war, much of the heavy industries were transferred from central Russia to the steppe, and factory towns arose like mushrooms after rain, built by convicts and 'labour armies'. These labour armies were recruited by the conscription of women and children, for the most part, and their conditions of life and work differed little from ours. In some cases they were even worse.

The commandant of the penal settlement would often come to inspect our work in the fields, where he toned down his official air and would even chat freely with the various prisoners. He often talked with me as he was interested in life west of Russia and asked many questions about it. From time to time he would speak of his own life with naive simplicity.

He told me that until he was seventeen years old he lived in some out of the way Russian village where he looked after the cattle and was completely illiterate. He did not know that there were other nations in the world and, in his ignorance, was sure that the whole world was peopled by Russians alone. He was pressed into the service of a small detachment of the Red Army during the Revolution in 1918. He did not know why he had to fight, or why there was a civil war on. He was even ordered to fight his fellow countrymen, his brethren, as he called them, so he fought and that so valiantly that he was awarded various medals for his part in this fratricidal strife.

When the fighting ended he did not return to his native village but began his schooling and with great diligence extended the range of his knowledge. He graduated not only from the compulsory school but also from an agricultural secondary. He became a Party member and was shortly afterwards posted to the agricultural estates run by the secret political police, the NKVD.

I must state that he treated the prisoners much better than other commandants did and did not discriminate against the political prisoners. He made it a rule to seek out the more educated people among them, enjoying talking with them and questioning them about scientific matters. In secret from his superiors, he took lessons in mathematics as well as Russian language and history.

Finally, be it stated, he saw to it that the bunkhouses were kept clean and that we had a bath every ten days but, as far as the food ration was concerned, there was nothing he could do.

When the crops had been harvested I returned to the sewing workshops and began to knit sweaters. I unravelled old, torn ones and made 'new' ones out of the remains. This was an absolutely new branch of production and I was the only one to do it. I became a very useful member of the labour force, but this does not mean that I received anything over and above the normal food ration. The only advantage was that for a time there was no hard, physical labour for me.

Two years in this strange rhythm of life had passed as mere hardship and sheer existence, when I began to experience the current day as such and to lead what I called a 'double life'. I began closely to observe not only myself but also the external features of life in others and their reactions.

The next step was to examine the transmutations of these reactions into moral concepts. Gradually I began to surround myself with this world and to combat the obstacles which cluttered up my road. I was restricted in terms of space and action, but I made a significant discovery which led to an understanding of real freedom. I found the limitless world of thought.

My longing for my children was still very strong, and I realised clearly that physical impotence barred me from inter-rupting it by rejoining them. Every thought of them caused me real pain, and I felt that a continuation of this approach would certainly not help them, but harm me to the extent that I would never see them again. I made it a rule to extend my conscious-ness towards their upbringing, and made it a daily practice to 'transmit' to them all my solicitude and best wishes, and somehow these manifestations of heart and soul assumed the form of prayer.

'Though bound by age old love, the power of enemies has torn us apart . . . fellow men have cast me into Siberia and led my children out into the great unknown world . . . dear little hearts, trembling souls, suddenly motherless, fatherless, homeless. Thou has willed it, O Lord. May Thy will then be my will, but hear me out. Thou that art within me and over me, grant that their young, receptive souls be upheld, give power to my distressed thoughts. Grant that they flow to them with the power of the pure love of a mother's heart, and grant that they guard them as if a granite wall against the access of muddy waters.'

Only thus was it in my power to do something for them, as I called them up in my thoughts.

Real hunger very often afflicted me, and it was only rarely that I could get something beyond the standard ration. Many prisoners starved to death. Small wonder that at meal times I began to concentrate ever more attention upon eating and in my thoughts concentrated upon every crumb of bread so that it would yield some of its strength to help me endure this life of privation. Drinking plain water I begged it to share the energy within it and, conducting deep breathing exercises every day, I consciously strove to absorb health and strength. I lived with the conscious realisation of every vibration which could be felt around me.

There were sometimes hateful external blows which struck at me painfully, but these were gradually transformed into a calmness which yielded a great sympathy for the people who suffered with me, as also for those who so brutally trampled the human dignity of their fellow men. I sorrowed that this attitude would be handed on by them.

There were about two hundred women and over a thousand men in our penal settlement, the number of political prisoners increasing every month. The bunkhouse in which I lived was the liveliest one in the evenings. The women came in from work, related the events of the day, including such important things as what eatables had been 'found' and picked up. The women with many years of confinement behind them gave life in the bunkhouse a certain rhythm which enabled the new-comers to fit into the established customs and routine more easily. On the whole, however, every woman lived her own life and did not pry into that of her neighbour.

Personal habits required much understanding for others so that they would not clash. As a result, despite the great variety of characters and intellectual level, our co-existence was peaceful on the whole. Little groups would establish friendly relations with others and extend mutual aid. In such ways, our life extended its scope and acquired a richer content. We found it brought relief to talk about ourselves and mutual help yielded a satisfying emotion which linked with the ties of inner solidarity and proximity. The very thought of giving pleasure not only to oneself but also to one's friend enhanced the energy needed to disregard the menaces of authority and repression. It was really a delight to scrounge food and share it with a friend.

On one side of me, Lusia had her bunk. Auntie Liza slept on the other side, after whom came Mikolayevna and others. Auntie Liza came from a village deep in Ukraine. Though she spent all day in the hut, she always tried to take up as little room as possible. She had been a prisoner for some years and during the first few of them had been allocated the heaviest work with the result that she over-strained herself and suffered from a badly descended uterus. All she could do now was to help in keeping the hut tidy.

Auntie Liza had five grown up sons, three daughters and so many grandchildren that she always got their names mixed up. Her sons were fighting at the front and she had received no news of them since the war broke out. She was a shy woman and made no friendships with the other women. She would sit on her bunk and spin wool and yarn for the commandant as she looked at the photographs of her children and grandchildren. Gazing at them, she would pick up the photographs of one or other of her sons and, uttering his name, would sigh, 'Oh my dear falcon, where have you flown? May God bless you.'

It was at one of these moments that I sat down beside her on the bunk. She swiftly slipped the photograph under her rug and looked at me with suspicion but, when I spoke to her in a friendly way, she shyly showed me the photographs of all her 'falcons'. To the surprise of everyone else we became close friends from that time on.

Resting side by side, Auntie Liza would tell me all that brought her joy or sorrow, but she was happiest when she was telling me about her children and grandchildren and, strangely enough, why she had been arrested and sentenced.

It appeared that she had received a letter, many years before, from a relative in America and, during the purge, someone in the village remembered this event and told the secret police about it. She was arrested on the charge of 'espionage'. Auntie Liza was illiterate and had never heard this word before. When the examining magistrate said she was charged with 'espionage', she calmly answered that if '. . .' (she could never pronounce the word) was some prohibitive medicine for horses, she had never bought any. The magistrate smiled and replied, 'It doesn't matter whether you bought it or not, you'll pay for it'. She was paying for it with ten years of hard labour.

The other prisoners had explained to her what 'espionage' meant, but to the very end she could never understand why she had been arrested and sentenced to penal servitude. When I was leaving that particular settlement, Auntie Liza was still gazing steadfastly at the photographs of her 'falcons'. We parted as good friends, and I never saw her again, but I often wondered whether any or all of Auntie Liza's 'falcons' returned safely from the war.

Afina Mikolayevna had a large head and dense, grey hair cut short. She was always bubbling over with the most fantastic news as she bustled about the penal settlement with enormous vigour and energy. She was a barrister by profession, the daughter of an eminent barrister in Odessa before the Revolution. She bore the fine French surname of Rousseau, and always liked to brag that not only Russian and Polish blood flowed in her veins, but also Greek and French. She gave everybody sound legal advice and wrote innumerable petitions and applications to Moscow on behalf of herself and hundreds of others. No reply was ever received.

When I was there, she was working on the weaving of mats with such energy that no one could equal her output and she won a larger bread ration than the others.

She dressed in an old-fashioned jacket with large pockets, in which she reminded me of an eighteenth century French burgher. She always had grain in her pockets, or sunflower seeds, and was eternally chewing something or other. She would approach one of the women in the hut and tell her, under the strictest conditions of secrecy, every latest and 'genuine' piece of news she had picked up. She would put her hand into one of her pockets and offer a piece of sunflower seed cake or the like. I must say she invariably tried to inject some of her optimism into others.

As she wrote petitions and applications of all kinds, she had close contacts with those having something to do with the food supply. She most liked to visit the dairymaids' hut, where they always fed her well, and from where she could secretly bring something to eat for her fellow prisoners. This she did so cleverly that the guards never noticed. She had a kind and noble heart, and was always ready to help others. I will never forget that, when I was lying prostrate with malaria, she and Auntie Liza took it in turns to tend to me as if they were my dearest sisters.

I was sent out with Lusia one day to a little farmstead some three miles away. It had only three buildings, two barns and a small hut. The women lived at one end of the hut and the men, who were nearing the end of their sentence, at the other. Just behind, there was a largish pond with swarms of mosquitoes. All told, there were eighteen of us, women working in the barns whilst the men mowed grass. Lusia's task was to mend and patch sacks, whilst I had been detailed to watch the harvester at night.

It is the custom, in the Soviet State, that any machine left in the fields must be watched at night in case of attempted sabotage. The harvester was nearly two miles away and it was late in the day when I was told to set out, with a general idea of the direction I should take. As this was the first time and dusk was falling fast I walked off at a sharp pace. I walked for a great distance but could not catch sight of the machine.

It was getting really dark now. The bushes assumed strange shapes and, as I looked back, gleaming points here and there seemed to be following me. My scalp began to creep. It had been said that there were wolves in our vicinity. Simply sweating with fear, I covered my head with the rug I was carrying (from an American gift parcel, by the way), stretched out my arms and ran blindly ahead, although I cannot today give any logical reason for running about with my head swathed in a rug. The wind lifted the rug a little and to my intense relief, the harvester loomed up just in front of me. I joyfully ran up to it and clambered into the seat.

For some reason it seemed to offer absolute refuge from all the terrors of the night. Chance sometimes plays strange and not always unpleasant tricks. In this case, it led me straight to the harvester despite my panic stricken flight through the darkness. It was mere chance, or possibly some sixth sense, or providence – or possibly, when the senses were being paralysed, intuition began to work.

I hardly slept that night, certainly not after midnight or thereabouts, when the wolves gathered around the harvester, albeit at a respectable distance, and howled away in blood-curdling fashion.

I had never before heard the howling of wolves and had not imagined it could be so terrifying. They seemed to be coming closer. I was now really frightened, when I suddenly recalled the paradoxical 'there's nothing more frightening than fear'. I jumped down and, picking up an iron bar, began to bang it against the harvester in an effort to drown the howling. As my blows reverberated, the echoes came back from afar so that the whole steppe seemed to be in an uproar. I stopped only when my arms were so tired that the bar fell to the ground. The last echoes died away. All was quiet again, and the wolves could no longer be heard.

The convict labourers came very early in the morning accompanied by an escort. The leader of the latter, a Kazakh, rode up on his horse and exclaimed, 'So the wolves didn't eat you after all. I can't understand how the Chief could have sent you, a woman, into the steppe alone. I'll tell him to transfer you.'

I begged him not to trouble, explaining that I had volunteered for that work.

Some of the prisoners came up to me later and confidentially told me the latest news. 'There was a regular cannonade last night. The Germans must have been bombing Karaganda.'

Alas, I had to disillusion them and related how I had scared away the wolves. When I returned to the camp and told the women about my nocturnal adventures, they were not impressed. They had heard my clamour but it had not worried them for, they assured me, wolves never attack a human being in the summer, and rarely do even in winter.

I went out a little earlier that evening and found the gang still at work near the harvester. I collected some ears of wheat and prepared the grain for cooking. Wolves again approached me, howled and came closer until I frightened them away with my banging. I found the howling less terrible this time. Long drawn out, it seemed infinitely sad and poignantly longing, inexpressibly distant though so near. As I longed in utter sadness for my far off native land and loved ones, I felt a fellow feeling in their wailing, plaintive lament.

Thereafter, I would often lean back and gaze at the marvellous firmament of Kazakhstan. The stars there seemed larger, enormously greater than elsewhere and much nearer. They stand out in high relief against the dark blue background of the sky. Lost in delighted admiration, I looked at the constellations majestically sweeping across the heavens, unfailing in their constant course from horizon to horizon.

The Great Bear stayed over my head as if guarding these denizens of space. Cassiopeia, to the east, opened her gates and moved slowly along. Below her, Pegasus, Andromeda and Perseus swept by in eternal pursuit. The Pleiades gathered together, cheerily winking to one another while, in the east, the Swan with outstretched wings swam along near the charmingly modest Northern Crown in the company of Gemma, my favourite.

Memories arrived of those quiet starry nights when, as a schoolgirl, I used to drag out a ladder and, tomboy that I was, climb on to a barn roof, spread out a rug, lie down on it and stare at the infinity of space, with charts of the night sky to help me to seek out the constellations.

This universe was now somewhat closer to my heart. I felt nearer to God and to my children. The stars were no less inaccessible, yet I hoped my thoughts speeding to the astral bodies might flow thence down upon my little ones, illumined by the self-same rays at this very moment.

My soul prayed to God in adoration and I felt, as it were, the breathing of higher beings and a sense of one-ness that extended to all above me. I remained intent on the enormous calm and silence of the steppe, the quiet that reigns when God speaks only to our innermost self.

Engrossed in the profundity around me, I sensed peace and thoughts not my own. I began to understand, looking at the unknown worlds, the gigantic constellations vibrating and pulsing in their being, that a wonderful order and harmony governs all. Pulsing, vibrating life surrounds each of us. Yet these vibrations are but forms which pass through many changes.

It is strange indeed that we should have conceived the tenet of having been created solely for happiness. Life is a unity composed solely of vibrations, as it were of various wavelengths, some pleasant and some unpleasant. Lacking tranquillity we seek feverishly here and there until some relative happiness is attained and then, all too soon, lose interest in it. The never ending search goes on. Thus do we act as individuals, but there are also certain political systems that strive to impose their 'relative happiness' upon us, regardless of consequences and the immolation of their victims.

Such systems clash with the rhythm of the universe and distract its eternal laws, and for this reason peace and harmony cannot be found in our world. An ever broader consciousness arose within me as I understood that this order and harmony can be found in one's heart. It is necessary only to reach to the depths of one's innermost being, to control oneself and one's attitude to others. Only this can enable us to find an explanation for all around us. 'He' exists in every being and speaks to one and all, but it is essential that we have the will to hear and listen.

The experiences of these nights brought me a plenitude of energy and tranquillity. Transferred to other work after three months, I knew that those nights had not been wasted, that their teaching would endure as a gain in spiritual strength which enabled me to fortify the faltering spirit in others and, incidentally, to increase the sum of human amity.

CHAPTER 12
Life in the camps

Another detachment of newcomers arrived, this time consisting exclusively of children, from nine to fourteen. They were homeless children who had occupied themselves with robbery and violence. The boys were at once sent to the men's huts and the girls came to ours. Their occupation had been that of prostitution, and they were so feebly developed that they looked scarcely eight years old.

The chatter of children's voices could be heard in the whole camp and, I'm sorry to say, these voices used the foulest possible language. The boys were driven out with the men to work, and to simply keep them out of mischief. They feared nobody and refused to carry out orders. They would not work in the fields and wandered about the whole camp, plundering whatever they could find.

The commandant was helpless and moved heaven and earth to get rid of the youngsters. Finally, to everybody's satisfaction, he succeeded and the youthful delinquents were taken somewhere that efforts could be made to reform them.

There were other young boys, who had run away from the labour camps, but they were village boys and quite another element. They had been conscripted and forced to work hard in the munitions factories where conditions were very hard. The boys could not get accustomed to life in town or to work in a factory, so whole groups of them escaped and tried to get back home. They were usually caught and sent to ordinary hard labour camps.

I worked with some of them for a time, collecting hemp. One

of them, a fourteen year old boy, polite and very nice, kept close to me and finally became attached to me as if I was his mother. His name was Valentin, and he told me that he ran away from the factory because he was afraid of the work. It terrified him, he was hungry all the time, and longed for his mother and his native village. He looked badly undernourished, coughed constantly and became weaker by the day.

I persuaded him to rest frequently and sometimes let him drink my soup ration. He always refused shyly at first, knowing I would not get any more, whilst I was ashamed that I could give him so little. Sometime later he was sent to the 'Death Point' to recover his health. One of the doctors paid him special attention and, from time to time, she would let me know how poor Valentin was getting on.

Towards the end of autumn, a large contingent of newcomers arrived. They were for the most part the worst type of habitual criminals. Every commandant of a penal camp did his best to rid himself of these elements and seized every opportunity of transferring them to some other camp.

The criminal convicts were therefore constantly being shuttled from camp to camp to the vast relief of the sender and the profound resentment of the recipient. I remember how our commandant once received such a 'bouquet'. He cursed long and furiously, but had to accept the unwelcome prisoners. The guards were doubled and stern reprisals imposed on the criminal gangs. To no avail, the bandits did just as they pleased.

Life in the barracks suddenly lost its monotony. Incessant noise became the key note, songs, quarrels, dancing, men coming to visit their mistresses and leaving them. The criminals stole from us. They broke open the food store houses and what they had no time to eat was buried or hidden in the haystacks on the steppe. They once even cached their loot in the commandant's building and, for good measure, stole his clothes and boots at the same time. These were later returned and the trick accepted as good clean fun.

Examining the female criminals in general, many characteristic features could be noticed. First of all, their faces and movements brought to mind various types of rodents, or cats, snakes, or simply monkeys. Some of them were pretty, some ugly. Whether aged eleven, twelve or in their sixties, all of them had an animal cunning and were quick-witted. Nearly all of them had something that distinguished them from other women.

Their way of life seemed to have branded them in some way. Only a few looked dull or betrayed signs of degeneration. They all loved singing and dancing. One of their favourite recreations was to make themselves up as Charlie Chaplin. They imitated him splendidly in mimicry and movements, as they danced the *chechotka*. They had a special cult for the poor little man who was eternally young and of current interest. For that matter, there was much sentimentality and melancholy in their songs, regret for lost childhood, for their mothers, for the lover sentenced to death by one's own father, the Public Prosecutor, leaving the maiden plunged in tears and all alone.

Their life was always shameless, with a superabundance of sexual experience. The presence of other people in the barracks was no deterrent to their sexual intercourse. They were apparently never jealous of each other since they belonged to nearly all the male criminals.

The men, on the other hand, were quick to show jealousy and I often saw them publicly punishing their mistresses for 'betrayal' with another man. They would rip up their clothes, slash their arms or breasts with razor blades, or simply thrash them. The given woman did not in principle resent such treatment. She would proudly exhibit such marks of affection to her friends, who would thereupon exclaim, 'See how he loves you!'

The women criminals looked down upon us. They disdainfully called us suckers and, for the same reason, the exclamatory, 'Princess Turandot* she thinks she is' was used to express the utmost contempt. True, they called us various foul names too, but these were not meant to be insulting. It was only their way of accepting us at their level.

From time to time, one or other of them would have a bout of profound discouragement and depression, *handra* as they called it. She would then sit on her bunk for hours at a time, cursing her fate and sobbing. Simply grovelling in self humiliation, she would somehow express a longing for better things that were quite unknown to her.

Sometimes such a sufferer would sit down near an impromptu prayer meeting and giving one of the participants a piece of bread, saying, 'Here you are, Lovie! Pray for my soul. This is the kind of life I have'. Then, as if nothing had happened, she would return to her usual ways.

Many of them were epileptics. Epilepsy in fact seemed endemic among the denizens of their strange world. It sufficed for one to have an attack for a number of others to follow. They writhed, foamed at the mouth and uttered inarticulate cries. There was no medicine available and all we could do for anyone was to hold her limbs firmly and put a spoon into her mouth to prevent her biting her tongue. If there was some steel object nearby, it would be placed in her hand or applied to her body. It was believed this would draw off the convulsions, but whether it actually helped I cannot say.

I was very sorry for these unfortunate women and girls. I wanted to help them in some way, but all I could offer was a friendly word. Such was their level of consciousness, and they could never attain any other. Society had turned away from them. Their environment enabled them only to develop this

* A Puccini opera based on a Persian fairy tale. Princess Turandot is never to lie with a man. Although a cruel woman she is finally won over by a prince.

consciousness whilst imprisonment could never teach them a better way. They have to be isolated, for they are a terrible community, dangerous yet so pitiful.

Two women ruled over this nether world, Valentina of Odessa and Nina of Moscow. Both had great reputations for their exploits in banditry. Dressed smartly, with faces made up, they issued orders to their well disciplined subjects.

In spite of various penalties, this criminal element refused to go out to work. One day, the camp commandant had Valentina and Nina brought to his office. He spoke with them most amicably and persuaded them to organise a labour brigade or battalion. More food would be provided and all of them would get new *telogreyka* and quilted trousers. He made Nina our tutor and promised to report on her favourably in her records. Valentina was appointed brigadier and one after another the criminals agreed to work outside the camp.

Nina was at first pleased to have been thus singled out. A cultural educational instructor came to the camp, told her what to do and left a few books. Thereafter, she strolled from barrack to barrack with a book under her arm, resplendent in a new white *tielogreyka*. As could have been expected, she never spoke with us on any educational topic, and in fact spent most of her time in the milkmaids' quarters where she was always sure to get some extra food. None of us had previously been allowed to enter that barrack.

The commandant strutted about full of pride, certain that he would reform these women and thereby attract the favourable attention of his superiors. Alas, the idyll was short-lived. The women returned to their former ways within a month. These criminals can work well when they feel like it, being strong physically, but cannot stand systematic work, just as they cannot bear staying in one place for long.

It was rumoured soon after that a large contingent of criminals would be sent from the Karaganda region to the far north. The women were beside themselves with joy. True, life in the arctic could be unpleasant, but the prospect of change was always a great attraction. They stopped even any pretence of work and discussed the coming journey all the time. One day, the healthiest and most dangerous were selected for transfer.

Before the departure they shook hands and begged us not to remember them with grudges. They marched across the steppe singing and shouting, bursting with vitality and eager for new adventures. From the commandant down to the least notable political prisoner, the inhabitants of the camp heaved a deep sigh of relief. Peace and quiet again reigned amongst us.

Valentina's 'adjutant' was Zenka, an hermaphrodite. Of all those in this category in my camp, she was the only one whom I classified as being objectionable. She was tall, inclined to be corpulent, and very strong. Her figure and movements were very mannish. One of her legs had been amputated at the knee and she moved about on crutches. She boasted that she had 'more than one life on her conscience', and she was always despotic and evil. All the women criminals feared her profoundly. If any one of them failed to carry out her orders at once, she would immediately fall into a fury and belabour the delinquent mercilessly with a stick.

The only person who could control her at such times was Valentina. It was enough for the latter to say 'Zenka', or even to glance at her for Zenka to calm down at once and go up to her leader humbly. Zenka was always ready to carry out even the slightest wish expressed by Valentina. We were sure that if Valentina were to demand the head of the commandant, Zenka would bring it to her sooner or later. This was not some flight of fancy on our part. There were well authenticated cases of bandits gambling for the head of a camp commandant, the loser being obliged to deliver the given head or to forfeit his own. The criminal fraternity was very strict on the point of paying such debts of honour.

Zenka was a very cunning type and soon after her arrival

organised her own 'procedure'. The young hooligan girls robbed whatever they could from us, excepting bread, and if the owner wanted to recover her property she had to go to Zenka. Zenka would then demand a quantity of bread, depending on the nature of the stolen object, and would tell us in a whisper which of the young criminals had the loot. Taking the bread, Zenka would shake her stick and threaten, 'If you give it away that I told you, I'll kill you'. The duty warder would be called and the stolen goods restored to their rightful owner. Zenka would share the bread with the culprit and so the procedure went on time after time.

The gong beat out the alarm one day. All the convicts were lined up in ranks and counted several times. The guards anxiously searched the barracks, and finally the order to dismiss was given. We guessed there had been an escape and spoke of little else. The women prayed for the well-being of the fugitives, a Russian and two young Azerbaijanis, but they were caught after three days and brought back to camp to be flogged in front of morning assembly.

It was a terrible sight as they were mercilessly beaten with knouts until life barely pulsed in their torn and wasted bodies. Dogs had ripped their clothing to tatters and the fangs of the fierce animals had left many a gaping wound in their bodies. When they were untied one of them collapsed. A guard ran up and brutally struck him with his rifle butt, shouting, 'Stop shamming! Get up!', but the poor man lay motionless on the muddy ground.

The camp commandant turned to us and shouted, 'Look at these scoundrels. Look well! That's what will happen to any one of you that thinks of escaping from the camp.' We were dismissed and, as we women trudged away in gloomy silence, our eyes were full of tears. I looked back at the poor men and my heart bled for them: they looked, not like human beings, but like tattered, lifeless scarecrows. (Berazniki, 1943 or 1944).

On another occasion, one of the convicts had escaped from the camp. Though efforts were made to keep this secret, we soon learned who it was and how he had escaped. The camp authorities had trusted him because he had been sentenced for a criminal, not a political, offence, and made him overseer of hay-making. Having considerable distances to cover in these duties he drove a light cart from place to place.

One day he loaded it with bread and uncooked food for his subordinates, who were busy at work on the steppe, but never arrived or returned to camp. His men returned at the end of the day and asked why no food had been brought and it was only then that the camp authorities realised something was wrong. They announced he had lost his way and perished miserably before he could be saved.

He was caught four years later and sentenced to an additional 15 years penal servitude. He was also exhibited at all the neighbouring penal camps as living proof that every escapee would be recaptured sooner or later. The convicts looked at him with contempt and laughed at his stupidity for it had come out that, having successfully evaded pursuit, he had sold the horse and cart, and using his real name, settled in Uzbekistan where the local authorities identified him as an escaped convict.

My fame as a specialist in knitting sweaters had spread to the other penal settlements, and I was ordered to transfer to another camp. I said goodbye to my fellow prisoners and set off in a wagon drawn by two oxen, with my kitten on my knees.

We stopped to rest at Death Point and I dropped in to the hospital in order to visit my friend, Valentin, but the doctor told me that the poor little fellow had died a fortnight before. The news made me very sad. I put the piece of bread intended for Valentin back in my bag and left my kitten with the doctor.

By now I began to feel unwell. My limbs and my head ached.

I ate something at noon and set off alone with my sack on my back walking fairly slowly. It was a good road and the air was crystal clear. Here and there, along the way I saw clumps of *karaganik* covered with red berries and from time to time a lone bush of white rose. As I trudged along, I felt weaker and weaker and began to shiver. I hurried but soon had to slow down until I could go no further. My temperature was soaring as I staggered to a clump of bushes, lay down and fell asleep or lost consciousness. I must have caught my first bout of malaria.

From time to time I awoke and called to my children by name. I thought I saw my husband leaning over me and drifted back into my sleep with a feeling of pleasure for I do not know how long. When I awoke and opened my eyes the full moon was overhead. I felt cold and was covered with perspiration and did not at first realise where I was. I recollected seeing my husband's face just before I fell asleep and began to look around but all I saw were bushes, the bare steppe and the sky. I realised that, of course, he couldn't have been there. He had remained in prison in Lwow and I was on my way to a new settlement.

I became very sad. I felt so poor and forlorn and longed to have somebody I loved by my side. I got up but staggered, and had to sit on the ground for a while until my strength returned. I was very thirsty and my lips were parched, but there was no water anywhere. There were some large dew drops on the grass so I licked them off and gained some relief. Finally, I got up and, step by step, very slowly trudged on to the settlement.

I reached it and went into the hut, but all the bunks were occupied as the women were asleep. I didn't want to awaken the duty prisoner, so I spread my rug on the clay floor near the stove and lay down fully dressed until morning when the women greeted me in a friendly way.

I lost consciousness again and when I recovered it was dusk and the women were moving about like phantoms in the

163

darkness. Little by little, I came to the conclusion that I must have gone through a second bout of malaria just before my arrival. The women came up to me and asked whether they could help me. I was very weak and felt a great longing for some very sour drink, but there were no lemons in the penal settlements. One of the women brought me about two pints of very sour cucumber juice which I drank eagerly. I felt great relief immediately and when I woke up in the morning, found I had fully recovered.

A few days later, I began to shiver again and felt that another bout of malaria was on the way. We had no medicines and, without any process of reasoning, I jumped into the river. To my surprise, the shivering stopped and I felt quite well. I applied this treatment several times and to this day I have never been troubled by malaria again. When I told my companions of my treatment, they laughed and said that the malaria must have been scared of the cold water and cleared off.

For that matter, nearly every prisoner, faced by the lack of medicines, had to practice her own method of curing illnesses. If I were to describe these curative remedies, the orthodox medical world would reel with horror, but they were nevertheless effective. Apart from pellagra, there was very little sickness in the penal camps.

As an experienced convict, my first task on arrival was to amass all the information available regarding the camp. It was a new one, still in process of being extended. It was situated on the bank of the River Nura and, looking northwards, we could see an *auyl* of 'free' Kazakhstan far away on the horizon.

Rather less than a hundred hectares of land were cultivated under vegetables. A special station pumped water from the river and led it along ditches to the fields. There was also a large dairy farm and store houses for vegetables two kilometres away where punishment squads of men and women worked in a desiccated vegetable packing plant.

It might seem that, with all these vegetables about, nobody should go hungry, but, conditions in this respect were worse than at Berazniki. The camp commandant allocated only the very worst vegetables to the prisoners' kitchen, whilst he sent out all the sound vegetables to nearby Karaganda where he sold them for the benefit of his own pocket. Both he and his wife simply hated the 'political' prisoners, and both were equally greedy for money.

Although the commandant's wife officially ran only her own household, she really directed the whole penal camp. It was she who decided which of the prisoners was to work and often forced them to labour for her private benefit. It would often happen that when a gang of prisoners returned from the fields or store houses, she would stop them and make a personal search to make sure they had not pilfered some of the food. She was most unpopular amongst the prisoners.

Soon after my arrival, she called me in, shut and locked the door, drew the curtain over the window and went up to a large trunk standing in a corner of the room. She raised the lid and I was surprised to see that the trunk was full of stockings. She pulled out several pairs of various colours and asked, 'Can you make sweaters out of these?' I had never heard that sweaters could be made from stockings and in my confusion made no answer. She added, 'Because if you don't know how, you'll be put to general field work.' I immediately assured her that I could certainly transform the stockings into sweaters.

It was wearisome work. I had to unravel the cotton stockings into individual threads, then twist up to twenty of these into a single thick thread, and then make little blouses. I could not imagine why she needed so many of them. The wives of the other camp officials asked me time after time when I would be able to knit something for them, but all I could do was to send them to the commandant's wife. She gave them no satisfaction and shortly afterwards one of them conducted a private investigation and found out that she was selling the blouses in Karaganda for a good price. She paid a few kopecks into the official fund, and kept the rest whilst I received absolutely nothing.

It must be admitted that I did once receive something from her. I had brought one of the knitted blouses and found her busy packing shredded cabbage into a barrel for the winter. There was a large pile of cabbage cores on the floor. I was hungry and my eyes rested on the heap and, as I stood before it, I remarked that I liked cabbage cores very much. She gave me two and I ate them ravenously, they were sweet and sound. As I was going out I picked up a few for my companions, but she came up and snatched them from my hands, crying, 'No, no more. I've got to leave them for the cows'.

When I told my companions about this incident, they were most indignant. None more so than the bandit molls who went about cursing her with the extensive repertoire always at their command and, typically for them, left a pail full of excrement in front of her door a few days later.

These street girls always reacted very sharply against people's greediness and miserliness, and against the wronging of prisoners. They would make no secret of their indignation and loudly cursed the culprits at great length with considerable obscenity. They would be incarcerated in a punishment cell, but this made no difference and they would return still more bitter and full of hatred.

The commandant was sentenced to a prison term for various embezzlements a few months later, and his wife liquidated her 'business' and departed.

A sudden thaw began soon after May 1st. The snow melted so quickly that the soil could not soak up the mass of water in normal fashion. All the steppe streams around us, dried up in summer, were now cold, raging torrents. The situation was menacing, particularly as we were surrounded by the swiftly rising flood and all communication with other centres was interrupted. There was no question of help from outside.

The water soon reached the barracks. One of them was evacuated as it began to collapse. Some of the buildings on lower ground were nearly submerged, and several huts with clay walls disintegrated as we looked. The women sat on their bunks in the barracks and prayed aloud or whispered to each other, but none broke under the strain. I and a few others sat on the roof, watching the water reach our barrack walls and then rise steadily. We could hear the cattle lowing with disquiet. The sun blazed above us in a cloudless sky. Just as I had lost hope, the waters rose no longer and began to subside.

All the prisoners were mobilised on the next day to tidy up the settlement. Everything was soaked and blackish. The barbed wire fences were askew, and most of the buildings were very battered. We trudged through mud up to our knees for some days thereafter as we repaired the damage. Finally, all was done, communication with other penal settlements was restored and new batches of prisoners again began to arrive.

Apart from Russians I met women of various Caucasian nationalities: Lezgians, Chechens, Georgians, Azerbaidjanis, and so on. Most of them were the wives of political prisoners. They lived in a separate hut and worked together as a group in charge of given vegetable fields. There were also very many Finnish women, deported from the Finnish territory annexed by the Soviet Union after the Soviet-Finnish war of 1940. They were very resolute and stood up for one another. They were chiefly engaged in transport duties.

All the women were allowed to go about the penal camp at will, but the men political prisoners were kept in a pen surrounded with barbed wire.

One day the rumour spread that an epidemic of cholera had broken out somewhere in the camps. The authorities denied it, and threatened that anyone repeating this rumour would be incarcerated in the punishment cell. Nevertheless, the rumour spread and finally we were all unexpectedly and painfully inoculated against cholera.

Before this took place, we were ordered to bring excrement in a piece of paper to the sick bay, and so a serious problem arose. There wasn't a single scrap of paper for our needs in the whole camp.

The commandant was a clever fellow and knew well how to find a way out of every difficult situation. He ordered the prisoners to go on the steppe and find leaves of appropriate size. His idea pleased us greatly. Instead of going to work we wandered about the steppe and looked for leaves. It was no easy matter to find leaves of sufficient size and the whole matter afforded us a little light relief.

Paper was a valuable commodity and was used in the camp only for important matters by the office. All other matters that needed recording were inscribed on thin wooden boards which were scraped clean with pieces of glass so that they could be re-used.

I made the acquaintance of Judith Hakanin during the second year of my incarceration in the camp and we at once became great friends. She was in her fifties, strongly built and ruggedly healthy. She abhorred prevarication and had a keen sense of justice. She had been in the penal camp already for some years, yet she always worked hard, with strange determination. She invariably took on the hardest jobs: digging, carrying stones and boulders and so on. In the dairy farm she carried heavy milk cans besides working on the pasteurisation and processing of *ayran*, a kind of milk. She had enough to eat as she was allowed as much milk and groats as she wanted. Nevertheless she would come back from work quite tired out. I would often say, as I helped her to undress, 'Judith, why don't you stop working so hard? You must think of your health. At your age, they'd certainly give you lighter work if you asked for it.' Her invariable answer was, 'Serves me right. I wanted such a life and I deserve what I've got'.

As we lay in our bunks side by side, we would often talk of the past. She was a U.S. citizen by birth, of Finnish parentage. As a qualified nurse in a hospital she had been quite well off, but she became an active member of the Communist Party of the United States. She implicitly believed Soviet propaganda and rejoiced that at least one country in the world had happily solved the problem of the working classes, as she thought.

She felt ill at ease in the United States. She considered the standard of life among the workers to be too low so, when she and some fellow Communists were invited to the Soviet Union, the invitation was gladly accepted. Their party was greeted enthusiastically and, surrounded by a whole retinue of interpreters and officials. They visited various centres and farms in the Ukraine. Charmed by all she saw, Judith decided to stay in the Soviet Union. She was given a splendid, well paid job, and for a time all went well.

She began to interest herself in the real conditions of life and work in the country: she often spoke openly of her observations as had been her custom in the United States. She chiefly criticised, according to her, the system of having shops reserved for special categories of the population, such as her own, shops where even luxury articles could be bought. On the other hand, the shops accessible to the rank and file of the workers usually had nothing to sell, though at rare intervals inadequate supplies of foodstuffs or textile products appeared and were immediately sold out.

The authorities took it amiss that Judith did not keep her observations to herself. She was invited to the offices of the secret police after a few months and told that information had been received that she was really an American spy. She was then, under normal procedure and without trial, sentenced to ten years hard labour in a penal camp.

Judith told us how she used to visit her Communist colleagues in American prisons. They had all been sentenced after a fair trial and on the strength of indubitable evidence. She assured us conditions in the U.S. prisons were good. The inmates had fresh clothes, could use the library, read books and newspapers, write, see friends and relatives, and even play tennis. The Soviet women listened with astonishment finding it hard to believe that any country in the world treated its political prisoners in such a humanitarian way.

I was transferred to another penal settlement a few months after meeting Judith. We parted with sincere regret, and never met again. Most probably she was transferred with the other Finns to Karaganda in 1946 or 1947.

CHAPTER 13
Volkovsk

The men beyond the zone looked terrible. They were in rags and were badly under-nourished. The mortality in Karaganda camp was very high at that time, so high that the central authorities of the NKVD in Moscow were intrigued. Various commissions came along to investigate. We knew, of course, that the real cause of this abnormal death rate was the stealing of our food supplies by the camp officials, and the neglect and bad faith of these dignitaries.

They always had several days' notice that a commission was due to arrive and feverish activities were at once undertaken. The commandant tore about issuing orders, often inconsistent and sometimes diametrically contrary to one another. Buildings were hastily repaired, huts whitewashed and bunks scrubbed. White sand was brought from afar and spread around buildings and on every patch the members of the commission might use. A day or two before the event an old horse or a bull, which will have been fed only a little better than the prisoners, would be slaughtered for the kitchens.

As the prisoners had nothing but rags to wear, and should not offend the eyes of the dignitaries from Moscow, they were all driven to work outside the camps when the great day came. This likewise demonstrated how efficiently the camp was run, and how zealous the workers were. The only prisoners left inside were those who worked in the office, in the workshops and in the store houses. Scouts would be posted along the roads and as soon as one of these observers saw the carriages on the horizon, he would dash back to the camp shouting,

171

'They're coming'. The commandant and the other free men, dressed in their best, would assemble before the office or march off to the entrance gate 'to welcome the guests'.

It happened once that a scout saw some carts in the distance and at once reported the expected inspection team was in sight. The commandant and his aides came out in full parade to greet the visitors. Unhappily, these were only a group of emaciated prisoners sent to our camp as being incapable of work. There was much last minute scurrying about as the newcomers were led into the fields or hidden among bushes where the commission would not see them.

An inspection team from Moscow was usually comprised of two or three high ranking NKVD officers and, when they reached Karaganda Camp, they would be surrounded by a crowd of senior and junior camp officials. I counted thirty-three of them on one occasion. The inspectors would be taken on a conducted tour of the camp buildings and shown only what it was thought safe to show. They would go up to a prisoners' hut, that had been carefully prepared for their inspection, and hear the head woman report how many prisoners were housed there and how many were out working.

The first question was invariably, 'Any bugs here?' It had been firmly impressed upon everyone beforehand that there was not a single bug in the whole camp, and the inevitable answer was prudently couched in the same terms.

The second question was always, 'Do you get boiled water here?'

They looked at a bed or two, went to the kitchen and asked the cook whether she received the full quota of food and whether she used it for the allotted purpose. Her answer was always in the affirmative. They examined the bill of fare and sometimes even tasted the prisoners' soup. On such inspection days, the dinner was a gala. There were even 'meat' dumplings. Finally the members of the inspection team walked around a few huts and entered the administration building where a simple though satisfying banquet awaited them.

In principle prisoners were entitled to present complaints and also personally to hand over pleas and applications to the higher authorities. No complaints were ever made in all the time that I spent in the camps. It appears complaints never produced any results apart from the malcontent being made to rue his temerity bitterly when the inspectors had gone.

For the most part the inspection teams had no contacts with the mass of prisoners simply because they never went on to the fields. On the first occasion I told them I had been sentenced to ten years penal servitude without any proof of guilt and that I had written to Moscow several times without receiving any reply. One of them was kind enough to retort that a ten year sentence was not enough for the likes of me. There could be no answer to this beyond a shrug of the shoulders so I went off, never troubling again to speak to any member of a commission of inspection.

I remember once, when an inspection team was expected, I went into the hut to sit down on my bunk and eat my dinner. To my astonishment I saw a table covered with a clean, white sheet. I sat down joyfully on a bench and, for the first time in four years, ate at a table.

The camp doctor and cultural-educational instructor (in one person, and not a prisoner) came in. She looked at me in amazement and snapped, 'How dare you eat at the table when the commission is about to arrive? You know very well that when we are receiving visitors you're not allowed even to breathe!'

I answered reasonably and with mild surprise, 'I learned a song in this country of yours and it goes. ". . . there's no other land in the world as here, where we can breathe so freely . . ." and the fact that I'm sitting at a table and eating can only impress upon the commission that the educational instructor

173

has provided such cultural amenities for the prisoners. They don't know that we always eat on our bunks.'

The doctor gave me a nasty look and went out without a word, but she stopped releasing me from work when I didn't feel well. Our relations soon improved after I made her a nice sweater. For that matter, camp inmates very soon pass over wrongs inflicted on them by others.

After the inspection team left, camp life quickly returned to normal, until the next team was reported due. In the meantime, the commandants of the penal settlements did just as they wished with us, quite rightly affirming 'Moscow is far away'.

Not far from our work shop there was a lone building surrounded by several high barbed wire fences. This was the so-called Isolation Zone, which housed convicts who refused to work as well as the most dangerous and violent criminals. One afternoon, we heard piercing screams from that direction. When we ran out to see what was happening we saw a terrible sight, an absolutely naked man scrambling around the isolation area on all fours while a guard mercilessly belaboured him with a knout from head to foot.

Some of us ran up to the outer fence and began to shout at the warder. Senior officials and other guards hurried up and ordered us away. They then entered the zone and immediately dragged the poor man inside the building, whence his screams and moans continued for long after.

We were assembled next morning as usual before setting off for work, when the same man was led out of the isolation building. He was still quite naked and his hands were tied together. His body was severely bruised and criss-crossed with ugly weals. With guards and dogs around him, the unfortunate man was run out of the camp, as we later learned, to the main camp six kilometres away.

The full story came out a few days later. It turned out that criminal convicts had stolen his clothes and he would not leave

174

the building to his work until his things were restored to him. The guards had thrown him some disgustingly dirty and tattered clothing but he refused to put it on, still demanding that the criminals be made to return his own things. It was for this that he was so inhumanely punished.

Everybody liked 'Auntie Pola', a decent, kind-hearted peasant woman from Russia. She was quite illiterate, but full of wisdom, the wisdom of plain, sincere people living close to nature and understanding.

She endured her incarceration calmly and without protest. She would often state, 'Thy will be done, not mine.' She hand-spun the yarn I used for making sweaters for the camp commandants and we would often sit side by side as we worked. She would then relate memories of her life, and these included the events that had led to her arrest.

Shortly before Germany attacked Russia in 1941 she had several dreams that seemed to have a bearing on the political life of these countries. In one of these she saw Stalin with an overcoat thrown over his shoulders. As she always related her dreams to the family at breakfast, on this occasion she said to her son, ' Vasia, I bet half a litre of vodka that we'll have war in the land very soon'.

As she had seen Stalin with an overcoat over his shoulders and this obviously meant that some other country would force something upon Russia. According to her, no other interpretation was possible, but her son replied, 'You're raving, old girl. How can dreams decide about war?' They all laughed and forgot about it.

When war broke out Auntie Pola recalled her dream, went up to her son and said, 'You see, Sonny, you've lost your bet. My dream has come true.' Vasia went off to the front three days later, but not before the half litre of vodka was drunk. Auntie Pola bade farewell to her son and, in accordance with ancient custom, sewed the 91st Psalm, written upon a scrap of linen, to his greatcoat as a protection against all the hazards of war.

Auntie Pola's daughter-in-law was not a good woman. She wanted to live without restraints so, deciding to get rid of Vasia's parents, went to the NKVD and told them her mother-in-law had known the war would break out some months before the event. The NKVD men came, searched the cottage and put Auntie Pola and her husband into prison. When she was asked in a preliminary investigation how she had fore-knowledge of the war she frankly told them of her dreams. Everything she said was written down, and two or three weeks later, she was informed that she and her husband had been sentenced to ten years penal servitude.

Auntie Pola bowed to all present and thanked them for letting her know her fate, and asked, 'It may well be that according to your laws I am guilty because I had such dreams, I don't know. I can't read or write. Perhaps that is God's will, and I accept it, but, tell me Judges, why are you putting my husband into prison? It is I who dreamed, not he.'

The reply came pat, 'Because he listened when you spoke of your dreams and did not report them to the NKVD'

We parted soon after, but three years later I was transferred back to the same penal settlement and found Auntie Pola sitting on the edge of her bunk and looking mournful. She was glad to see me but could not overcome her sadness. She sobbed out that she could not help it. News had been received a few days before that her husband had died in a labour camp.

Very often some of the women, including me, would experience intuitive knowledge of events to come: new repressions by the camp authorities, sad news, and even atmospheric changes. The symptoms, observable forty-eight hours before the event, say of a sudden severe sandstorm, included an increase of nervous tension, irritability towards others, even towards close friends.

One day, when the weather was hot with a dry south-eastern breeze, but the normally bright sun and clear blue sky had for two days been veiled by a light rosy mist, I and several of the women felt that something new would that day break into the monotony of our lives. I looked at the sky but could not understand the portents. The prisoners had gone off in the morning to their various tasks as usual. Some were building new huts. Others carried clay mixed with straw to the brick kilns. Some were up to their knees in water, opening and closing the irrigation ditches watering the fields. Others were bowed down digging the soil or weeding. Some were spraying the potato plants and cabbages with insecticides. All of us, prisoners and free labourers, irrespective of nationality and creed, and the guards watching us, were waiting for the midday gong so that we might throw down our tools and get our bowls and spoons ready for the coming meal.

As it happened, we heard the gong that day much earlier than usual, and the signal was repeated with ever greater urgency. We downed tools and trudged back to the penal settlement, striving to guess what could have occurred. Those with less experience of penal servitude wondered whether an amnesty had been proclaimed. Others thought someone had escaped, and some whispered to their closest friends, 'Perhaps he's kicked the bucket'. When we entered the settlement, there seemed quite a panic on foot.

Senior and junior officers dashed about excitedly, issuing and countermanding orders. Horses and oxen were being harnessed to carts.

At length, when most of the prisoners had assembled, we were informed the steppe was on fire and that the blaze was racing towards the wheat fields and the settlement buildings. We were to go out at once, armed with spades and besoms made of steppe grass. I had never seen a steppe fire and my interest was aroused. I shouldered a besom and marched forward to fight the conflagration. On the way, we passed the wheat fields with their steady rustle in the breeze and wave-swept surface. The same breeze was fanning waves of fiery destruction in front of us. Some of the prisoners stayed just beyond the wheat fields, and began to dig wide strips to stop the fire.

The smell of smoke became more and more overpowering as we advanced, and the distant crackling of the fire could be heard. Half an hour or so later, we reached the fiery front where we began to fight the flames as in some eerie and fantastic dance. There we were with hands wrapped in rags and faces covered to the eyes, brandishing besoms as we moved backwards and forwards, striking at the tongues of flame stealing along the ground.

At times the fire would creep close to the ground and with a stealthy rustle come up to our feet. Again it would reach high dry grasses up which it would climb, crackling and spurting flames. It would sometimes hesitate for a moment at some solitary wide rose bush, but flames would envelop the base and slither up among the leaves and branches. The bush would hiss and writhe in the heat, become more and more transparent, and finally be engulfed by a dancing, flickering flame. With a roar, burning twigs and leaves would be scattered around to fall slowly as grey flakes to the ground, as greyish tatters. Very soon, the bush disappeared and nothing would be left save the greyish black memory of what it had once been.

The protective zones in front of the wheat fields did not help. The wind threw great sparks over them to the yellow wheat which began to blaze in many places at once. There were times when the fire was all around us and we retreated to the other side of the wheat fields, desperately fighting the streams of fire as they outflanked us.

Our ranks were now thinner as we spread across the steppe, beating out fires caused by wind borne sparks from the wheat fields. The flames in the corn gathered into one huge sheet that swept across the whole field in the twinkling of an eye, then another puff of black smoke followed by a blaze of fire, as the next field was attacked and the conflagration swept on.

We had managed to save the settlement itself and that was, at least, something. As I looked at the burnt out fields where the golden corn had murmured and rustled to the melody of the winds I experienced the regret that every lover of country life must feel in such cases, but the thought soon followed that this, too, is nothing. It was ordained and in any case next year would see the good earth enriched by this martyred generation with the gallant seeds producing crops taller and stronger, more beautiful than ever. We returned to our camp as from a hard fought battle, blackened by smoke, tired out, with scorched hands and very hungry.

Fifteen or more women worked in the sewing shop during the winter. No two of us were of the same nationality or character, but we remained in accord and solidarity.

Patching the old, dirty rags of the prisoners, we related various events in our life, and so time passed quickly 'from one bell to another'. Sometimes when we knew that the guards were distant, each of us would sing her national anthem and long for her native land.

Eloranda was a Finn. She was always quiet and, as it were, cut off from us. Her pale face, with its delicate features, bowed over her sewing machine all day long. She sewed only for 'freed' prisoners and Hilda, a Swedish girl of tall robust build, the wife of the Russian consul in Sweden, who also had been arrested, helped her. Eloranda slept next to me in the bunk for some time and, after she had got to know me better, began to tell me of her life.

She came from Helsinki where she had been trained as an expert cutter of valuable furs. Her husband was a mechanic and they had earned quite a lot together. There was an only child too, a little daughter. Communist propaganda was very active in Finland for a time. Under its influence, she and her husband decided to acquire first-hand knowledge of the 'wonderful' life of workers in the Soviet Union.

They slipped across the frontier together with a few other people and were received enthusiastically by the Russians. They were shown only the best and most striking sights, and given well paid jobs. Shortly afterwards they experienced the real nature of life in the Soviet Union. They were trapped, however. They could not return to Finland, and lived a vegetative life under constant fear of being arrested.

Barely a year after their arrival in Russia, their daughter was taken away by the authorities and Eloranda and her husband arrested and sentenced to ten years penal servitude. She had been in many a penal camp since then. For that matter, she merely encountered the fate that overtook nearly all those who left their own countries in search for a supposedly better life in the Soviet Union. With no news of either her husband or daughter she concentrated all her thoughts on the child, writing to the most varied institutions and authorities in the Soviet Union but never receiving a reply.

One day she did not turn up for work. Though she showed no signs of being ill in the morning, we thought she must be feeling unwell. After a time I began to worry about her and went to the hut only to find her joyfully packing her things into a little bag.

'Eloranda, where are you going?' I asked.

She smiled strangely and, jigging from one foot to the other, whispered, 'Do you know? The commandant came into the hut during the night and told me that my little one had been found. She's not far away and I am to go to her at once'.

I looked at her closely and understood. There had been nobody during the night, and Eloranda quite obviously was no longer normal. I went off to call the doctor but on our way back we noticed Eloranda at the gateway to the camp. A sentry was holding her back and she was in tears, crying out that the man would not let her go to her child.

We persuaded her to return to the hut where the doctor gave her a sedative and she fell asleep. She stayed in the hut for a few days but never recovered her sanity. Day and night she unpacked and re-packed her belongings, peered under all the bunks and corners of the hut and ceaselessly sought her daughter. She assured us constantly, 'I know the commandant has hidden her, but I'll certainly find her'. Finally, she was transferred to another settlement where there was an asylum for the mentally ill. She should have gone free within a year, but I don't know what happened to her. Perhaps she recovered her sanity.

CHAPTER 14

The war comes to an end

The snow storms, *purga* or *buran* as the natives call them, are the chief hazard of Kazakhstan winters. They often last from several days to a fortnight without interruption. All communication is stopped and the 'white death' is the fate of any traveller distant from a place of refuge. In 1942, some one hundred oxen and fifty drovers left the main penal settlement. They were overtaken on the way by a snow storm which lasted several days and buried them all, leaving not a single survivor.

Visibility is down to nil during such a storm. If you hold your arm outstretched, the hand cannot be seen even in the day time. The swirling snow sped by the powerful wind encloses one in a dark quivering world of white darkness. The snow presses its way into every cranny. It plasters down the eyelids, the nostrils and the mouth so effectively that breathing becomes difficult.

No sense of direction is left and the traveller at once loses his way, actually he walks in a circle. Fear seizes him and becomes sheer terror. He shouts, calls for help, but the wind moans and whistles so loudly that it drowns very other sound. The victim is bathed in sweat from his own exertions. The drifts are deep and the snow moist and he is soon exhausted. He knows it is fatal to stop and so struggles on. Finally, however, his exhaustion is complete. He sits to rest, longing to close his eyes for a while. He feels warmer now, apathy overcomes him and he is soon asleep never to awake.

The snow goes on falling, without cease, one day or two, or three, sometimes for another eleven or twelve days. At length

182

an enormous drift covers the victim completely. He will be found in the spring when the snow melts away.

A seven day *buran* came on our penal settlement one year. The weather reports had forecast it some days before, and the camp authorities had made some preparations. All the convicts were called in from the steppe and no outgoing transactions were allowed. No unaccompanied prisoner was allowed to leave his or her barrack, even for a moment.

Fatigue parties of volunteers went to the kitchen for bread and other food sufficient for all the women in each barrack. Visibility was poor during the first few days, and we held each other's hands tightly as we trudged to the kitchen and back. It became worse until we went roped together like a mountaineering party, holding desperately to another rope stretched from the kitchen to the barrack area. The wind howled fiercely and would often blow us off our feet.

Conditions became so bad that we were ordered to stay in the barracks. Salted fish, uncooked groats and bread were left at the doors. The snow became ever deeper and one day we woke up to find it had reached the roof, blocking up all the windows.

The sixty women in my barrack rather enjoyed the situation at first. They could rest and sleep as long as they pleased, making up all their arrears in this respect. The criminal types sang and danced, but our little smoking lamp soon ran out of paraffin and left us in pitch darkness. To make matters worse the three day ration of food was consumed too quickly.

We tried to keep up our spirits and did our best to reduce the depressing monotony of life in complete darkness. A group would get together and relate jokes and funny anecdotes. We exchanged recipes for making tasty dishes. Someone recited a poem or two, and Sonia told us some short stories she had read somewhere or other. Finally, we ran out of topics and the silences grew longer.

The Long Bridge

The mounting tension and disquiet of the women could be felt as the darkness became increasingly oppressive and entered into our very beings. We lost all count of time. There was neither day nor night, and no hours to while away, nothing but an unchanging existence that seemed to have already lasted long and longer. It was even more difficult to take a deep breath, or to think, and we slipped into some lethargic heavy sleep. The bandit women were the first to fall into this state and they lay in the most apathetic silence.

Long after, possibly whole days and nights later, faint sounds could be heard outside. We livened up and began to listen. Snow was being shovelled away. The sounds came nearer until, suddenly, there was a clatter of glass and a ray of light entered through a broken window pane. Even the most apathetic of us jumped up with excitement. Some clapped their hands with joy and called out exultantly . . . some even jumped up and down like little girls.

More and more light streamed in, with ever more delight for us. Prisoners from other barracks had dug a way to our door and this was opened wide to the accompaniment of enthusiastic cheers. It was a quiet, sunny day outside. We had been snowed under in darkness, three whole days and nights. The kitchen was opened up, and we at once received hot soup and groats. A fatigue party was organised from amongst our number and began to help in the liberation of other barracks. Deep ravines in the snow, tunnels almost, provided communication routes within the camp area.

The building housing the baths and laundry was situated some distance from the barracks and administrative offices. One of the convicts acted as washer woman and lived there permanently, all alone. When a passage was dug to the door of this building, we could not find her inside. We went on digging outside until, pushing the snow off the roof, we found her there. Lightly dressed, she was frozen stiff. We supposed she had gone out for a moment, could not find her way back and wandered about until the white death overtook her lying on the roof of what should have been her refuge.

Our work was not done. We had to dump the snow into the nearby river and then hastily repair the damage to all the buildings blackened and shattered by the frost, desolate and miserable amidst the white wilderness stretching away as far as the eye could see.

Again, somebody escaped from the settlement although we were counted often and locked in the bunkhouses at night. This time it was a young Azerbaijani student who had made a lone escape. Though allotted to the punishment zone he managed to gain the confidence of the camp authorities and of the guard detachment by helping to run the books in the office. He was allowed to leave the punishment zone every morning to work all day, besides being allowed to move about freely within the camp until evening.

As it happened, his absence was not noticed until the morning of the second day. This was because a dummy had been placed in his bunk and the guard who counted the inmates at night did not notice a prisoner was missing. One of the others must have helped to cover his break for freedom. The escaped prisoner was a merry, intelligent youth and got on well with everybody. We all liked him and were worrying about his fate.

Alas, he was brought back to the camp a week later, and it was difficult to recognise him. He had been beaten mercilessly and could barely stand. He had become a piece of bluish red meat, swollen and nearly dead, a human rag. Only his black eyes, dark and flashing before, could be seen as dull and tired. An enormous pity came over me, yet I had to restrain myself from screaming in protest against such degradation of a human being. On the other hand, terror seized me that human beings could so mistreat a fellow human being.

We had to hear out the vile speech of the commandant. He

assured us that the same fate would overcome us if we tried to escape.

One of the guards began to incite the dogs to attack the prisoner, but they would not obey and continued to lie around him. Suddenly one of our number, a young girl who always bragged she had belonged to the young Communist pioneer organisation, and who was strongly suspected of being an NKVD stooge, ran up to the poor boy and struck his face with her fist. All the women shouted in protest and one of us, the youthful bandit moll Marusia, leaped upon the girl with a curse, clutched her throat and began to choke her.

This took place so unexpectedly that she was barely alive when the guards managed to release her. They began to flog Marusia with their whips, the dogs arose in great excitement and barked frantically, the women began to shout and scream and indescribable chaos and turmoil broke out. One of the guards fired a shot in the air and we were hurriedly herded to the bunkhouses and locked up.

We were all so moved by what had happened that none of us could eat our dinner, though it was the basis for our day's work. The 'zealous' girl did not return to our bunkhouse and, in any case, all the bandit molls loudly proclaimed they would kill her if she turned up. The commandant transferred her to the bunkhouse of the clerical staff and sent her to another camp some days later.

We now thought to ourselves how Marusia could be helped. After having been severely flogged, she was thrust into the punishment cell. I asked the girls to get some milk from the dairy maids and undertook to deliver it and any other food we could get.

One of the guards was a Tartar with whom I chatted when none of the others was near. He was a middle-aged man and treated us with humanity, even with politeness. When he entered our bunkhouse he would always wake us without shouting, merely saying, 'Girls, get up! The pancakes are waiting for you, and if you are late the boys will eat them before you'.

We all liked him and were grateful that he made the unpleasant act of getting up so relatively mild by his kindly words. After evening roll call, I went to him, and said: 'You must help me. I want to help Marusia by giving her a little milk. Please don't lock up the punishment cell at night.' He scolded me indignantly and ordered me to return to the bunkhouse immediately. The women were very disappointed when they saw me return with the can of milk.

It must have been one o'clock when I quietly left the bunkhouse with the can of milk in one hand and another one of water in the other. It was a dark, moonless night and the only light was that of the stars.

The punishment cell was about three hundred yards away. I carefully passed the guardhouse and saw the duty warder dozing in a chair in the dim light of a small lamp, and was soon in front of the dark cell. I could hear nothing but the beating of my heart.

I was sure there had been no mistake in my choice of a confidant. The Tartar, I told myself, was so humane and kindly whilst he had officially to call me down and reject my request. I waited there and felt very uncertain of myself, just as if I had done something wrong, but then I realised that it was not I but Marusia, a social outcast, thief and prostitute, and nobody else, who had courageously reacted against the degradation of a fellow human being. I put my hand on the latch, but did not have the courage to press it down afraid of what I might find. Finally, my heart stopped racing and I pressed.

The door opened, and I whispered, 'Marusia'. She answered faintly and in the pitch darkness, guided by her low moaning, I found her lying on the clay floor in a corner. I touched her face and could feel a crust of blood, whereupon I began to wash her wounds with the water. I told her all the latest news, and also that the Pioneer girl had been transferred to the office personnel building. Through her clenched teeth Marusia muttered time after time, 'Doesn't matter. I'll kill that bitch all the same'. I gave her the can of milk which she drank greedily and then, leaving her a wadded jacket, I returned safely to my bunkhouse.

On the next day, my Tartar was sullen and angry. He would not look at me, nor did I 'notice' him, but, during the nights when he was on duty, I could always take Marusia something to eat. I was passing the punishment cell during the afternoon before Marusia's last day there when she appeared at the barred window and called out to me, 'I'm frightfully thirsty – let me have a pot of water'. So I returned to the bunkhouse, filled a pot with water and tied it to a long stick.

Just as I was lifting it a group of senior camp officials on camp inspection noticed me. They summoned me and asked, 'What right have you to hand water to that prisoner?' The only answer I could think of was rather inadequate, 'The right of my heart', whereupon they ordered a guard to incarcerate me in the punishment cell with her.

Marusia, I am sorry to say, was very glad to have company. She had fully recovered from the flogging and until late at night related her bandit exploits with pride and from time to time sang thieves' ballads to entertain me. Finally, we lay down on the clay floor and slept until morning, when we were released and returned to our bunkhouse.

Rumours that the war would soon end became more and more frequent. There was an atmosphere of excitement from the early spring of 1945 within the whole penal settlement. We awaited official news from day to day and then, on May the 8th, in the morning, as the prisoners were setting off to their allotted work, the gong summoned us to assembly. We hurried back and saw that the red flag was flying over the administration building. We met some people who shouted joyfully, 'The war's over!'

The war comes to an end

When we were all assembled, the commandant and his suite appeared before us and delivered a patriotic address. When he finished, everybody gave two cheers and we were excused from work for the rest of the day.

There was little enthusiasm among the Soviet citizens amongst us. I was surprised and asked them why this should be so. Somebody answered, 'We are very glad that brotherly blood no longer flows, but the mere fact that the war is over will bring no change in our own life, unless the huts become more crowded than ever.'

'Why?' I asked, 'there will be an amnesty for political prisoners . . .'

'Yes,' was the answer, 'There'll certainly be an amnesty, but not for us. That privilege in our country is only for the criminals. As long as Stalin is in power there's no hope for us and, what's more, we don't believe they'll release you foreigners.'

I could not believe this to be possible and all the other women from countries occupied by the Russians agreed with me. For our part we were quite overjoyed. We were quite convinced the Russian authorities would release all the political prisoners and so we enthusiastically awaited a change for the better.

That day was a real holiday for all of us. The women put on their best clothes, and the men tidied up their clothes too, besides having a long needed shave. The food ration was larger than usual and we were permitted to approach the barbed wire fence around the punishment zone and speak freely with those inside.

The guards looked on indifferently on this particular day. There were more than a thousand men behind the barbed wire, most of them political prisoners, working class, intelligentsia, journalists, civil servants, professors, poets, unskilled factory hands with a leavening of common bandits from every hole and corner in this enormous country.

Some senior officers of the NKVD turned up with a group of musicians in the afternoon. Each of the officers delivered an ardent speech on the subject of the victory of the Red Army, and then the musicians began their concert. So that the prisoners in the punishment zone could likewise enjoy the music, the concert was held in the open between the zone and the rest of the camp.

A large number of privileged prisoners gathered on one side. They were given more freedom of movement and could from time to time 'organise' some extra food for themselves. On the other side was a collection of seemingly human beings, in rags, haggard and miserable. We all experienced something together, standing or sitting on the ground. We listened to really beautiful music for the first time in many years, played by a young violinist from Riga. He played melodies familiar to us all, and each item recalled some episode in our past life.

Memories of the past appeared, homes full of love, friends, pleasant work, concert halls and so on. We felt a wave of powerful emotion, and as I looked at those around me their faces, intent on the violinist, betrayed their feelings. Very many of the men and women had tears flowing down their faces. It was absolutely quiet all around. Even the cows and calves grazing in the nearby field stretched out their necks and listened. The violinist finished but we stayed in our places, still lost in our memories until, suddenly, the sharp command, 'Dismiss'.

The other non Soviet women and I waited thereafter for freedom: weeks, months, and then years. Our Russian friends were quite right. The prison camps became more and more crowded as the years passed.

CHAPTER 15
Karadzar

Before I could finish knitting sweaters for all the 'free wives', I was transferred to the base settlement and again had to take leave of my friends.

This settlement was the centre of nearly a score of penal farms and was equipped with offices, store houses and granaries, mechanical workshops, living quarters for the NKVD and so on. Our bunkhouses were some two kilometres away and I was at once struck by the careful regard to cleanliness and order. There was even a small canteen next to the kitchen so that we could eat at tables. In short, everything here was splendidly masked.

There was no morning and evening assembly, no marching columns of ragged, starving prisoners from the punishment zone, and no visible bandits lording it over the others. Everyone had allotted work, and after morning roll call the workers set out in small groups or singly. My detachment of transient prisoners did not pass through this camp. The only new arrivals were prisoners with some speciality who had been asked for and the habitual criminals were kept in isolation in the local prison.

The workshop in which I was to knit was a large one, equipped with several sewing machines and a shoe repair workshop. Between twenty and thirty people were able to work there at the same time. It was managed by an energetic Latvian woman who was close to the end of her fifteen year sentence. A middle age woman, tall with beautiful blue eyes and nice complexion, she was a friend of our tailor, who was

Polish but born in Russia and was going to be released in six months. He suffered from a gastric ulcer. Zenia looked after him carefully, and after being released decided to settle in neighbouring Karaganda, sending him parcels and waiting for him there to get married.

We sewed only for free people although from time to time, as we had a lot of material, we sewed donkey jackets and trousers for ourselves, the specialist prisoners. In the workshop shabby shoes were repaired for prisoners. The mechanic entrusted with repairing the machines, which broke down often, was a 65 year old engineer who had quite recently arrived. He had left Russia in 1918 and had settled in Bulgaria which had in time become his second motherland. Immediately after the war, when the Soviet forces invaded, he was arrested with all the other Russian émigrés who had not succeeded in escaping to the west in time. These 'repatriated' Russians were then distributed among all the labour camps in the Soviet Union, most of them with 10 year sentences.

Most of the prisoners in this camp had the political 'paragraph'. The office workers and the senior specialists were better fed and clad. They also lived in separate bunkhouses, and were called 'office rats' by the others. Fearing to lose their privileges, they kept strictly together and would not contact other prisoners. In addition, they distrusted one another as there was always at least one of them serving as a stooge for the authorities. As can be imagined, the result was that they deprived themselves of the consolation of sincere friendship, which we in the outer settlements could enjoy.

I was astounded when I entered the bunkhouse in the evening and saw Lila there. I had not seen her for more than three years and was certain that she had been released long ago. We greeted each other like sisters and she at once arranged for me to sleep next to her.

She had changed greatly. She was no longer the merry, witty girl I had known but a woman depressed and without hope of ever regaining her freedom. Her intelligent face was no longer vivid, her eyes showed nothing but fatigue and apathy. Though she longed for manly friendship, she had not been able to decide on a new 'lover' since that first time.

Up to the year 1948 when political and criminal prisoners were mixed in the penal camps, the problem of sex was easily resolved for many of the women. Most of them were between eighteen and fifty and so of an age to long for family and life. Up to that year women moved about the penal camps freely and the same applied to those men who were not subject to a 'special watch'.

The prison conditions always for some time damped down the sexual urge, but further years of confinement brought on a dulling of sensation and life flowed on as if 'normality' existed with the result that, despite prohibitions, the two sexes did manage to attain intercourse.

Women had different reasons for choosing their sexual partners. Some desired not to satisfy the sexual urge but to get extra food. These women sold themselves, as it were, for a piece of bread or a pot of potatoes. In every penal settlement there were men who managed the food supplies and they could pick and choose and often changed their women. When the situation was reversed the women were invariably more faithful to their lovers.

Other women sought a 'lover' with the perfectly understandable purpose of bearing a child. The younger women very often really longed to have a child, although they were not always successful. Life in the penal camps was so monotonous and empty that having a child yielded great emotion and satisfaction, besides freeing the women for a time from all hard labour.

Then there were women who simply wished to have a companion to whom they could speak of their friendships and experiences and who could extend mutual aid. Such friendships arose when men and women worked together, and I knew many cases of such couples remaining faithful to each other after both had been released from camp.

Provided such couples were reasonably discreet, the camp officials in principle did not interfere, for they worked together and were more productive than single persons. Moreover, they were reasonably certain not to try an escape.

There were some incidents of lesbian love and sometimes intercourse with hermaphrodites, but rather sporadic. I also know of great, devoted and fine loves in the camps, but of these quite another book could be written. The majority of the women though, lived in celibacy. They preserved their moral principles, were faithful to their husbands, and with constant thought of their children, repelled every thought of letting themselves go. Within the confines of our small penal world they simply vegetated.

One day, Lila confided in me that she would like to have a baby. With the onset of long evenings in the autumn, we organised theatricals with the participation of many of the younger folk. From time to time too, we had concerts.

Lila had a very beautiful voice and took part in these events. She met a young actor with whom she kept company, but only for a time. As soon as she knew she was pregnant she threw him, abandoned him, managing the whole affair so discreetly that nobody knew. She would now stay in the bunkhouse every evening and, sitting next to each other, we would relate our thoughts and memories. She was again the same joyful girl whom I had met four years before.

In the spring, as soon as the snow began to thaw, we spent all our free time from work sitting on the river bank. Fresh islets covered with variously coloured pebbles appeared daily in the stream and the dense thickets of willows began to sprout leaflets. There, concealed from the eyes of the guards, we would sit in great content and listen to the quiet murmur of the river and its age old rhythm of rushing waters. The banks were winding, and various obstacles had to be overcome, but they interrupted that rhythm only for a while, so that the river flowed on, heedlessly carrying her pure waters to their northern destiny.

'Do you know,' said Lila, looking at the water, 'I think I've found that age old rhythm within me too. Can there be anything holier in the life of a woman than giving birth to a child. I feel that marvellous mystery within me and love that awakening life with all my soul.' I nodded with understanding. 'It's nine years since I was thrown out of normal life,' she went on, 'and yet that mighty urge has come upon me, not only my body, but something much higher. I feel this is something I must accomplish. I can see an objective in life.'

Lila was a painter and shared my liking for nature. This common interest doubtless caused us to be happy in each other's company. She often longed to have brushes and paint, but this was an occupation forbidden in the camp and she had to satisfy her longing for artistic endeavour by collecting many coloured pebbles which she arranged in ever changing designs and fantastic pictures upon the sand. We would often be so engrossed in this labour of love that we would completely forget where we were, to such an extent that we would not hear the gong for evening roll call. In such cases, we would have to spend the night in the punishment cell.

Some time later, I was forced to give up my 'light' work. I calculated that ten to twelve hours of knitting daily needed up to 20,000 movements of the hands and years of this occupation finally produced repercussions. Often my heart would flutter painfully when I began knitting and sometimes a bout of weakness would overcome me during which I could not even speak or keep the knitting in my hands. The doctor advised me to seek a change of employment.

It was just at this time that the woman who received the milk on the farm fell ill. Lila somehow arranged that I take over the job, hoping that the rest would do me good.

The dairy farm was at its summer grazing grounds near Kirgitaz, some thirty kilometres from the penal settlement. Thus early one morning I took leave of Lila and set off in an 'ark' drawn by two bulls. The drover was a Kazakh with slanting black eyes in a round face, always smiling and looking well content. His work consisted of bringing the cans of cream from the farm to the settlement and taking back the empties. He liked his work, the more so in that it differed very little from what he had been doing in his *auyl* before his arrest. In fact, every Kazakh feels happy when he can move about freely on the steppe. Sitting on his cart as it jogged along slowly, he submitted to the rhythm and sang in a monotonous voice during the whole journey, about the events in his life and that of his family, about his friends and about the friends of his friends.

He would from time to time get down, crack his whip and shout at the bulls, '*Cep cebe!*' The animals never changed their slow steady pace. Suddenly withdrawn from the great assembly in the camp, I was quite glad to enjoy a little loneliness now. Half lying in the cart, I looked at the far distances of the steppe, and of my own heart, and in my thoughts was again with my children and my dearest ones. It was a beautiful day. The air was clear and visibility very great. The faint wind caused the grasses and bushes to move rhythmically, and the whole steppe was like a great ocean upon which peace and quiet reigned.

I got down from the cart at times and strolled up to the wild rose bushes with delight and, altogether, this journey was for me a rare pleasure, a real feast. Nothing here reminded me that I had lost my freedom.

It was about noon when my likeable companion decided it was time to eat. He unharnessed the bulls and let them graze. We lay down on the grass and got out our provisions. All I had was a small piece of bread and a pinch of salt but he pulled out a pot of groats and milk from under the hay and invited me to share and so, for only the second time in four years, I drank milk and savoured its pleasant taste. I extended greetings and homage to all the cows in the world.

While we rested after eating Ambayev, that was the Kazakh's name, told me the story of his life. Up to the Revolution, his father had been a rich bey (leader of a small tribal group). He owned large flocks of sheep and led a nomad life. When spring began and very soon after the snow melted away, the whole family would set out with shepherds and flocks, moving across the plain and never having their tent in one place for more than a few days. They lived on mutton, milk and cheese, had tea and rice in abundance, never using bread but sometimes baking oatcakes in covered utensils or saucepans placed among hot ashes.

When the system of collective farms was introduced into Kazakhstan in 1928 most of the Kazakhs opposed it and many of them escaped to China, Afghanistan or Persia with their flocks. They were just about to cross the frontier when the Communist authorities seized the convoy and exiled them all to a distant part of Siberia.

My Kazakh's parents died some years later, and he returned to his native haunts. He found his auyl burnt to the ground, covered with weeds, with wolves having made their lairs amongst the ruins. So he went on to the neighbouring *auyl*, married there, and worked on the local collective farm, but there was next to nothing to eat on that farm. Crop failures and exorbitant levies imposed by the authorities forced the collective farm workers to secure food beyond the regulations. They would from time to time kill a sheep on the steppe and share the meat, but, as was bound to happen sooner or later, someone denounced them to the authorities and they were all sentenced to ten years hard labour.

He assured me that life in the penal camp was better than on the collective farm as far as he was concerned. He not only got his normal food ration as a prisoner but also, as he was working on the dairy farm, an abundance of groats and milk. His wife visited him every year and brought a new child with her every time. She brought six of her children when she saw him last. It is rare to encounter a large Kazakh family, infant mortality is so great. He told me how long he still had to serve: winter-summer, winter-summer, winter-summer and so on. I finally lost count, but that is how the Kazakhs always calculate their years of penal servitude.

After a good rest, we proceeded on our unhurried way. Ambayev returned to his monotonous singing with fresh energy, this time lauding the virtues of his wife, Murdzia, and all their children while I remained sunk in thought until, in the early evening, our destination came in sight, an area of hilly country. When we reached the top of one of the hills, a familiar scene spread out before my eyes although, of course, I had never been there before. On the right were the little white houses so well known to me, the familiar roadway, the bushes. On the left, the old, boulder clad hills, to one side of which there should have been the glass house through which one went down to the coal-mine, but I could see no trace of this building. When we reached the next hill top, here, too, I saw and recognised a familiar panoramic view. On the distant horizon one could see a spreading, white town, Karaganda.

At the time when I was observing the view, the whole scene was flooded with the rays of the setting sun, the colours and the shapes of which were also familiar to me. I was immediately reminded of the dream I had a few years ago in which I saw the view I was facing now. The buildings were there for centuries and I had the feeling that they were waiting for me. I, like a pilgrim, only walked by. Later I also learned that under this hilly landscape lies the second largest coal deposit in the Soviet Union.

We started our descent at the highest speed that the oxen were capable of. When we reached the bottom, we also reached our destination, the state dairy farm and I was allocated a place in the bunkhouse with the milkmaids.

Most of the prisoners on the dairy farm were women from kolkhozes, some of them with political paragraphs (Article 58 paragraph 10)* and others who had been sentenced for criminal infringements of the law, quite savage sentences for what were really petty misdemeanours. I met an eighteen year old Kazakh girl sentenced to seven years for having eaten seven radishes from the garden of a kolkhoz. Others had been sentenced to ten years forced labour because they had stolen one or two kilograms of wheat to be boiled for the better nourishment of their children.

The women looked quite well fed and healthy, and it can be stated that by and large their work here was the same as when they were living in freedom. I noticed, too, that the women here worked much better than the free workers on the collective farms. It was noticeable that they were great friends with the cows and every one of them had the ambition of 'her' cow being the best looking in the whole herd. They tried to secure the best fodder and even stole grain from the store houses to increase their animals' rations. They kept them very clean and well groomed, always chatted with them and stroked them with enormous affection, just as if the cows were dearly loved and close to them.

My allocated job was to receive the milk from the maids and to record the amount produced by each cow. I also had to keep the milking records of each woman which determined how many grams of bread she would receive the next day. I passed my records to the manageress who would copy my figures in her book. In readiness for the next milking I would erase my records, kept on a flat piece of wood, by scraping off the data with the sharp edge of a piece of broken glass.

There were about 250 cows on the farm and it was the first time that I had been with such a large herd. I observed their ways with great interest. I very soon noticed that every cow

---

* Propaganda and agitation against the Soviet Union

had her own individual character, habits, caprices, and friendships. Cows are on the whole mild creatures and live peacefully in their herd, politely making way for one another. There are selfish and unsociable ones, though very few. One of the cows in the herd here was a very nasty type. As she wandered along she would use her horns to push aside another cow or seize a better patch of grass from a more peace loving companion. When the colder days came on in autumn, she would go up to a cow which had been lying on the ground for some time and push her away.

I soon noticed two cows who appeared to be great friends. They would never be far from each other, would lie down side by side and often lick each other. One day the farm manager transferred one of them to another herd. The same day they began their longing for each other. They were restless, bellowing, and after a few days their milk dried up. When they were finally reunited everything returned to normal.

I remember another occasion when the same manager separated a calf from its mother who had a fighting spirit and went berserk. It took a few days to calm her and it appeared that she eventually forgot her calf. Some days later the manager returned and entered the cows' enclosure. She immediately spotted him and went for him. It took a long time but we finally succeeded in rescuing him and sent him to hospital in a serious condition.

The women in the bunkhouse discussed this and praised the cow for having fought for her rights since all of us, in an inhuman way, had been torn away from our children.

The first milking began at 4am and, to be on time, we had to get up an hour earlier. For three months, as I set out across the steppe to meet the cows, I daily welcomed the rising sun, the most beautiful time of the day. The huge eastern horizon stretched out before us and the first wonderful hues of dawn began to appear against the dark blue sky, shy and subtle, flowing lazily as if just awakening. The colours became stronger as they spread over more and more of the sky, mingling, changing, trembling, they ever more swiftly painted new colours on the heavens.

Then, just above the horizon, there appeared a golden mist. The hues of dawn began to fade one after another, ever more quickly. The golden mist rose higher until the sun came up in golden glory. The sky became peaceful, and the sun rose higher and higher. The earth now began to take on life and awaken. Huge drops of dew trembled and took on all the colours of the rainbow. The grasses and shrubs of the steppe glittered as if hung with jewels and our eyes were dazzled by the brilliant colours. The flowers slowly began to open up their chalices

Aroused by the sound of their names being called the cows arose from their warm places and ran towards us, each to her 'mistress'. There were mutual greetings, caresses and chatting. The milkmaids stroked the cows and spoke to them kindly, whilst the animals licked their faces and hands and answered with their soft lowing. Each of the milkmaids milked from ten to twelve cows and these were so trained that they came up for milking in turn without having to be called.

The cart would drive up with the cans, and milking would begin in earnest and of course, the drinking of warm, fresh milk. No milkmaid would drink the milk of another one's cow, and the milk was never mixed.

The milking of the cows always seemed to me one of life's mysteries. I listened intently as the milk flowed into the pails, and the gushing rhythm became associated by me with some higher power, one that distributes its gifts eternally to all that live, though to some less and to others more. The cows stood there quietly and gladly gave up their milk to humanity, and it was very tasty milk, very nourishing. I drank up to eight pints of it a day, and I felt very much stronger as a result.

We were ordered in the autumn to wander out further into the steppe. We advanced from place to place, spending about a fortnight on the river bank, living in huts dug in the ground.

We cooked for ourselves. We moved on and spent the nights in the open, although these were getting colder. We cuddled up against the cows which warmed us pleasantly but, in spite of this, we often awoke covered with hoar frost.

The steppe changed colour, and assumed greyish chestnut hues which quickly became most monotonous. It was livened only by the sunrises and sunsets, and from time to time by mirages. A cold wind whistled across the steppe and we all recalled with longing our warm, lost homes. We moved on with the cows towards the *otdelenie* (the central camp buildings) and impatiently awaited the order to return until, one day, the 'white flies' of snow fell. We slept with pleasure in a warm bunkhouse that evening.

The commandant of this farm was a simple, uncultivated man, but a Communist Party member. He could not bear political prisoners and as far as I was concerned I was for him nothing but a member of the 'decadent intelligentsia'. He used to visit the summer farm from time to time to make an inspection, as well as something for himself on the side, so I did not always encounter him there. Here we met every day and he invariably picked on me to express his dissatisfaction with something or other.

I finally got tired of his attitude and, when he once quite unjustly started cursing at me in the most vulgar manner, I threw my little tally boards and told him I would not go out to work anymore.

I was transferred to my previous bunkhouse until some decision was taken as to what to do with me. I lived with Lila during this time. The matter was being examined and for the time being I ran errands between the little settlement and the branch establishments.

Lila looked calm and well. Nobody in the settlement knew she was going to have a child shortly. She had kept her pregnancy strictly secret as she did not want the authorities to investigate who the father could be. Shortly after my arrival she woke me and said, 'The pains have started. I'll have to go to hospital.' I got up and dressed as quickly as possible, after which we both went outside quietly so as to waken nobody. It was about three kilometres to the hospital, but luckily it was a bright night as the moon lighted the way for us very effectively.

Lila leaned heavily on my arm. She was suffering keenly but uttered not a single sound. Perspiration flowed down her face and I stopped from time to time to wipe it off. The pains came more frequently and I was afraid she would bear the child on the way. We hurried until Lila had to stop every so often. We could see the hospital lights not far off when the birth pains came on still more sharply and she lay down on the ground.

'I don't think I'll be able to get there,' she said, so I took off my jacket to cover her and ran to the hospital as fast as my legs could carry me. The woman doctor was at once aroused whilst I and one of the nurses seized a stretcher and ran back, and very soon after Lila and her child were lying in the hospital bed.

The news that she had borne a child was the sensation of the next day. The whole settlement spoke of little else. Both the free and the penal workers were loud in their appreciation of Lila's smartness in having arranged everything so well. The women folk cudgelled their brains in efforts to guess who the father could be, whilst the very inquisitive ones even went so far as to visit the hospital in order to inspect the baby and then work out which of the men it resembled. However, everything remained in the domain of conjecture. When Lila was up and about again, the commandant summoned her to his office and ordered her to reveal the name of the father but she categorically refused.

Shortly afterwards my case was re-examined and as a result I was transferred to a punishment settlement. I barely had time to take leave of Lila.

CHAPTER 16
Zavod

'Greetings to you, girls,' I proclaimed from the threshold of the punishment bunkhouse.

Half naked bandit molls sat about on their bunks and smoked their vile tobacco . . . under the so-called 'forty' system. The girls got up and, seeing that I had been well nourished, asked, 'Oh Auntie, come from the farm to visit us? Played them some trick, did you, and they sent you here to have a good time?'

'Well, girls,' I replied in the approved style, 'one doesn't drink cream all the time in the camp, one has got to try the prison soup too. Anyhow, aren't you human beings? Why shouldn't I enjoy my visit here?'

'Oh Auntie, you're a real fellow. We'll get on all right,' one of them called out. 'Want to have a smoke?'

I thanked them kindly and explained that I did not smoke, and again praised their hospitality. In such wise I made a good start with my new companions and very soon was treated by everybody as an old friend.

Apart from the molls there were a few educated women from Leningrad, Moscow, Tallinn and Riga, besides several 'nuns', these being women who had been sentenced for the political offence of their faith in God. These non criminal prisoners worked within the camp for the most part. They made room for me in their section and the molls came to have a look at my belongings but very soon drifted away disappointed.

This particular punishment settlement belonged to the Volkovsk complex, from which I had left some eighteen months before to the branch establishment. Although it was the season for desiccating vegetables, the factory was still under repair. We had no light at night and the majority of women had no work to do.

The men's bunkhouse was opposite ours but separated by barbed wire. Actually this wire was no obstacle to the young hooligans since they would come across and sleep in our bunkhouse with their molls, though the latter sometimes slipped through to the men's bunkhouse. Therefore, until late at night, there was an indescribable hubbub in our bunkhouse, singing, curses, dances, free fights and orgies made our life far from monotonous and, as one of the molls remarked, 'it couldn't be merrier in hell'.

The molls had no older leader to keep them disciplined and, moreover, some fifteen or sixteen were pregnant and did whatever they pleased, knowing full well that the authorities would not punish them.

One night, a bandit prisoner sleeping with his moll had an attack of epilepsy and fell from an upper bunk to the ground with a loud bang, accompanied by shrill screams from above. We all awoke, terrified. Many of the molls were likewise epileptic and they now, one after another, fell victim to epileptic attacks.

It was a terrible scene. The girls fell from their bunks to the ground in convulsions, jerking and twitching as they uttered inhuman, animal like cries, like butchered cattle. Some were pig-like, others like the whining of dogs or the caterwauling of cats. The hubbub was equalled only by the utter confusion. Half dressed men ran out of the bunkhouse, whilst the women prisoners began to cry and bewail their fate. Shrieking with terror the 'nuns' began to recite psalms and the holy words mingled with the hoarse rattle of the epileptics and the horrible, foul curses of the other bandit molls. It was only with the greatest difficulty that I pressed through the heaving bodies to call up the 'sanitary' orderly who came with a little oil lamp, like Florence Nightingale, and lit up the scene of horror. Things now became worse as visual impressions were added to the others.

The women became still more terrified and a wave of hysteria swept through the whole bunkhouse. Finally the guards turned up and matters were quietened down a little. They picked up the unconscious bandit and took him off on a stretcher to his bunkhouse. I and the orderly sister, together with the calmer prisoners, now started to tend the poor girls on the ground, but there was little we could do to help them apart from lifting up the twitching bodies and putting them back on their bunks.

Things were much better for three or four days after this, the most unpleasant night that I had spent in a Russian penal camp. The molls soon began to lead the same life as before. In addition they had grown tired of this particular camp and decided to force the authorities to transfer them. They made life a misery for the commandant and his subordinates and proclaimed that they would get paraffin by hook or by crook and pour it over the political prisoners and set fire to them. Whenever a political prisoner received a food parcel from her family, they would seize it from her and sometimes even kill the poor woman.

The authorities looked through their fingers at all this but one day the molls attacked a guard who had entered the bunkhouse. There was a terrible crash and screaming, but the guard took out his revolver and shot in the air, whereupon the girls scattered. Eventually they were transferred to other camps, one by one, and conditions in our bunkhouse calmed down.

A large group of political prisoners arrived to take the places left vacant by the bandit molls. The newcomers came from Latvia, Estonia, Ukrainian, and from Poland's pre-war eastern provinces. There were also some Red Army men who had been repatriated from prisoner of war camps in Germany.

Zavod

I was crossing the assembly ground on my way to work after my name was read out at roll call. A prisoner came up to me and asked me in Polish, 'What are you doing here?'

I looked at him and, not very sure of his bona fides, answered curtly, 'The same as you'.

'Don't you recognise me?' he asked.

Again I answered curtly, 'No'.

'Why, I'm from Rawa,' he said, 'and I used to go to school with your brother. My name is S.'

I recalled the name and at once lost all my reserve. I was so glad. We went in to the factory and he occupied a work place at my table. It appeared he had been arrested four months before and in a short time, without any trial, deported from Rawa. He had come as a newcomer to our camp the day before (it was now 1947). I asked him for news about my family and my home town.

He told me that my father had died of sorrow soon after my deportation to Russia.

My younger sister had perished in a Lwow prison and her husband of a heart attack when he heard the news.

Another of my brothers had been arrested and there was no news of him.

In 1941, when the Soviet-German War began the prisons in Lwow were full of political prisoners arrested by the Russians. They were murdered by the NKVD just before they evacuated the city in the face of advancing German forces, and my husband was one of these prisoners.*

Half the houses in Rawa were burnt down by the Germans, but my home remained. The Germans murdered all the Jews in

* This news that he died in the Lwow massacre of June 1941 was incorrect. The official documents relayed by Polski Memorial in 1995 state that her husband, my grandfather, prisoner number 2022 was shot in Zamarstynow Prison, Lwow on 5th March 1940. This was probably part of what is now known as the Katyn Wood massacres, carried out at various sites by the Soviets in an attempt to eliminate the Polish professional classes.

Rawa, around 7,000 of them, in a nearby forest and there they were buried by Ukrainian 'helpers'. Some of my Jewish friends and their families took poison.

All this sad news was relieved by only one bright item. My mother and the rest of the family had survived and when Rawa was re-occupied by the Russians in 1945 they had moved to western Poland and settled there.

The food in this settlement was disgusting. The soup we received stank so terribly, with worms in the rotten, salted herrings and vegetables. Even the chronically under-nourished prisoners could not bring themselves to eat it. This left us solely with bread and hot water as our diet. Many of the men began to swell from starvation and the death rate among the prisoners rose sharply. It was with real relief that we finally learned that the factory had been repaired and that we could begin to work.

The prisoners at once livened up in preparation for more abundant food. Every one of us now exerted every effort to acquire a piece of tin plate from some old can and then, with a nail, to transform it into a grater. Peeling the vegetables for desiccation, we could eat some, but there is a limit beyond which the raw materials can be stomached, although with the help of a grater an additional quantity of the raw vegetables could be eaten. Imagine eating eight raw potatoes every day, as I did, or up to thirty a day as some of the other women did, and even more as several of the men could do. It was far from pleasant but grated raw potatoes, properly seasoned, could be eaten with pleasure and certainly seemed more nourishing. Here is the recipe:-

'Grate the raw materials (of course, so that the guards will not notice), add some onion and a little salt, then spread on a piece of bread and really enjoy it.' Things were not so good when we passed from potatoes to onions and all the prisoners wept and were hungry.

We worked in one large hall together with the men who, not so long ago, had still been free people. Most of them were soldiers and officers of Red Army, who had been taken prisoner by Germany. In two shifts of twelve hours each we scraped carrots and potatoes. One of the men, a likeable Russian school teacher, would sit by my side and chat with me. I was really interested in his story, because he had managed to survive the war campaign and now suffered as a result. His personal experience was a general history of thousands of Soviet captives, coming back from Germany to their motherland.

He had been sentenced to penal servitude because as an officer of the Red Army he had allowed the Germans to take him as a prisoner of war. He was a sincere Russian patriot and very conscientiously carried out his duties to the State and to his fellow men.

When the war ended he was, firstly, nourished by American occupying troops. Once he recovered he found work in a factory in the American zone for a time and found life pleasant as never before. In spite of this when the summons came for him to return to his native country he immediately applied for repatriation. With hearts full of joy the prisoners of war journeyed back to their homeland, to their sweethearts, wives and children. They were greeted at the frontier with great enthusiasm, a military band played rousing, merry tunes, and they were well fed, almost feasted. Great was their disappointment when, instead of returning to their homes, the whole train load of repatriates was directed to Karaganda and scattered among the various penal camps.

We all had high hopes that conditions would improve after the war, that there would be an amnesty for prisoners which would, as Stalin described it, 'astound the whole world', but more prisoners arrived and the bunkhouses became ever more crowded. When the factory ceased production again, the slow process of starvation began again.

The Volkovsk's commandant came to the punishment zone

one day in order to 'recruit' some women to work in his camp on specialised jobs. So, without any hesitation, I announced that I was a skilled dressmaker and to my rather relative joy, in spite of all, was accepted. The chosen women left the next day and as we passed out of the zone, the men and women we had left behind crowded up against the barbed wire fence bidding us goodbye and good luck. I could hardly raise a smile, as I looked at their emaciated, pale faces.

I was returning to my previous settlement at Volkovsk. It was not far off and we were escorted by one of the guards. The bunkhouse in which I used to live was unchanged, only the faces of the inmates were new with two exceptions. I was joyfully greeted by Auntie Pola and by Tania, the actress. After my stay in the penal zone, I now felt as if I had returned home after a long and tiring journey.

I enjoyed the relative freedom of movement about the settlement, running to bathe in the river that same day and thereafter, until the water froze over.

It soon turned out that I was no expert seamstress. When finally I admitted to the commandant that I had claimed to be one only to get out of the punishment zone, I was quite sure he would send me back, but he was a humane man and allotted me work at the distribution point for sending water along the ditches. It should be recalled that vegetables cannot be grown in Kazakhstan without the help of irrigation.

This commandant was one of the most humane men I encountered during my sixteen year long stay in the Soviet Union. I never heard him use foul language to prisoners, which was a rarity in the penal camps. He often inspected the kitchen and the quality of our food. He saw to it that decent vegetables from the fields were supplied to us, often over and above the standard ration. He also made sure that we had regular baths and kept the settlement spick and span, and he respected the doctor's recommendations that the sick be excused work.

The morning allocation of work took place quietly, without shouting and unpleasant episodes. While he was in charge of the camp, life proceeded as if in a small village where everyone knew his job. The prisoners here were not in such a state of depression as in other camps. This commandant was a Party member and an ardent Communist, and he explained his attitude to us in the light of his Communist views. Unfortunately, the higher authorities considered his treatment of the prisoners was too tolerant, and he was transferred after a year.

My task was, from May to October, to distribute the water from the main ditch to the smaller ones. Our bread ration depended upon the amount of water that passed through the 'station'. A pole in the water showed the requisite levels of water in the main ditch for the various vegetable crops under cultivation. It was I, too, who calculated how much water was supplied daily by our 'station'. The work was light and even pleasant. I built myself a little hut of turf and a sundial which I decorated with pebbles shaped like a colourful mosaic. During the season I often slept in my 'hut' because the labour gangs worked on three shifts whilst I worked alone without a substitute.

The penal settlements with irrigation installations usually stand out because they have trees and bushes on the fertile land, and thus differ widely from the surrounding monotonous steppe. The fields are divided into areas of several hectares each, with a whole network of minor irrigation ditches. It was the task of the prisoners to stand in the deep mud for eight hours a day, opening and shutting the gates controlling the flow of water.

I had much free time now and was glad to be on my own, observing with interest how the crops grew around me. I would spend whole hours observing a carrot or an onion and seeing how they would grow from little ones into ever larger ones, but I cannot frankly state that I ever noticed the actual increment of growth taking place. The plants had to overcome great difficulties to grow at all. The soil had to be swamped with water but very quickly dried under the burning rays of the sun. It would then become as hard as concrete, so hard that it required a great effort to pull a vegetable out. In fact, before harvesting the crops it was always necessary to flood the fields to loosen the soil and make it possible to dig out the vegetables. Often, however, even this did not help and pick-axes had to be used.

It can be imagined what a hard job it was for the plants to grow up and fulfil their purpose. In spite of all this the vegetables were fine specimens, juicy and none of them rotten. I thought to myself, we prisoners have also been pressed into this 'bent' rhythm of life, where with enormous difficulty we had to break our way through in order not to lose our personalities and individuality.

The first detachment of new prisoners to arrive in the spring of 1948 was a so-called special contingent which differed from the others in that it was surrounded by a more numerous guard.

We were not allowed to get close to the newcomers. The men were at once led off to the punishment zone, whilst the women were allocated to our hut. They were Germans arrested in Königsberg, now Kaliningrad. There were also some fifteen or sixteen German prisoners of war, and these looked very exhausted and ragged. In principle they belonged to a war camp, but Soviet authorities for unknown reasons provoked some of them and then, giving them a 'criminal paragraph', transferred them to NKVD camps. They were quite unfit for work and were therefore housed for a few days in the *Atatavonar* stationary, a kind of rest house with medical attention. Since this building was opposite our hut I could speak with the newcomers from time to time.

I established contact with Walter, a captain of the Wehrmacht, who had been educated at Oxford and was a real

European in his views. He was greatly exhausted and terrified by the life into which he had been thrust so suddenly. He knew no Russian and knew nothing of the customs in the Soviet Union. He could not make head nor tail of anything that he had encountered. I was very sorry for him and tried to help a little and so it turned out that, every evening, I found Walter waiting in his hospital clothing and wrapped up in a blanket, leaning on the wall and looking out for me.

We were both glad to have these meetings. He could speak German with me and break away for a moment from this nightmare life. I was glad that I could bring him something to eat from the fields or share with him any extra soup ration I had managed to organise. After all, I was a veteran prisoner and knew various subterfuges and tricks for occasionally getting more food.

We had to conduct our talks in secret from the camp authorities and so kept discreetly out of sight. I listened with interest to his accounts of international events during the war, of new inventions used by either side to deal out death to fellow men, and of the barbarity which had led us to a common fate. Eight years had passed since I last read newspapers or listened to the radio, so this was my first detailed news about the war. I told him about my work for the Polish embassy and that my children had been taken safely out of the Soviet Union but that I did not know where.

One day, Walter gave me his father's address in Germany as he suspected that I would be released before him. He wanted me to notify his father as to his whereabouts. I wrote the address with indelible pencil on a piece of white rag and sewed it to my rug. I kept it until 1955 when, caught by heavy rain between penal settlements, everything I had was soaked through and all the addresses I had written so carefully were washed away.

Once it happened that Walter was not at the usual place waiting for me. When I entered my hut, the women told me that some drunken young man had gone into the rest-house and had tried to kill him but the other patients had stopped him. The young man affirmed he had wanted to revenge himself on a German officer who had ordered his whole family to be shot. After this incident I saw Walter several times but he was shortly afterwards taken to the punishment zone. From time to time I saw him among the prisoners being driven to work in the fields. Towards the end of the summer I was unexpectedly again transferred to the punishment section for women just as I returned from work, and I never saw Walter again in that camp.

Some days after I was incarcerated in the punishment zone, a note was slipped into my hand. It was from my friends in Volkovsk. They wrote, 'You've been transferred to the punishment zone because N.M. told the authorities that you had said, in his hearing, that if you had a little money you'd have escaped from the camp long ago.'

It was quite true, and N.M. had chosen this way of revenging himself upon me for slighting his advances. In any case, I was soon to leave the camp.

How strange are the fates of man! It was Walter who was the first to inform my children, then in London, that I was still alive*. Some of the German prisoners of war were released in 1950 and Walter was one. The moment he returned to Germany he wrote a letter about me to General Anders. When he was given my children's address he made a special journey to London to tell them all he knew.

Eight years later I met Walter again, this time in London's Dorchester Hotel. I could barely recognise him. He was, of course, no longer in his hospital attire and rug. I was greeted by a very well dressed and healthy looking man. We sat down comfortably in the hotel lounge and talked freely, without having to look around cautiously in case some guard was approaching.

* A copy of Walter's letter posted to General Anders is on page 323

CHAPTER 17

The Way to Kingir Camp

When the war ended, there were stubborn rumours that great changes would ensue for political prisoners, but year after year passed and apart from detachments of new arrivals, nothing changed. I awoke one Sunday morning and said to my next bunk neighbour, 'I have a feeling that I am getting out of here.' I was very unsettled all day long, folded up my things and packed them into my bag, and waited. We went to our bunks after the evening roll call and my neighbour remarked, in lieu of a 'goodnight', – 'See, your intuition was all wrong'.

She fell asleep, but I still waited for something to happen. Everybody except me was fast asleep, when the door was opened, and the guard called out my name. 'Get out . . . with your things,' he said. The inmates woke up and my neighbour said with surprise, 'Why, your intuition was right after all'. When I entered the office building to settle the usual formalities, it was just fifteen minutes to midnight.

A guard took me and another prisoner towards Volkovsk in the morning. Some of the political prisoners were already assembled ready for the journey. Only one of the doctors was in our group, the others remained in the settlement. My friends who were staying behind wanted to come up to me and say goodbye but the guards would not permit this. One of them, Nusia, an Ukrainian from Poland, disregarding all bans, ran up to give me a hug and a bag of bread crusts. Among the German prisoners there was only one doctor. Walter and others stayed in the camp. We set off, heading in the direction of our *otdelenie* until, after 3 hours of walking, we stopped on the settlement outskirts. The final formalities were settled and dry provisions for the journey handed out to us. Other prisoners were coming in from all directions and we set out shortly afterwards.

Shortly after stopping I was overjoyed to see Lila with her son, now about two years old. She had been formally freed but actually had to remain in the settlement until further orders, as did all the wives who had concluded their sentences in 1946/47. They worked as free workers, living beyond the prisoners' bunkhouses but remaining under strict control. In time they would be fully released but without the right to return to their homes should they be one of the central towns of the Soviet Union.

Lila had known from documents she had seen that I would be coming to her place and waited with as much food as she had available, but we could not have a good chat as the guards forbade this. Soon after we had to part and we will probably never meet again, but she will remain in my memory for ever. After a few years I got to know that Lila had been finally released from the camp and allowed to settle in Kyrgyzstan.

In the evening, surrounded by guards and guard dogs, we set off again, some hundreds of male prisoners and about sixty women. When we were a safe distance from the settlement and could not be seen by any commandant, the guards did not keep order quite so strictly. We could mix with men and talk freely. I met many of my acquaintances from other camps. We were all greatly confused and wondered where we were being sent. It was the first time we found ourselves without the company of criminals and, for the first time, no-one was concerned that food might disappear from our poor bags on the carts.

When it got dark the guards ordered us to stop and we camped in the open, lying down one by one on the ground to sleep without undressing. The stars winked at us and with their quiet rhythm lulled us to sleep. In the morning we got to the next penal settlement, where more carts joined us. We were allowed to use these carts in turns and so moved faster towards Karabas. I knew this section of the road as I had travelled it seven years before when first on my way to a penal camp.

The vicinity had been deserted but was now full of prisoners' settlements, and in the distance the new town of Saranstoy could be seen. Dolinka, the main centre for the Karlagier district, had been built up beyond all recognition. There was an experimental farming station, electric lights were everywhere and a tangle of telephone wires, flower beds, and lawns. It was full of bustling NKVD officials, well fed and well dressed. We passed through all this luxury quickly, so as not to infect their fresh air with our bad breath and were greeted in the evening by lights and puffing locomotives. We were back at Karabas.

It was difficult for me to find my way about in this new Karabas. There were many new bunkhouses. It was much cleaner and, to my surprise, there were no bed bugs. The whole climate at Karabas was different. There were now two extreme and hostile worlds within it, the worst of the habitual criminals, often abetted against us by the authorities and that of the political prisoners, nothing in between. The criminals were waiting to be sent to the settlements left by us whilst we were to go on to the large isolation camps which they had left. The chaos of the two parties passing through, and over-crowding, was enormous. Every day thousands of prisoners arrived from different gulags.

We were led into a large hall known by the prisoners as the 'station' where we found sitting space only with great difficulty. The NKVD specialises in crowding a great mass of people together into infinite degrees of cramming, e.g. where a hundred people should normally be held, they managed to cram five hundred, and even then said it was quite comfortable.

The bandit molls circulated amidst this dense crowd, although they were supposed to live in separate buildings, but now they had their harvest. Elbowing and pushing, they brandished razor blades or sharp knives and went up to women sitting on their suitcases.

'Hand over that suitcase,' they would demand, the blade already touching the woman's nose. The woman would hastily hand over her suitcase. One of the molls would look through the contents and pick out all the best things. 'You can keep the rest,' the moll would say. 'It won't help you where you're going and you'll get your wooden jacket there anyhow.' Then, merrily, with song and witticisms the molls would leave the place.

The guards looked on all this with perfect indifference for the molls acted on the incitement of the authorities and we were quite helpless.

As soon as we were in Karabas the guards began to treat us with the utmost brutality, beating prisoners with truncheons for nothing. After a dozen days of this inferno, women weakened – sleepless nights in sitting position, frost and malnutrition took a heavy toll and the small hospital was overcrowded.

In our final days there we were led to a medical commission which, with remarkable celerity, certified us all as capable of the heaviest work regardless of our health and physical state. A search was made of our persons and belongings, and here again, the utmost brutality was used.

We were assembled in large groups in a room with a stage. In spite of the guards present we were ordered to strip and throw all our things in a heap. Then we had to go on to the stage where we had to execute a number of knee bends before the orderly. No exception was made, and some of the women prisoners were over seventy years of age. Calling us foul names, with special insistence that we were whores, was part of this degrading performance.

In the meantime the guards went through our belongings. They separated not only everything made of metal, such as buttons and spoons, but also wooden articles, such as bowls and mugs. Every one of us was sorry to lose these things, acquired with difficulty through the years often by dint of going hungry. It must be remembered that the penal camps never supply bowls and spoons. Hence to secure even a broken spoon of one's own was a great achievement.

The guards also seized our dearest souvenirs, such as the photographs of children and family letters. Even although they had been passed by the censors before they reached us. The women demanded that these souvenirs be returned. They wept, begged and implored to no avail and the guards roundly abused them in their usual foul language.

We were now allowed to sort out our property from the heap and so we wandered about, stark naked, searching and then walking out one after another, wrecks of our former selves.

This particular search has remained firmly in my memory as something most shameful on the part of those who planned and conducted it. The conduct and pillaging of the bandit molls was nothing in comparison with the conduct of the guards.

Breakfasts would drag out to dinner time, and dinners to supper time, even to midnight, for fewer than a score of bowls and spoons were allotted to several hundred women. As our bowls and spoons had been seized during the search, we had to wait in a queue to get the necessary things from women who had already eaten, and all this was done with premeditation, to break our spirits and instil fear in our hearts.

After nearly three weeks of this hell, we were given three days' dry provisions and loaded, like cattle, into railway wagons. As the doors were locked, we sighed with relief.

Some of the women had been sent to Spask, many kilometres away. Our destination had not been revealed but we supposed it would be the new political isolation camp at Dzesgark.*

Now in the wagon, for the first time in many years, we were not surrounded by members of the criminal world and the Soviet authorities and it was quiet and calm. We were vastly overcrowded, lacked water, but were relieved of tension. The guard would visit us only once a day, in the evening, to count us. We looked through the tiny grated window and observed the landscape as the train chugged along. We would often see in the distance the dark outlines of penal settlements, notable for the guard towers around them.

All these were branch camps, very densely established in the Karaganda area, one of the largest provinces of Kazakhstan. We passed Kazakh tents with their grazing flocks of sheep, and from time to time, we stopped at one of the small railway stations. As we moved in a south-westerly direction, the vegetation became more and more sparse, and sand dunes were encountered. We were now passing through the 'Bare Steppe'.

Our train stopped on the third day at Dzhezkazgan. It was afternoon and we could see through our window that it was a large penal camp, surrounded by a double fence of barbed wire. Many guard towers were on the perimeter and in each of them stood soldiers with rifles or machine guns pointed towards the camp itself which was brightly illuminated by searchlights.

It appeared that some misunderstanding had arisen. The camp was solely for men and the commandant at first refused to accept us. It must have been a long argument he had with the convoy for it was not until evening that the wagons were

---

* This correlates with a 1948 decree creating a group of 'special camps' for what were termed 'especially dangerous state criminals'. This was one of the Steplag, newly formed from divisions of Karlag.

opened and we were led to some isolated bunkhouses. The men prisoners looked at us with interest. They wore big fur caps and Japanese wind-cheaters called *trofea*.

It was evident that the bunkhouses had just been evacuated. Barely had we put our belongings down when we were ordered to line up and go to the kitchen for supper. The canteen was large and clean. Without cooked food for so many days, we ate the hot meal given us with a willing appetite. The short time spent in the canteen enabled us to establish contacts with the prisoners in the camp, and I even had a chat with some countrymen of mine. We learned that this place was a new political seclusion camp – all the prisoners were quite new and had been brought from different gulags throughout Soviet Union. I learned that former inmates had been German and then Japanese prisoners of war and was told that the region was rich in copper ore deposits and that the prisoners worked in the mines. The conditions of labour were very onerous and the climate was said to be unhealthy. The nearest penal camp for women was less than twenty kilometres away.

The next day we were again summoned for a medical inspection so that our 'high' rating for work capability could be duly certified beyond all doubt. I and a few of the other women somehow were not even examined. I did not even suppose that this omission would later result in a favourable turn in my affairs at Kingir. Lorries took us to the women's camp at Kingir that evening.

It was night when we entered the dimly lit prisoners' hut, a large one and half empty. Some women lying in their bunks, at the far end, got up and greeted us with a flood of epithets and foul language. This was nothing new. It was, after all, the normal speech of habitual criminals, but we were surprised to hear this scum call us 'enemies of the people', 'fascists', 'bourgeoisie' and 'traitors', the whole gamut of Soviet invective directed against political prisoners.

We had spent many years with such criminal elements. They always stole from us, but cared nothing for our political views and did not interfere with our way of life. We guessed these were to be transferred to make room for political prisoners and that they resented this, whilst the camp authorities had incited them to act in this way. We made no answer and quietly lay down in our bunks. However, sleep was impossible, the bandit molls kept up their noise all night and, to make matters worse, brought in their lovers.

It was still dark when reveille sounded. Tired by our journey and the sleepless night, we rose and stood in ranks. The guards came and pushed us into a large dining hall where hot soup, or rather soupy water, was served out. After this breakfast we were lined up in front of the hut and waited in the dark.

Dawn came slowly, and the silhouettes of the penal settlement became clearer and clearer. This camp differed from others. The buildings were larger, with whitewashed brick walls, and looked like army barracks. We waited a long time. The sun was already high when the local security police turned up with our papers.

They first of all looked at us balefully and called us fascists and enemies of the people. The next step was to read out our names, check the length of our sentences, work categories for penal servitude, and so on. It appeared my papers bore no work category and the same applied to another of the women. We were ordered to leave the ranks and told, with a choice selection of vulgar epithets, to go to the first aid ward for medical examination. The rest of the women were divided into labour battalions.

The guards, armed with tommy guns and assisted by dogs, surrounded the prisoners and with the cry of 'At the double!', drove the women through the gates to their work place. Some of the unfortunates were as much as eighty years old, some were very young, some in good health and some obviously quite sickly, often with cardiac problems. When the older women and the weak could not run fast enough, or fell to the ground, the dogs then ferociously worried them, tearing their clothes and ripping their flesh. Using the foulest language the guards urged the women on with their rifle butts. Not all of them could stand on their feet again, so stretchers were brought and they were taken to a nearby hospital. A group of officers, young and healthy, smartly dressed, looked on and laughed heartily.

The other woman and I went for our medical examination. A most charming nurse received us and while we were awaiting our turn, told us something of the women's zone. It had its own sixty bed hospital, and beyond there was a whole medical settlement with many hospitals and specialist wards, but the discipline established here was very strict. Before she could tell us much more I was called for examination. Two doctors looked me over and decided I was fit only for light work. The older one suggested I work in the hospital itself. I gladly accepted the offer and he arranged all the formalities for my immediate transfer to the hospital building.

It was quite by chance that I had missed assignment to a work category while at Dzhezkazgan, yet what had seemed a minor and unimportant omission now proved a most lucky and fortunate one. My allotted work was really light and in bearable conditions. Moreover, I had escaped the worst brutalities of the initial phases in the establishment of this isolation camp for political prisoners.

My first work was handing out meals to the patients, and dish washing. Two months later I was transferred to the hospital settlement where I tended the patients' shirts and bed linen. Sometimes, when the post-mortem staff were overworked, I helped in their department.

When I entered a sick bay for the first time, all the women glanced at me and I heard an exclamation, it was my name, 'ULA!' To my amazement I recognised Helena A. who had been incarcerated in the punishment cell before my leaving the prison in Alma-Ata. Both happy with our encounter we told each other our stories since the last time we met.

Helena, straight after my leaving, returned barely alive to our cell. Three days of incarceration in a special cell had been hard. She had been receiving only 300 grams of bread and a litre of hot water. Additionally she had had '*banya*' (a bath) done, which means that she had been locked in a stony narrow empty room with a small window hole. With her inside, the room had been filled with cold water up to her neck level. Helena had been shouting but nothing apart from warders' steps had been audible to her. Taken out wet, frozen and half conscious she had suffered a severe haemorrhage and landed in a prison hospital. A few months later she was allowed to set off for Karaganda. For the previous couple of years we had been as close as 50km to each other and did not know anything about it.

She agreed to work in a byre, which gave her separate accommodation, better rations of food and one litre of milk daily. After a while she was permitted to contact her mother and afterwards she would get food parcels regularly. Better nourished in the healthy climate of Kazakhstan, she fully recovered from tuberculosis.

When she commenced working in an office, she met a young prisoner – an agriculture engineer and a son of a minister, who supervised one of the biggest experimental stations in this camp. She fell in love, but her liaison did not last long. In two years Volodia died from pneumonia.

A few weeks later Helena was brought to Kingir and delegated to work in a quarry, where she suffered a heart attack and again landed in hospital. When she recovered one of the doctors allotted her to the hospital staff. She fulfilled the function of a ward maid.

The year 1949 ended Helena's ten years sentence. Her only dream was to join her mother, but shortly before her release she received a message about her Mum's death. She fell into extreme despair and we all consoled her.

When she was released she asked the authorities for permission of visit her mother's grave in Leningrad, but they refused and sent her to some sunken corner of Kazakhstan, where she vegetated.

It was interesting to observe my environment, the mentality of the patients and the attitude of the others towards them. I worked in the Medical Building, which apart from specialist wards also had an operation room. Exemplary cleanliness and the total absence of noise set the place off from the sordid world outside. Every convict, the men folk particularly, dreamt of lying in a hospital bed, even for only a few days because the hospital was the sole place where a human being could recover spiritual equilibrium, at least for a while.

Sick prisoners brought from the huts to a hospital ward often broke down with relief and emotion. I saw many a grown man cry like a child when installed in that oasis of peace and humane treatment. The sudden change to such conditions must have made a powerful impression on these unhappy people because the medical personnel, all prisoners themselves, treated every patient with the utmost solicitude and conscientious care, regardless of nationality.

When I started in the hospital all the staff consisted of prisoners. The chief physician was assigned to organise a new hospital somewhere near the Mongolian frontier. It appears he had required too much from the authorities on behalf of his patients. He was replaced by a non-convict doctor who, however, was just as conscientious in his efforts.

Working conditions for the doctors were far from good. There was a chronic shortage of medicines while some could never be secured and the stock of surgical instruments was limited. In spite of these shortages the doctors did all they could and, best of all, their patients had the fullest confidence in them. Thus was trust in beneficent humanity revived and the memory of a better world kept alive.

The Long Bridge

Doctor Shriter, of Swedish origin though born in Leningrad, worked in the Medical Department. He was a man of great erudition, learned and possessing a profound knowledge of people. The convicts and the free both liked and respected him highly.

He fell ill one day and, after many efforts, it was decided nothing but a blood transfusion could save him. Blood banks were, however, not supplied to the penal camps. When the convicts heard blood was needed for him, nearly all of them volunteered. I did the same but, to my regret, it was established that my blood group was not suitable. In any case, the good doctor received all the blood necessary and was restored to health amidst universal joy.

I must mention one of the finest people I have ever met in my life. Maria Afanasyevna, who was a surgeon in the hospital settlement. When the patients spoke of her it was as if she was some holy being. She was of medium height and her pleasantly regular features brought out the tranquillity of her face. She was a graduate of Leningrad University and had been convicted for once reading a forbidden author's poem. She had already spent fifteen years as a convict in penal camps.

Merely to look at her gave one the impression of something very pure and noble. She always reminded me of a day well washed by the rain, when the sky and air are so clean and the sun so bright. Unchangeably the same, she was withal always different. There were days and nights when she was so over-worked that her only respite was to doze off for a moment between one operation and the next. Even when most over-worked, she always looked fresh and was invariably courteous and patient, while she managed to carry out her tasks with unfailing vitality and energy.

I admired her intensely and at the same time pitied her. I enjoyed our talks, if only because they left such a profound impression. Often after a hectic day, I would drop in to her tiny study and start a conversation with her.

'Maria Afanasyevna, I can't imagine how you find so much strength and energy,' I exclaimed once.

'Well it's like this,' she answered, 'I am one of those who like to give. I am sorry, so sorry for all these prisoners. They are sick not so much physically as spiritually.' She pondered a moment, and added, 'I understand their sufferings. I too, was once swamped by a flood of murky experiences, but I'm probably stronger than they are. I swam out and pretty soon threw off that relative 'burden'.

'What I personally went through became easier to bear and I felt sure I could stand more than they could.'

I looked at her as she collected her thoughts.

'You see,' she went on, 'when I was young, an old Jew once told me of a prayer which goes, 'Oh Lord, grant not that I bear as much as I can endure'. It seems therefore, that one must be very strong to bear more than one can endure. I tried to draw still more strength from my inner being, and to give, disinterestedly, to give all that I could . . . to do *good*.'

She paused and then said slowly, with a smile, 'You see, all this work flows from my inner being, and I like it. I only add that tiny little bit of love. Perhaps that is the mystery, the dynamic that humanity must sooner or later attain. Don't think I get nothing out of it. My reward is lasting, eternal, and it's a hundred-fold. These little acts of mine give me an inner joy that nobody can destroy.'

Maria Afanasyevna had a special charm, never before encountered by me. Patients would often say they felt better the moment she entered their ward. Passing from bed to bed, it seemed she sensed and understood the innermost being of everyone under her care. She always left each patient with a friendly word and a smile. Small wonder they virtually worshipped her. Not striving for popularity, her life was such that she was universally respected, by both the free and the imprisoned.

She would never speak of her past life though, in case of need, she could always find some fact or analogy. Every day was an experience to be lived through intensely and to the full. She greeted and took leave of every day with a smile. For her every day was different, and everyone full of interest. Whether difficult or easy, whatever its nature, every day provided happiness and opportunities for helping others. This specific element of love gave her insight into all around, and in this understanding the firm conviction that every human being should bequeath his good deeds to posterity, and to eternity.

CHAPTER 18
The bull in the road

We could not trace the source of the rumour going round the camp that an amnesty would shortly be proclaimed. In any case, the signs seemed against this happening. New batches of convicts came to our transit centre in quick succession. More of the newcomers were freshly convicted and there were fewer transfers from distant penal camps. The newcomers included members of the intelligentsia, villagers and industrial workers from Moscow, Leningrad, and Kiev, most of them from those areas of the Soviet Union occupied by Germany during the war.

There was no pattern that we could identify. The 'crimes' of the convicts hardly seemed serious, unfounded accusations, imprudent remarks on the shortage of bread or clothing, or betraying dissatisfaction with 'unending queues in front of shops', were all very minor offences. Convicts from the annexed territories were sentenced to penal servitude because they had not fled to the interior of Russia before the advancing German armies arrived. The Kremlin fell into a kind of psychosis, isolating lots of innocent and good citizens of its country.

Nearly all the newcomers had been sentenced to ten years penal servitude and it was said that mass arrests were still being made.

Quite a number of the newcomers had been high officials in the Soviet Union, many working in the offices of public prosecutors, firm in the conviction that the sentences they had confirmed were invariably fully proven and just. Now their own fate, and contact with other convicts, brought them to a realisation of the truth. The reality filled them with panic-stricken fear.

A huge group of Ukrainians from annexed Eastern Poland, now called Western Ukraine, arrived in December 1948. Mostly peasant farmers they were a sound, strong, youthful element deemed excellent workers for the construction of the new industrial town of Kingir, as also for the excavation of the 'New Sea'. Having revolted against Soviet rule they had been deported from their homesteads and families. All had been sentenced to twenty-five years penal servitude.

Some of my countrymen were among the newcomers. After service in the Polish Armed Forces in Great Britain they had returned to Poland after demobilisation, but when their ship docked at Stettin they were seized by the Russians, packed into cattle wagons and taken to Russia. They were severely beaten up during interrogations as they would not admit to being spies. Their injuries had not yet healed when they arrived. Their supposed crime was aggravated by the fact that they had fought for the allied cause under General Anders, and for this reason they were called 'Anders' men' by everybody.

Among them was a large batch of Asians, Koreans arrived from the North, Japanese from Sakhalin*, and intelligentsia of every Asiatic and European nationality from Harbin†, including Dr. Harbinski, a famous specialist in children's diseases. Many other nationalities were represented, but in smaller groupings or as individuals, and more than enough work was found for them all. We had learnt from Soviet newspapers that the authorities had decided to construct Kingir, a great new city, in the 'Hungry Steppe' and wondered if this wave of arrests was simply to provide the labour force. The

---

* A large island in the pacific Ocean just off the Russian east coast.
† A city in NE China with a large Russian population of defeated White Guards in 1918.

newspapers also reported that this great work was being done voluntarily and with tremendous enthusiasm by valiant 'sons and pioneers' of the Soviet Union. Those 'sons and pioneers' were actually prisoners originating from the whole Soviet Union and all the other parts of world. I am sure that the Soviet public understood really well.

When inspection and investigation teams began to arrive from Moscow some of the bolder Russian women stepped out of the ranks and began to complain of the brutality of the guards, the unhygienic conditions and inadequate food. Although these braver spirits were transferred to the isolation zone after the teams left, conditions slowly began to improve. The most important gain was that medical boards now made monthly checks and allocated a lighter-work category to the weaker women, or a disablement, non-working category to the older. Each of us received 300 grams of sugar per month. Food improved, we were getting porridge instead of millet now, although those not receiving food parcels from their families remained under-nourished.

A radio set was installed and a library established where Soviet propaganda books and newspapers were available. The barracks were aired during the day, and the profound depression that had weighed so heavily on the camp gradually dispersed. The life of the convicts became, in some measure, stable, and the women formed friendship groups in which nationality or beliefs played no part.

The conditions of life for all the convicts, women and men, working outside the penal camp continued to be terrible. It was autumn now, and cold rain mingled with sleet. The convicts were forced to run to work, but from time to time on the way the order would come, 'Sit down', and they had to sit down on the spot, whether it was dry, muddy, or in the middle of a puddle.

Women worked in the open too, quarrying stone, clay and

sand for the manufacture of bricks, or for concrete for the new town. Unaccustomed to such work and with no proper precautions applied, many convicts were killed by falls of stone or earth. In particular, many women were permanently disabled by strain when lifting heavy stones and sacks.

The convicts would return to the camp wet through, shivering with cold and smeared with mud and clay, and at dawn the next day they would put on the same damp and dirty rags and be driven off at the double. Some prayed for injury and the hospitals were over-flowing. Sick and injured lay along the corridors and on the ground awaiting their turn for a bed, or the mortuary.

One frosty evening the stars were shining in the sky like diamonds as I returned to the bunkhouse from visiting A.H. and dreaming of how wonderful it would be to find on my bed a thick slice of bread, some sugar and butter. I could not stop myself from seeing an image of me taking my bowl, pouring hot water and sugar and adding butter and finally breaking bread. I was thrilled by those thoughts. After all, someone who has been hungry for many years knows these hallucinations, they come without any will and you can even taste the food.

The moment I opened the door of the bunkhouse all my imaginings stopped and I returned to reality. The bunkhouse was poorly illuminated, filled with stinky, stuffy air and buzzing as if over two hundred women were making the sound 'uuuuummmmm'. I squeezed past a forest of dirty legs sticking out to get to my own place where I noticed on my bedding a big bundle. Astonished I asked my neighbours whose was that? They told me that, the evening before, one of prisoners came in to the bunkhouse, asked for my name and left this for me. I opened the parcel and saw what I had been dreaming about a few minutes before, but a much bigger portion. I had a great feast with my neighbours.

A few weeks later, passing the zone I heard my name. It was an unknown face to me. He looked better than others and was better dressed. Smiling he asked: 'Do you recognise me?' and 'Do you remember Volkovsk? – I was in the penal zone there and you were knitting sweaters and in those days you knitted a sweater for a cook. You were getting additional portions of food from her and you were passing some to me. It was a big help for me'.

I remembered the emaciated man from Brest. He said: 'When I recovered, I was sent to Kingir, where I built this town. Hard work and under-nourishment weakened me again. In hospital I met an Armenian who helped me to get a job as a cleaner in this little kiosk and since then I have not been hungry any more. When women came to Kingir I asked for you and waited for you, but you never came. I thought that you did not have money and were in the penal zone with an empty stomach. I took the risk and managed to get to the women's bunkhouse with my little gift.' I was deeply touched by this.

The criminal convicts celebrated their last night in the camp by pillaging the store-houses containing the political prisoners' belongings. They took all the best things and then, with much shouting and whooping, with a song on their lips, they set off in lorries much to their own and our satisfaction. The camp authorities made absolutely no effort to recover the stolen goods.

A few of the female criminals remained with those sentenced for political offences, but they were now greatly outnumbered by the 'politicals' and consequently showed no aggressive tendencies. Thenceforth too, no more thefts troubled us.

Soon after the habitual criminals were sent away the senior commandant of our political isolation zone appeared. He enjoyed the rank of colonel and was said to have close relations with the Kremlin. All the convicts, men and women, were released from work on the day he came and as many as possible assembled in the great hall, while the overflow stood outside.

He began, 'You are all enemies of the nation. We have separated you from the criminals so you should not poison them with your venom. Don't think that we have brought you to a health resort. You are here to work, and rot. Don't count on any relief, amnesty or any departures from here. This will be your grave! For your vile activities you will be branded with a *kleymo*. Every one of you will get a number and you will be kept locked up in your barracks, as in prison, and let out only to go to work.'

He wound up with a long tirade of disgusting invective directed in particular against the prisoners of Soviet nationality. Strange to state the speech made a shattering impression upon these prisoners, the women especially. They had borne all their undeserved humiliations with patience and fortitude but now burst into tears on returning to their barracks.

Typical was the one who asked, 'Why does our country have to be so severe on us?' Others asked in vain, 'Why do our brother Russians treat us to badly.' Another called, 'We work hard and for nothing. We gave birth to heroes for the war and our sons' blood for the defence of the motherland, and now they're going to put numbers on us! Curse them all!'

As I listened, I could hear the sobbing and wailing of women coming from the other barracks too.

We foreigners did not take the commandant's speech so tragically. All of us lived in the hope that sooner or later our situation would change for the better, for when the governments of our countries would arrange our release. The poor Russian women had not even this slender hope. We tried to console them, but they remained terribly depressed.

A few days later, great chains and padlocks were installed on our doors and every prisoner received her number stencilled on several pieces of cloth, one to be sewn on the back, one on the skirt, on a sleeve, and on the cap. The settlement looked grotesque as we walked about looking like lottery advertisements. The women released from work outside the camp remained locked up in their barracks, unlocked only at meal times. It was very hard to get used to this prison system.

A large group of Yakut women from Kamchatka* attracted my attention. They always kept together, were slow to establish friendly relations, taciturn but invariably polite. They sat erect on their bunks like mysterious 'totems'.

Two of them were young school teachers and spoke excellent Russian. During the few weeks we were together I learnt something of the life and customs of their distant country. They told me that the Yakuts are very anxious to learn. They have many schools and hospitals, both male and female physicians, and engineers. Yet, although civilization is making rapid progress in their land, the old customs are still followed in the more distant and isolated *igla*. When an old man feels his forces are declining and he is becoming a burden to his community and family, he invites his closest friends to a feast in his *yurta*.

They sit around and he serves each one with tea and delicacies and talk of old heroic times and other pleasant topics. He rises towards the end of the feast and hands a towel to his best friend who winds it around the old man's neck and throttles him as the others look on. Refusal to perform such a last service is unthinkable.

Again, when a woman is about to bear a child the older women put her into a small, dark closet where she remains in absolute silence, without uttering a single sound, until the child is born. In the absence of these precautions, evil spirits might be attracted by her cries and, learning she is about to bear a child, enter the body of the infant.

Young Yakuts often go out alone, armed only with a knife, to hunt bears. The more they kill in single combat, the more they are respected and the greater their fame.

A new batch of prisoners had arrived. I was too late to see them come into the camp, so I went from hut to hut in search

* A 1250km peninsula in the far east in the Pacific Ocean.

of news. A beautiful young girl was lying in one of the bunks. She looked sad and engrossed in her thoughts so I approached her and for some reason spoke in Polish. She jumped down and, with tears running down her face, hugged me.

'How good it is to hear Polish again!' she cried, as her face lit up. 'I haven't heard a word of Polish for the last three years. I have just come in from an arctic camp where I was the only Pole.'

We at once became firm friends, and I introduced her to the other Polish women and to girls of various nationalities. She was universally liked and we all did our best to help her. Looking at this lovely girl it was hard to believe she had been sentenced to ninety years penal servitude.

Little by little I pieced together Janka's story and was astonished that one so young could go through so much and remain unspoiled. At the age of seventeen she and her brother joined the clandestine Polish Home Army, the resistance force of Poland fighting the Germans. She was at first a nurse in a field hospital in the forests, but was later transferred and ordered to enter the German intelligence service in Poland as an undercover agent. She became engaged to a colleague and in 1945, after the war, went to Baranowicze in Eastern Poland, annexed by the Soviet Union, to bring her mother back.

There she met some of her former friends, one of whom she had been engaged to before. The young man was apparently over attentive to Janka and the outcome was that his current fiancé denounced her to the NKVD as having worked for German intelligence. She was arrested, sentenced to twenty-five years penal servitude and deported to the far north without any attempt having been made to ascertain the facts. None but young, healthy prisoners were sent to these Arctic penal camps where she was forced to work in the mines and on railway construction in the tundra.

A mass escape organisation was set up in 1947 and Janka

was one of the first to join it. The idea was to break out and seek sanctuary in Finland. The organisation was good and there were high hopes of success, but the plan was betrayed by somebody a day before its realisation. However, Janka and one of the male prisoners tunnelled their way out of the camp and escaped to the taiga with only some dried bread, a little fat, matches and two small knives. With these meagre reserves, they spent close on three months in the northern forests, avoiding all human settlements as they trudged towards the railway line.

There were plenty of wild berries and mushrooms in the taiga in that season and these, apart from the tiny fish they dredged out of streams with the help of her apron, which they ate raw, kept them alive. Both she and her companion suffered from the attacks of mosquitoes and other blood sucking insects. Their faces were swollen and covered with sores. She encountered bears on two occasions when they looked at each other steadfastly, they with indifference and she half dead with fright.

Of course, it never occurred to me that I would have a similar experience.

Their strength grew less by the day. Their footwear finally fell to pieces and they proceeded barefoot through the taiga. Janka's companion was in worse condition than she. Complete exhaustion overcame him and he was racked by fever.

He told her one day, 'It's all the same to me. I'll probably die anyhow, I'm going into the next settlement we come to', and that was what he did. She was left alone in the wilderness and wandered another three days until, starving and unable to walk further on her injured feet, she sat down at the foot of a tree to wait for death. Then, unexpectedly, she heard the barking of dogs. The guards arrived and took her to prison.

Janka was sentenced to twenty-five years penal servitude for belonging to a clandestine organisation and a further twenty-five for escaping. Thus, after serving her first twenty-five year sentence and then the fifty years now added (there is no such thing as a concurrent sentence in the Soviet Union), she was to suffer fifteen years deprivation of civic rights. In theory this would be no special loss but in practice she would remain a prisoner. All told, therefore, ninety years. In addition, they imposed Soviet citizenship on her.

Janka was well treated while in prison, where her courage and endurance had gained her everybody's grudging respect.

In Kingir penal camp she was not allowed outside the camp enclosure and was directed solely to the heaviest tasks. The latest of these was the digging of sand for building construction works.

Some time later she sat in the sandpit to rest beside another woman convict. This woman, about thirty-two years of age, was just finishing a ten year sentence. Freedom awaited her in a few days time, she said, and then what happiness! She would return to her two children left with her sister when she was arrested. They were then such tiny tots. How she would kiss and cuddle them! But, all her joy was marred by evil premonitions, by some strange disquiet, throughout the last few days. Only that night, she had such an unpleasant dream.

Janka moved away a little to make herself more comfortable, and the woman began to relate her dream.

Before she could end her account, Janka felt a blow, darkness encompassed her and she could not breathe. The side of the sandpit had collapsed and buried them both. Women arrived with stretchers and doctors came and waited. Janka was the first to be dragged out since she was nearer the edge of the fall. She was unconscious but her pulse, though barely perceptible, was still beating. The other woman was dead, quite blue from asphyxiation, when the rescue party dug her out.

I was just leaving the hospital hut when the stretcher bearers came up, one set to the ward and the other to the mortuary. I returned, raised the sheet covering the body and saw Janka's face. It was a long time before she recovered consciousness and then spent several months in plaster of Paris, while everybody tended her with the utmost care.

I was sent to another settlement before her convalescence began. It was a real pleasure for me when she was transferred to the same place some months later. She looked healthy and as pretty as ever but she was no longer able to do heavy work. She stayed in the hut all day and embroidered her beautiful fantasies upon napkins for the senior officials of the penal camp, for their friends and the members of inspection teams.

This settlement had been built by German and Japanese prisoners of war. The buildings were well constructed with large light rooms and the kitchen was well appointed, with proper vats for large scale catering.

Some Germans were there when I arrived and I met a few senior police officers from Wroclaw (Breslaw before the war). The Japanese had gone but had left some splendid trophies and we dreamt of getting one of their fox fur caps and an airman's windcheater lined with down.

There were still two huts of men prisoners in the camp when we came, and as a matter of course, a lively bartered trade was at once set on foot. I did a splendid piece of business, though at the price of going hungry for a few days. The exchange of bread for an aluminium spoon, a mess tin engraved with the depiction of a tulip and the German saying, *alles ist vergänglich* (everything is temporary), and a little pot with the inscription *Domoy 1952*, (Home by 1952), just as if specially ordered for me. I thus became at one stroke one of the best equipped women in our bunch, and all my friends were glad if only because I had something to lend them in case of need.

A great attraction of life in this camp was the canteen. There were several large rooms, used by over two thousand women during the short break for eating, women of many a nationality, speaking over thirty different languages, assembled there. They came in groups from their work, took their places and ate, while others waited their turn. The highlight was that all the latest news from the camp and the outside world was exchanged and repeated.

At the hatch where the food was handed out, frequently there were heated arguments and conflicts between the various groups regarding whose turn it was to get served next. In general the canteen was always a lively place full of comings and goings, with the animated chatter of so many women. There was only one drawback. The canteen was never heated, so that in winter nothing but our body warmth and the steam rising from our bowls kept the place at a bearable temperature.

Our clothing was most fantastic and varied. Most of us wore wadded trousers and clumsy, but warm felt knee boots, or enormous *chuny*, thick rubber galoshes that were often made from old motor car tyres bound with rags. Our jackets were of various colours and usually torn here and there. Wadding would stick out from the tears and this served as an indication whether a given woman smoked or not. It was difficult to get matches in the camp, so the smoker would pull out a piece of wadding and wind it around a piece of wood and rub it on the boards of the bunk until it began to smoulder. Head gear consisted of warm kerchiefs or marvellous Japanese fur caps. The ensemble was set off by white brassards bearing the prisoner's serial number in black.

When evening came the animation and chatter would shift to the bunkhouses for a short time. When the final signal came, the women quickly fell asleep after the hard work of the day and all was silent.

There is probably no other country where satire and political witticism so strongly reflects the desires and thoughts of the population as in Russia. Witticisms circulate in the whole of that vast land but in discreet and very cautious fashion, concealing real expressions of public opinion. If repeated to another citizen of the country, a penal offence punishable by eight to ten years hard labour in a secret police concentration camp might follow. Paragraph 10 of the code, 'harmful conversations aimed against the State' being the one usually applied.

During the many years of my enforced stay in that country I heard so many of these satirical anecdotes that they would fill a whole volume. I relate, however, only three characteristic ones. I will try to remain very close to those versions heard directly from the citizens who had been sentenced for telling them to others.

ONE: It was during the Yalta conference and Stalin, Roosevelt and Churchill were on their way in a car. They were in a great hurry, but suddenly had to stop since a bull was standing in the road and refused to budge.

The three statesmen discussed ways and means of removing the obstacle. The first matter requiring a decision was to arrange which of the three would be the first to try and persuade the animal to make way. As Stalin was the host he yielded priority to his guests.

Roosevelt got out first, walked up to the bull and asked it to permit them to pass. Speaking tactfully and delicately he pointed out that they were hastening to a conference where the future of the world would be decided by the most humanitarian of accords. The bull looked at him with pity and refused to budge. Roosevelt, rather crestfallen, returned to the car.

Churchill now went to try his powers of persuasion. He energetically ordered the bull to clear off otherwise he would call in the London police to have him removed. The bull opened his eyes wide in surprise but would not budge, so Churchill returned to the car in great irritation and anger. It was now the host's turn.

Stalin got out, calmly walked up to the bull and whispered

something in its ear. The bull immediately swung round, raised his tail high in the air and galloped off into the fields.

The leaders of the world could now continue their journey to Yalta, but Churchill could not sleep at all that night. He called his chief of secret police early next day and ordered him to find out what Stalin had said. The Intelligence Service is well known for having the best spy system in the world and Churchill very soon received this report, 'Stalin said: "If you, you son of a bitch, don't get off this road right away, I'll immediately have you sent to a kolkhoz!"'

TWO: During the German-Soviet war one of the Moscow tramcars was more than usually overcrowded. One of the passengers, an elderly man, began to curse aloud, 'May he die miserably, that accursed devil! Got us into this war! It's his fault everything is so overcrowded, queues and nothing but queues. There's no bread, no sugar, no boots, nothing!' and so on.

His neighbours drew away and got out at the first stop, but he still went on, and more and more people prudently got out. Eventually the man got a seat and rode to his destination in comfort. He got out and was moving off homewards when a young fellow came up to him, flashed his police badge and said, 'You come along with me.'

The man went along with the secret police agent who asked him on the way, 'Who was it you were cursing in that tramcar?'

'Why, don't you know, comrade?' asked the man. 'It's all that damned Churchill's fault that we suffer so much.'

'Oh,' said the detective, 'you were thinking of him! That's another matter. You can go home. That's all right.'

The elderly man turned homewards but came back to the secret police spy and asked, 'Comrade, and whom did YOU have in mind?'

THREE: Stalin could not find his pipe during a conference at the Kremlin. The panic stricken ministers and commissars looked for it high and low but could not find it. Stalin was furious and told Beria the pipe had to be found at all costs.

Mass arrests began the next day, but without concrete results. Stalin called up Beria time after time on the telephone, but Beria could only report that they were on the track. More people were arrested until finally Beria was able to report to Stalin that the culprit had been arrested and that the pipe would be shortly restored to Stalin.

'Which pipe?' asked Stalin.

'Why, the pipe that was stolen at the meeting!'

Stalin recalled the incident and, laughing heartily, replied, 'I found that pipe long ago!'

Beria did not turn a hair but merely asked, 'What shall I do with the people I've already arrested?'

Stalin at once answered, 'Give them ten to fifteen years of hard labour for the NKVD'

CHAPTER 19

Spask

Vigilant guards, punishments, hard work and under-nourishment, even a six foot barbed wire fence could not keep the men and women apart when there was a will. Many of the women became pregnant and the camp authorities were obliged to fit up a maternity bay, and an outside settlement where the children could be brought up.

The babies were, it was argued, free citizens of the Soviet Union and could not therefore be kept behind barbed wire. A building outside our zone was set aside and an eminent gynaecologist, a Jew from Harbin, was put in charge. The mothers were allowed to keep their babies only as long as they suckled them. They were not then allowed contact and, after two years, the children were transferred to state orphanages. Families of the prisoners could also take children away.

The climate in Kingir was most unhealthy and many of the women, including me, suffered from the sudden change on our arrival. Movements were slowed down, hearts beat faster and blood pressure rose. Some kind of flu arrived with the spring, attacking the heart and lungs, causing virtually no rise in temperature but leaving the patient enfeebled and unable to work. After some time the authorities decided they would get rid of the 'ballast' and called in a medical commission, with the result that some of us were sent to a special isolation camp for the disabled at Spask. Mothers with babes in arms and the doctor left with us.

After three days' journey we alighted at some sidings near Karaganda and were marched to a clearing not far away. It was a fine, sunny day, the air was bracing and pure, and we could smell the mown grass on the steppe. The improvement in climate made itself felt almost at once.

There was a fair sized town not far away with white houses against a backdrop of the usual little hills. It seems that Karaganda is one of the largest coal mining areas in the Soviet Union.

The women appeared to be in good shape on the whole, but the men were exhausted by the hard labour in the copper mines of Dzhezkazgan and the harsh climate there. They looked very tired and under-nourished. Many of those leaving the wagons were so enfeebled that their companions had to support them, whilst quite a number were carried out on stretchers.

The transit group was a large one, over four hundred women and about 1000 men. We all sat down on the green grass, with a sigh of relief that Dzhezkazgan was a thing of the past. The women, as usual, began to tidy up their external selves, whilst the men pulled out their small mahorka-bags and smoked cigarettes with profound satisfaction. Such a moment of waiting by the wayside gives one relief from tension, knowing that nobody will drive us off to work for the present. After a long wait, lorries drove up and began to transport us, group by group, to Spask, the invalids' camp.

Spask is about forty kilometres away from Karaganda. It was at that time a typical camp for convalescents situated in slightly rolling country, about 750 metres above sea level. Up until 1918 an English company had a concession for the mining of coal and various metal ores and several brick buildings and an Anglican Church have survived from those times. Now they serve as a prison camp. The wives of arrested Soviet dignitaries were kept here in 1937.

Forced labour camps in all parts of the Soviet Union now sent prisoners to this place, political convicts no longer capable of further hard physical labour. Here they would either recover their strength or die. The food was better and more plentiful than in other camps. Oatmeal and fish were given more often than millet, but in spite of this the mortality in the men's zone remained high, the chief cause of death being *destrofiya* (pellagra), caused by inadequate diet. Special gangs were put to work doing nothing else but digging graves.

Those whose health improved were given first category and sent off to the hard labour camps whilst newcomers arrived in their place. The weaker ones worked in the market gardens cultivating vegetables and irrigating the ground. Those on the way to recovery worked in the quarries, brick making, or on the construction of new barracks. Many of the men and women were still incapable of work, but there was not a quiet day when the guards did not rout them out of the huts and drive them off anyway. They might be set to shifting piles of stones from one place to another, and in winter it was their task to go through the vegetable stores, selecting those suitable for use and clearing away those which were spoilt.

The camp was well guarded. Surrounded by a double row of barbed wire fencing and watch towers with armed soldiers faced the interior of the camp. During state holidays and celebrations the guards were doubled and machine guns set up in the towers. The population was composed of about 2000 women and over 18000 men, but groups of prisoners were constantly arriving or leaving and it was difficult to estimate how many inmates there were at any given time.

The sanitary conditions at Spask were much worse than at Kingir. There were no wash basins and the supply of water was restricted. In the women's zone there were for a long time no bath installations, and no well. The women were led into the men's zone every ten days, but only at night so that they would not meet any of them. Dysentery was always rife in the summer and in 1950 there had been a serious outbreak of jaundice among both men and women with many fatalities.

Those responsible for sanitary conditions in the camp did all they could for us, but always encountered the resistance and carelessness of the NKVD police and, in the end, there was little they could do. There was a small hospital in the women's zone and a very large one in the men's, where eminent medical specialists were among the prisoners. Not all of them were Soviet citizens and many came from the European countries occupied by the Russians after the war. There were very many Hungarian doctors and surgeons in particular.

Our huts were large and light, with barred windows. All were filled with high tiers of bunks and crammed full of women. By this time there were no lice in the political part of the camp, but the bugs survived the frequent disinfections and the mice were a plague. The barracks were kept clean and tidy, except for one thing. There was no toilet. As long as it was warm the windows could be kept open, but in winter with 300 people per hut, the smell was unbearable. When we arrived in the camp, indescribable chaos set in.

The commandant of the two zones was a habitual criminal prisoner from Rankar. He strode about the camp with a gang of his kind and did just about as he pleased. All the bandits and their molls were treated as privileged prisoners and did what they liked. They did no work and the political prisoners had to make up the difference.

The men's zone was separated from the women's zone by a barbed wire fence through which it was relatively easy to pass. This amenity was allowed only to the criminals, who made the fullest use of it with the result that prostitution flourished in the camp quite openly. When anyone received a food parcel from home, the 'commandant' and his retinue were always present, exacting whatever 'tribute' he wanted in such cases. He was extremely brutal to prisoners who could not bribe him, and drove them out to work regardless of their category or inability to work.

The camp authorities looked at all the misdeeds of their

'trusty' with indifference, but brutality and exploitation of the weak has its limits. One fine afternoon when the 'commandant' was bullying one of the prisoners, another man came up to him and split his head in two with an axe.

A commission of investigation arrived and the governor of the camp was changed. Conditions thereafter improved greatly. The chief trusty in the women's zone was a most energetic woman, the wife of a Soviet general who had been sentenced for political reasons.

Advantage of this was taken to conduct barter across the barbed wire, make friendships and even establish affectionate relations expressed in the form of correspondence. Sometimes, one of other of us would find acquaintances from pre-war days or people from the same district and, very often, such meetings developed into sincere friendship.

It was most touching when some of the women found amidst this mass of miserable prisoners their long lost husbands, brothers, and fathers. This had to be concealed for fear of the camp authorities finding out. In such cases they at once transferred one or the other to another penal camp. In the meantime, depending on which side was better off, mutual help was given. The women were more adept at this since they had better opportunities to secure extra food since they worked in the kitchens and in the food stores.

I encountered the husband of a friend of mine who had been left at Kingir, and told him that his wife had been arrested but that his two small sons had been sent out of the country by the Polish embassy to Iran. Words cannot express either the joy that appeared on his face or the sorrow that his wife was in a penal camp. There he stood, on the other side of the fence, the tears of joy and sorrow trickled down his face as he heard the news with calm resignation about his own fate.

Some of the women were returning to Kingir soon after, so I sent news to his wife, who was really far from strong. She arranged for the medical board to transfer her to Spask and in actual fact she turned up two months later together with some other women. We held a conference to discuss ways and means for her to meet her husband.

A gang of women went to the men's zone every day to bring water for the kitchen, and we arranged matters so that she was allotted to this gang. Her husband arranged to work drawing water from the well and filling the buckets brought by the women. In such manner, though the women were carefully guarded by sentries, he and she could meet several times a day at the well without anybody knowing they were husband and wife. They could speak to each other only while he was filling the buckets brought by the women. However, the women shortly spread the rumour that Halina, that was the name of the wife, had found herself a boyfriend. The rumour did no harm, but when it was supplemented by another, that the boyfriend was her husband, the camp authorities immediately sent her back to Kingir.

She returned after some time, but there was now a high brick wall between the two zones and she was not allowed to work in the water gang. For that matter her husband was sent off to a distant camp soon afterwards. It is pleasant to relate that both were freed under an amnesty for Poles in 1955 and were happily reunited in Poland.

There was another encounter in the camp at Spask, but a more tragic one. A shot rang out and when we went to see what had happened, could not see anything amiss. We were hurried back into the barracks and the doors locked. It is very rare to hear a shot in a penal camp and, if there is one, it always means someone has been killed or wounded. The fact that we were hustled away and locked up indicated that something unusual must have happened. The bush telegraph in every camp works efficiently and swiftly. Nothing can be kept secret and we always knew in advance when new regulations were being introduced, medical commissions were expected, new groups of prisoners were on the way, and about new means of curtailing the little liberty we had. No one would or could say how the news spread and nobody asked. It sufficed that we knew everything.

Thus, we very soon found out all about the mysterious shot. A warder stationed on one of the watch towers had committed suicide. He was a young man who had entered the service of the NKVD police after demobilisation from the army. Standing on guard on the tower, he recognised his father among the prisoners. The father recognised him too, but gave no sign of this. The young man could not stand the thought that he was guarding his father as a prisoner and shot himself. The father became insane and died soon after.

We had been locked up so that we should not see the body being taken down from the tower and put on a sleigh. Officially the authorities stated the warder had shot himself accidentally.

The hut in which I lived during the last two years before being sent to the taiga had many of the features of a small, bustling town. Over 300 women of various nationalities, age and religious creed lived there, mostly with a non working category or one for a four hour working day. The hut was large with tiers of bunks, the younger sleeping in the upper layers and the older ones below. For that matter the bunks were used not only for sleeping but also for various occupations: eating, doing needlework or knitting, the writing of letters, praying, and the receiving of visitors and guests.

Our whole life and thoughts were for many years revolved around these bunks, particularly in winter. Surrounded as each one of us was by a large group of other women, we could find solitude there or revert in our thoughts to those we loved. In the camp, the bunk was our 'home'.

For seven years, I slept on bare boards lined with the clothing I wore during the day, but in the political camps, we received palliasses stuffed with straw or dried steppe grass.

The reveille gong sounded before dawn and the barracks were opened by a mixed group of male and female guards. We washed and dressed often in complete darkness. A second gong called us to the morning roll call. We lined up in rows, the guards counted us, called out our names and we answered giving our Christian names and patronymics. The roll call was held in the huts during the winter and in the open air from early spring. We were then dismissed and had our breakfast. A gong again sounded and the women were allotted to work-formed gangs and went off to their places in the fields or brick making, ditch digging or quarrying stone.

The gangs working the fields outside the zone were always more heavily guarded and they were not allowed to pass outside fixed boundaries while at work. Anybody who strayed outside these boundaries was liable to be shot on the spot. These work teams returned to the zone for dinner at noon, and after an hour's rest, those whose work was to last the whole day went back to their work place. The six o'clock gong marked the end of the working day and supper time. Finally there was the evening roll call, and we were shut up for the night. For many years of our life in the Soviet penal camps this was the order of daily life.

The best part of the day was when the guards locked us up after completing all the due formalities. Here and there one always heard a sigh of relief and someone exclaimed, 'Thank God, we are free at last!'

There would at length be relief of tension after the long day's various 'unpleasant surprises' and every one of us could do now as she pleased. We knew the guards would not now make an unexpected inspection, would not take away our scissors, eavesdrop on our conversations, or make us carry field stones from place to place. If it was winter the stove would be besieged for each of us would be anxious to cook what she had managed to pilfer from the vegetable stocks of the camp. The other women would lie in their bunks, rest, talk and visit each other and the hut would hum as if it were a beehive.

I liked to walk along the narrow 'streets' between the bunks, to linger near the sleeping places and listen or observe what the women were doing or saying. There was no dearth of subjects. The women would speak of their children, husbands, of their dreams and of their intuitions. They exchanged tasty recipes, and spoke of the difficult conditions of life in freedom. They read letters from home to their friends repeatedly and, here and there, a small group would be listening to a story. Another group would be in their bunks doing needlework and showing each other new motifs for embroidery. Again, others recited poetry or listened to a lecture on Russian literature or history by professional teachers.

I never heard any political discussions although the women could more freely express their views here than when at liberty. They simply did not like the subject. I noticed yet another interesting thing in the various huts and even in the whole penal camp. The women never talked scandal or ran one another down. The reason for this is simple, we lived openly and in all sincerity, the mask of hypocrisy had been removed and there was nothing to hide.

There were differences of opinion among the women, of course, but each would express her opinion and co-existence remained unimpaired. Though the women were from various spheres and intellectual levels it was indeed rare to hear voices raised in anger. Naturally, all this does not apply to the bandits' molls who lived their own, separate life.

The final gong would ring at 10 pm and the women then hid away their knives, scissors, razor blades and other valuable items for it was never sure that the guards would not make a snap inspection during the night. In fact, they very often did so, explaining that this was to help us remember that we were in prison. We would tuck ourselves in, the light went out and all would be silent in the hut after the day's bustle and hum. True, now and again, someone would utter a beloved's name or one of the molls would spit out some obscene word in her sleep. So ended our day. Dawn would bring the next.

One night was really dark with a heavy snowfall. An electricity station was being renovated that day and we had no light in our bunkhouse, so we went to sleep earlier.

Suddenly we were wakened by a rustling sound. I sat up in my bunk and saw moving shadows here and there and I could discern male voices: 'Marushka . . . Ninka . . . Zoyka . . . where are you? Make a sound.'

Awakened women whispered amongst themselves, 'What's happening? Who's there?' After a while we realised that the men were criminal boyfriends of some of the bandit molls.

They had used the cover of darkness to force their way through to the female zone, breaking the lock of our bunkhouse to spend the night with their girlfriends. Our bunkhouse was large, 300 women stayed there. Sometimes, before these men found their own lovers, they woke up other women saying, 'Take pity on me', looking for sex with any female.

We women wised up to the situation immediately and used the darkness to our own advantage. Those approached for sex would wrap rags around their heads and lisp, 'Go away, my son. I am an old witch, you could be my grandson', etc. Our fear took over and the noise level in the bunkhouse rose. The one man who had agreed to act as watch then threatened that if any of the women tried to get away or call for help, he would kill them. We knew well that each man carried a knife. Finally their girlfriends, having now wakened, gathered their lovers, while we lay in silence with hammering hearts, waiting for what would happen next.

In the morning we heard an alarm and double the number of guards came into the bunkhouse with lights. They approached the bunks in search of men. There was commotion and after a while, at rifle point, the guards led out the 'bravest' lovers.

That same afternoon they were led out from the isolation

cell in the female zone and taken to the male zone. Because there was no passage between the two zones, ladders had to be put up on each side of the fence. As each 'bachelor' arrived at the top of the fence, proud of his achievement, he would wave his cap in triumph to his girlfriend before descending to the other side.

The women had come out from the bunkhouse to clap and admire the bachelors' bravery and cleverness for managing to cheat the guards and, without ladders, to cross three lines of barbed wire on each side of the barrier between the zones.

During this and the following day there was great excitement about the events of the previous night. The fear had gone and was replaced with good-humoured accounts of the event.

Some women were completing their sentences while others were just beginning. Those completing their sentences, stayed in prison waiting for a 'special disposition' or resettlement to another place of exile. Since 1950 people were sent mainly to colonise places such as the Krasnoyarsk region and some provinces in Kazakhstan. I met some Russian women who had already spent twenty-two years in the penal camps, the most beautiful years of their life wasted to no purpose.

The women whose sentences were ending were tranquil for the most part. No repressions, chicanery or brutality by the camp authorities could disturb their inner equilibrium. They worked in order to have something to do knowing that, while excessive physical labour destroyed human beings, inaction killed them. During the years that I spent in the camps I met many people who quickly broke down under the stress of their experiences and the first symptom was always their refusal to work. They fell into a state of apathy and losing their spiritual energy suffered a loss of physical energy at the same time.

At first, they would be forced to go to work, but on arriving at the spot, they sat about or lay down throughout the day. The guards would sometimes beat them up, lock them in a cell, or starve them, but without result. These prisoners did not react to such treatment or, for that matter, to anything else done to them. Their muscles became flabby, apathy overcame them, and they lay in their bunks for days and months on end, powerless to arise even to attend to their physiological needs. Finally they were taken to hospital where most of them died.

The women for the most part stood the hard conditions of life better than the men, and the mortality amongst them was lower. They were more enterprising and bold while adapting to the conditions. They would often loudly express their dissatisfaction to the authorities. The men could not dare to use such sharp words as we women for the slightest protest was punished by incarceration in a punishment cell or by a beating. Whoever harboured a firm faith in anything had a better chance of survival.

There was another category of prisoners in our camp, political prisoners singled out for the severe regime known as *katorga* and they bore the letter K alongside the numbers sewn on to their clothes. The *katorga* system has been handed down from the Tsarist times with the implication that the prisoner was condemned to very hard labour and more suffering than others.

They were courageous and bore their lot with pride. They did not fear the commandants of the penal camps nor their guards, saying they had nothing to lose as they were practically sentenced to life incarceration. They worked in the quarries and on hard labour but their clothing was better than ours. Their living accommodation was also better as they were not so crowded. When they lined up for their food, the cooks always gave them larger portions.

It might seem at first sight that the huts in our zone were all the same. Whitewashed walls and ceilings, clay floors, and tiers of tightly packed bunks, with all the prisoners dressed in the same way, but the atmosphere in every hut was different. Every section of the larger huts differed in some way. One could feel as if each group of women was surrounded by some inexpressible 'field' within which something imperceptible was happening. When the inhabitants of such a group changed, the atmosphere changed too.

There was no need to be particularly sensitive to the environment when one entered the hut inhabited by the sectarians, for instance, one could feel almost tangibly that these women's thoughts were directed along different paths. They never thought of themselves as prisoners for they lived within the full freedom of their thoughts and feelings and independently of conditions.

They were a strange type of woman, all the more surprising to encounter because they lived in a Communist country which had, for over thirty years, fiercely combated all religious beliefs. They were quite unjustly called 'nuns' in the camp, for they were lay women most of whom had husbands and children and who were simply members of the various sects which exist in the Soviet Union to this day. As religious beliefs are not punished under the Soviet constitution they were sentenced to hard labour on the strength of Paragraph 10, a political one, to at least ten years imprisonment 'for harmful talk against the state'.

These rebellious martyrs for their faith were at first scattered throughout all the penal camps and after the summer of 1948 were concentrated in the political isolation zones, constituting a sizeable group in each. It cannot be denied that they gave the camp authorities a tremendous amount of trouble and even the most severe repressions seemed to have no effect. They would not collaborate during roll calls, refusing to be counted. They did not answer to their names but hid in odd corners, even under the bunks. They stubbornly clung to their principles and ideals, and nothing could break their spirit.

I remember there were some who refused all medical attention and others who blankly refused to profit by the bathing facilities. From time to time the guards would drag them off to the baths by force but even so with little result. I often visited them and we chatted quietly in the peaceful atmosphere of their huts. Their clothes were always tidy and clean and they wore white headscarves.

During the ten years that I observed them, not one of them gave up her convictions even at the cost of health and life. Some of the sectarians refused to do any imposed work though others among them might if they felt like it. Finally, the camp authorities gave it up as a bad job and left them in peace.

In the particular barrack which I have in mind, there were one hundred women belonging to as many as sixteen sects. Most numerous were the Baptists, followed by the Old Believers, the Witnesses of Jehovah, and a specifically Russian sect known as the Tolstoyans, who followed the principles of Leo Tolstoy and would not resist evil.

There were also some Methodists, the Spiritual Worshippers of Life and sects which revolved round the ideals of a monarchy. There were many who represented the Russian Orthodox Church and called themselves 'The Christians'. On Sundays, they would arrange hymn services attended by many Russians from other huts. Sometimes even the women guards would stroll up and stand in the doorways. Perhaps they were praying, who knows?

Every sect in every hut kept to itself. The members lived as a community but showed great tolerance to members of other sects. They prayed at various times of the day and night, and seemed to be busy with something or other all the time. The Holy Spirit Believers would often hide in the quarries where they prayed fervently and after a time fell into a kind of trance during which they produced inarticulate sounds. According to them this meant the Holy Spirit had entered within them and was speaking.

The sectarians received many parcels from their families,

and probably also from their co-believers at liberty. Everything they possessed was common to all the members of the given sect. They worked hard to convert others, not without some success, and their attitude to authority was either quite indifferent or tinged with scorn.

There was one sect which struck me as being most strange. It was a very militant one with marked monarchist views. It was headed by a woman of remarkable individuality, aged between fifty and sixty. Her features were regular and she looked very austere. Her eyes were large, dark and betrayed a masterful and despotic character. She had a small lump on one side of her back and had a strong resemblance to a witch of the Middle Ages.

She knew very much about life, but only in so far as it applied to the contrary aspects of the existing laws and order. Anything not in accordance with her ideas was the object of her hate and her aim was to destroy it. The world had to become what she wanted it to be. I asked her the name of her sect, but she made no answer and merely stated that it is life which must be destroyed and built up anew. According to her, the sole power in Russia should be the Romanoff family. Her co-believers adored her, obeyed her implicitly and I often saw them washing her feet and kissing them. They would comb and plait her dark hair every day. Parcels received by members of her sect were distributed as she ordered. She never went for her own food, leaving this to her subordinates who, for that matter, believed she was the incarnation of the Archangel Michael and the daughter of the last Tsar, Nicholas.

Her group numbered only fourteen women and they all hated the Communists. She always told the camp authorities she would never submit to them, since their authority came from Satan. Their rightful authority was that of the Romanoff Tsars. They began their day by singing 'God save the Tsar' and ended it with the same national anthem. I once saw what happened when a visiting team of secret police officers entered their hut. She ran up to one of them, tore off his officers' epaulettes and shouted at the top of her voice, 'You've no right to wear them. You've stolen them from the Tsar.'

The officers were so taken by surprise that they cleared out quickly, and the only reaction was that she was punished by three days in a punishment cell. This, of course, did not cool the ardour of this strange sect.

Shortly after, when hundreds of women were standing in the zone parade ground, one of the members dashed up to the commandant and kicked him so violently that he fell to the ground. We all thought he would shoot her on the spot, but he did nothing of the kind. They were not allowed to shoot when in the zone, as she well knew. They overcame the fury of her attack and dragged her away to a punishment cell. Some of the members of this sect would from time to time break into the camp offices and smear the portraits of Communist leaders with excrement.

In their most fantastic exploit they joined forces with the Worshippers of Life and put on long black skirts with white pinafores, the necessary material had been sent to them in parcels. This was not so bad, but they embroidered upon the pinafores a phallic symbol with the words 'For Holy Russia' and the 'Golden Cunt', and paraded about the camp for several days. The camp authorities ordered them to remove the phallus and the inscription, but they firmly refused. The commandant thereupon had them all brought to his office where the guards removed all their clothes. They left the office stark naked and were then surrounded by armed guards and dogs and taken to the punishment cells. As they marched off the women strode proudly with heads erect, shouting insults at the Communist authorities, calling them 'devils' and worse, and wound up with a spirited rendering of God Save the Tsar.

Shortly afterwards a public prosecutor came from Moscow and drew up an indictment against the more aggressive members of the sect. A public 'trial' was held in the women's zone, witnesses were heard out in due form, and finally seven women and two men were sentenced to death. They were informed the right of appeal was due to them. Not one of them took advantage of it but, nevertheless, an appeal was filed as a matter of routine. The persons sentenced were at once removed from the zone to another prison elsewhere. After some time, the leader of the sect returned as her sentence of death had been varied to twenty-five years penal servitude.

As far as I can remember, all this happened towards the end of the summer of 1951.

Our life acquired a special state of health during the season when the vegetables were ripening in the fields. We followed the example of the rabbits and ate incredible quantities of raw vegetables while we worked there. Potato digging season was particularly appreciated and the utmost cunning applied to the kindling of a smokeless fire at which potatoes could be baked without the guards noticing. Of course, some extremely zealous guard would occasionally notice a thin column of smoke from our lines. He would then stamp out the fire and mash the potatoes into the earth. On the other hand there were other guards who somehow never noticed our clandestine operations.

Another branch of our potato operations was to collect as many as possible before work ended for the day and smuggle the vegetables into the bunkhouse. The *urki*, the bandit molls, were easily the most skilled in this procedure. Some of them hid 9kg or more of potatoes on their person and got away with it. The dangerous point for this smuggling was the guard house at the entrance where snap searches were sometimes made of the workers returning from the fields, but the only ones to suffer were the first few ranks.

By the time the searchers reached the other ranks there was nothing left for them to find, for the rear ranks had already thrown all their potatoes across the fairly wide barbed wire barrier fence. On the other side companions picked up the flying potatoes and took refuge in the bunkhouse. The guards were never able to make a clean sweep of the potatoes looted from the fields. In the evenings, after the bunkhouses were locked for the night, the women cooked the potatoes and prepared a real feast. The appetising smell pervaded the whole bunkhouse and we could hardly bear to wait until the food was ready.

Tobacco was also an important commodity for many of the prisoners. Smokers either gave up the habit altogether on imprisonment, or became more strongly addicted. In the latter case, their health and ethics often suffered. Many a confirmed smoker, though under-nourished and weak, would exchange his or her ration of sugar or bread for a little tobacco, thus further undermining health and often hastening death. Some of them exchanged their 'conscience' for tobacco, reporting to the authorities any dissatisfaction expressed by their companions in misfortune.

Mahorka, the commonest and lowest grade of tobacco, was smoked. It was difficult to get factory prepared tobacco in the camp, so the prisoners dried and cut the leaves themselves. These would first be slightly dried, then rolled up and cut into thin slices, after which the process of drying would be completed. No cigarette paper was available, and newspaper was therefore used.

Tobacco was always in short supply so, when anyone acquired a little tobacco and lit up a cigarette, someone in the vicinity would always call out, 'Let's smoke' or 'Forty' and silence would fall on the assembly. The owner of the cigarette inhaled deeply several times and then passed it on to his or her neighbour. The cigarette now passed from mouth to mouth, without a single word being spoken by the smokers. Each inhaled twice, and for a moment profound satisfaction would appear on the smoker's face, after which the cigarette passed on to the next person.

Any differences between the prisoners were forgotten now.

The worst of the criminals shared their smoking with the intelligentsia, Communists with Fascists, Asians with Europeans. Every political and religious creed, every race and nationality fraternised during this ceremony and smoked the 'pipe of peace' in the utmost amity and goodwill to all, although the non smokers suffered a little as the blue, evil smelling smoke filled the barrack and made breathing unpleasant for them.

On the whole few of the women smoked, though the bandit molls were chain smokers, but then, I never saw them bartering bread for tobacco. They either stole the tobacco or were given it by the men.

CHAPTER 20
Christmas and New Year's Day

This Christmas Eve was my tenth in a Soviet concentration camp, yet it is the one most vividly remembered by me.

The camp zone for political prisoners housed a medley of nationalities, races and creeds. It was not always possible for each of the various groups to work and sleep together, yet I never noticed any signs of racial or national antagonism. Exemplary solidarity and tolerance was the rule.

Christian and other holidays provided an occasion for given groups to assemble, but Christmas brought the closest contacts and every Christian women kept up at least some of her homeland's traditions. New Year's Day was, on the other hand, a universal holiday.

The period just before Christmas was a particularly sad one for the women since it reminded them of family gatherings and increased their nostalgia. Each of us recalled those happy days and all the more strongly felt the loss of home life. Plunged in such memories the women worried about their children and other loved ones so, though sadness and longing afflicted us deeply, we tried to spend Christmas in the company of our own country women.

As early as the beginning of December those who received no parcels from home started economising their rations, pieces of herring or other dried fish, bread and sugar, hiding all this away so as not to offend the official eye. It mattered not that the hoarder went on short rations for a time. She would eat her fill at Christmastide and invite some friends to the feast.

When the long awaited day arrived the Christians who

263

celebrated this time began a feverish activity: the Catholic Poles, Lithuanians, Austrians and Hungarians, Germans, Latvians and Finns. Women walked from hut to hut with food hidden under their wadded jackets. Those who had not gone out to work bustled about in the huts, took out their hoarded victuals and made up their minds about the dishes to be made from the available supplies. Also some of them took out dresses from their bags to be dressed unusually that evening.

We knew our countrymen in the men's zone would send us Christmas greetings and of course we had to reciprocate, so I kept an eye open for our water carrier, a senile ox who dragged the water barrel cart and served as our secret postal service. It was my duty, at an appropriate moment, to extract the men's letters from one of the ox's enormous ears and secrete ours within it. When the cart stopped, some women, busy fetching water to the kitchen, would hover about the ox, talking to him nicely, stroking his ears, and pulling out little rolls of letters and placing their own letters to friends in other zones.

The hut in which I lived was the largest one. We were very anxious to arrange a Christmas Eve party at which all the national groups would assemble but, owing to the lack of tables, this idea was abandoned. Not all the Polish women lived in one and the same hut and thus not even we could get together. The huts were locked up at the end of the day and everyone had to be in her hut by that time, so we decided to meet after the last official meal at the quarry in our zone, cautiously assembling one by one, like the first Christians in the catacombs. All the Polish women and some Lithuanians were very soon there, about thirty-five of us.

It was very cold, the thermometer stood at 42 degrees centigrade below zero. Our breath condensed into vapour so that we were as if within a cloud of our own. In the sky we could see three enormous bands forming a cross, a common phenomenon in that climate during prolonged frosts and, above the horizon, the broad shimmering streamers of the aurora borealis. Its subtle rosy, light blue light was reflected on the snow and gave the whole region a strange feeling of calm and softness.

Dressed in our rags, all of us looked towards the west and for a moment there was silence as in our thoughts we joined our loved ones. We knew that in every home in Poland they would be praying for us, and sending us their best wishes. The eldest in our group, Antka, for many years Commissioner of Girl Guides in Vilnius, was the first to speak as she began to say the Lord's Prayer, and we repeated its beautiful words with her in a whisper. We then turned to the distant sprawling burial ground for prisoners, and said a prayer for the dead.

This done, we broke dark bread in accordance with Polish custom, forgave any grudges we felt and wished one another good health and a speedy reunion with loved ones in Poland. We again looked longingly to the west, and then sang a Christmas carol.

As our feeble voices died away, the Northern Lights and white celestial columns faded and the darkness of night came on. The stars came out, and the winter constellations rose above the horizon. Around the camp the solitary watchtowers reared up, the guards in enormous fleece coats pointing their guns at the prisoner quarters. The signal for evening roll call rang out and we returned, one by one, each to her hut.

When I hurried into mine the other women were already lined up awaiting inspection. With this formality done we were locked up for the night and could again breathe freely. The hut immediately became a hive of activity, merry yet tranquil. Some of the women busied themselves with the stove, others tidied up the bunks, pulling out boxes which served as tables in the narrow passageway between the tiers of bunks.

Some sheets served as tablecloths, and we began to set our 'crockery' upon the 'tables': clay bowls, chipped enamel plates, salvaged tins, and so on. There were no spoons as each of us had her own, knives and forks were not used in our circles. We had long ago been weaned from such luxuries by our guardians. Finally all was ready and the nationalities that celebrated Christmas on that day sat down at their tables here and there in the big hut. We had even a Christmas tree. German girls picked some branches of broom, supposedly to make brushes, and soon a 'decorated' Christmas tree was standing beside our table.

It may be of interest to record our menu of skilfully prepared dishes from the most ordinary camp fare: dried fish of various kinds, potatoes with herring, garlic rubbed bread, pudding made of groats and sugar. There was even a cake made of dried black bread with layers of sweet groat filling, the work of an expert in the culinary art to celebrate what would be my last Christmas in the camp.

Having taken the edge off our hunger, we sang our national carols, one national group chiming in as another ended. The Soviet women quietly lay in their bunks and looked with evident pleasure at our Christmas festivity.

From time to time, a sentry would bang at our door with the butt of his rifle and shout, 'Shut up!' The singing stopped until he went off on his beat, and then we started carol singing again. Eventually the guards lost patience and switched off the lights and we sat in the darkness, chatting with each other and relating our memories. Finally we lay down in our bunks but it was long before we fell asleep. From time to time, a deep sigh or quiet sobbing could be heard. We paid visits to Polish women in other huts on the next day and invited some friends of other nationalities to our Yuletide table.

The camp authorities locked up the huts for the whole of New Year's Day and opened them only at meal times. The Polish women formed a delegation which visited the senior members of the other nationality groups and transmitted our best wishes for the coming year. The other women liked the idea and each group selected its delegation which followed our example amidst universal goodwill and international amity. New Year's Day was celebrated by all.

For some days past, the radio and newspapers had been announcing that there would be an eclipse of the sun on a certain day and that it would be total at Karaganda. Astronomers from various parts of the Soviet Union came to a locality nearby to study the phenomenon. The camp authorities naturally provided us with no facilities for observing the eclipse but we managed for ourselves. We extracted a window pane from its frame, broke it into small pieces and, without the guard noticing, smoked it with a borrowed candle some days before the event.

Finally, the great day came. I had for many years got up with the others for morning roll call before sunrise and, while we waited for the guards, I would observe the sky and land. Mornings in Kazakhstan are mostly cloudless, fine, youthful and fresh, the most beautiful part of the day. It was as if they provided me with energy for the whole day and kept my mind clear. Anybody who does not see the rising sun loses much.

On this morning the day broke as if very tired, the pre-dawn haze was a reddish coppery colour and not the usual gold. When the sun appeared, it was likewise colourless. It was almost as if it felt that something sad would happen to it on this day. This sadness affected us too. After roll call the women did not go off to breakfast in a murmur of voices but gathered their pots together in silence.

The sun rose higher and from time to time coppery little clouds passed swiftly across it, making its countenance still more melancholy. I went off with the others into the fields and looked at it from time to time through my glass. Then I noticed at length that the moon had 'bitten off' a piece of the sun and was now greedily devouring the rest. It quickly reached the middle and the earth ever more quickly became covered by a dirty, coppery grey veil. Nothing but a crescent remained and finally even this disappeared. A curtain fell across the earth and the day became like night. Stars appeared here and there.

The cattle in the fields behaved very nervously. Cows stretched out their necks and lowed. Horses crowded together and lowered their heads, neighing and pawing at the ground. Sheep gathered in a compact flock and baa'ed away miserably. Jackals in the distance began to howl.

We too felt a strange disquiet in our hearts. Some women made the sign of the cross, and the bandit molls sat quietly with their jackets over their heads. There really was an atmosphere of terror and fear. Eventually the sun reappeared but to the end of the day it remained as if maimed and sad . . . our souls as well,

In the isolation zone for political prisoners we were allowed to send only two letters a year. On the other hand, there was no restriction on the number we were allowed to receive, and this likewise applied to parcels. At one time the camp authorities encouraged us to ask our families to send us as many food parcels as they could. I could not use my quota for outgoing correspondence as letters addressed to a foreign country were not accepted, whilst any letters sent to me were not delivered. I therefore passed on my quota to women who had families in the Soviet Union.

Thus I was surprised to receive a letter plainly addressed to me, yet in a handwriting I could not identify. Greatly surprised, I opened it and read the first words, 'Dear Penelope,' It was a letter written in a distant camp, full of love and endearing words, expressed the solicitude and longing of a husband . . . but not mine. I called out, 'Penelope, Penelope, here's a letter for you.'

A Lithuanian hurried up and it turned out she was one of those to whom I had passed on my quota so that she could write to her husband more often. I asked her why he called her Penelope when her name was Janina. She smiled and explained, 'That's how I always sign letters to my husband. Aren't we all modern Penelopes? Don't we long for years, and don't we faithfully await reunion with our husbands?'

I answered, 'You're right, but we modern Penelopes live in prison camps, dig ditches and canals, quarry stone, knead clay with straw for bricks, work hard in the fields. Who knows whether we'll ever again meet our Odysseus. Their hard labour is even worse than ours.'

Later, I heard from her that her husband, a doctor, had completed his ten year sentence and had been sent to the Siberian Arctic region where he died three months later. His Penelope still had five more years to serve.

CHAPTER 21

Ten-Year sentence ends

Once we had passed New Year's Day in 1952, every day swiftly brought me nearer to the end of my ten year sentence of penal servitude.

The camp authorities assured me I would then be immediately deported to the Polish frontier. I was under no illusions in this. I knew they were lying, for I knew, as did all of us, that a law had been passed under which all freed political prisoners were to be exiled for compulsory settlement in Siberia, regardless of their nationality and citizenship. For this reason nobody in the camp felt any special joy when his or her sentence finally ended.

The continuation was merely another form of imprisonment. Also, despairing letters were received from freed prisoners who had been forcibly settled in Siberia and they were not reassuring.

The very way in which the final formalities for restoration to 'freedom' were put through was far from pleasant. Most often it was painfully brutal and heartless. Most of the freed prisoners found that their clothes were tattered and torn beyond repair or, if these had been stored in the camp warehouse, had been badly damaged by mice, or simply stolen. Prison clothing would be taken from them, if in good condition, and a set of rags issued instead.

Freed prisoners would be most indignant that after so many years hard work they had to return dressed in rags and many would refuse to accept these apologies for clothing.

On returning to free life they would have to walk about in these rags for a long time before they could earn enough to buy something decent. Sent off to the place of their compulsory settlement 'in freedom' they were heavily guarded, just as if they were on their way to prison instead of leaving it.

It was touching to see how the 'old timers' took leave of their companions in misery. Every one of them had dear friends made throughout the years in penal camps, and each would give her a memento, some trifle made by herself. Whenever a prisoner left the camp but had nobody to receive her in freedom and not a single kopeck to her soul, we would make a collection to cover at least the expenses of her journey. Some of us even sold our bread ration.

Before she left, her companions would come up and share in her joy at leaving, and everyone wanted her to write. They said: 'Remember us, when you reach your country, and there, where a window is more open tell them about our life here'. Immediately she left the camp, one of the women would, mindful of the prevalent superstition, sweep the floor near the door with a besom to prevent her ever returning. Her neighbour would move her own belongings to the vacated bunk, so that she would follow in her footsteps as soon as possible.

It was thus that my dear companions took leave of me when the time came for me to leave. They knew that my whole family was abroad and that I could get no parcels or money from them. After ten years hard labour in the penal camps, I was given not more than 200 roubles, the price of 3kg of butter at the time, but everyone wanted to give me something from their things. A group of my countrywomen brought me a cambric fabric for a blouse as a present and wrote on it the inscription, 'May the way in Siberia be as rosy as the colour of this blouse'.

I will never forget how they parted with me and blessed me

on my way when, finally, one fine morning in April 1952, I saw them for the last time. They were standing, formed up in work gangs on the barrack square, awaiting the order to go to work, while I was standing in the lorry with a few others, ready to leave the camp for the unknown once again.

Our train came to a stop on a siding of the Krasnoyarsk railway station. After prolonged formalities between the guards, our new masters took us under their 'caring wings' and bundled us into canvas covered lorries. Looking through holes in the cover we saw that we were passing through a town of widely separated wooden houses with verandas. We knew that this was characteristic of Siberian settlements.

At last the lorry stopped and I heard the dragging sound of a heavy prison gate opening. When they removed the covers, we found ourselves in a yard with a large stone building emitting foul and disagreeable odours. We disembarked and were quickly separated from the women who had not yet finished their prison term. We were led along meandering corridors to a large dismal cell without even wooden bunks but with only a concrete floor to sleep on. It was already occupied by a group of women from other prison camps who likewise had completed their sentences.

Looking at their faces I caught sight of the pretty but sad countenance of a young girl sitting on the floor. Her features reminded me of a friend I had parted with in Spask. Spurred by this impression I approached her and asked her name. She looked at me distrustfully and turned her head away. I sat beside her and started talking loudly to myself, 'I come from a prison camp in Karaganda. I left there a German friend, called Marta. She told me that in 1947 she and her 15 year old daughter Helga were arrested in Krolewiec (Kaliningrad). For a time they shared a prison cell but were parted when their sentences were read. The mother got 10 years and the daughter 5 years of 'educational labour' in a NKVD camp. Since then she has received no news of her daughter, is filled with sadness and thinks of her day and night'.

As I was relating my story the girl slowly turned her head to listen in silence. When I finished she said in a trembling voice: 'She is my Mother. I also have had no news of her during the last 5 years'.

Her cheeks flushed and her eyes filled with joy and happiness. I gave her the camp address and Helga immediately began to write a letter. From then on we became great friends and she would not leave me even for a moment.

I continued to join the ranks for the roll call in the prison yard every morning and evening, wondering how many thousands of times I had replied with my name and that of my father, Urszula Mikolayevna. Who really needed this information?

Male prisoners stood some distance from us in long rows. We always observed each other with interest and I noticed that among them were many Japanese and other oriental faces.

A week after our arrival we were called to the prison office individually. There again they read me a document stating that I was now released from prison, but because of a special order I was being settled for the rest of my life in the Krasnoyarsk Region.

I was ordered to remove my prisoner's number and that was it. I was 'free'.

Not long afterwards we were marched from the cells into the prison yard with our possessions. There we were allowed to mix with the men who were also set 'free' and, for the last time, I answered in my own and my father's name. They led us through the heavy prison gate and I watched, strangely uncaring, as it was closed behind us. I remember to this day the grinding of the key in the heavy lock and the clinking of the chain. Here and there one heard loud swear words from the men and some of the women crossed themselves.

The Long Bridge

We all turned our faces away from the prison. This was in May 1952.

Covered lorries were waiting for us outside the prison. The guards were no longer armed and we set off towards the railway station to board a passenger train bound from Moscow to Vladivostock. We settled in the last two reserved coaches and set off eastwards.

We were not returning to our homes, and yet there was a happy atmosphere, laughter, lively chatter, greetings and expressions of good wishes for the new found 'freedom'. Men and women were allowed to talk to each other and the guards did not take any interest.

For the first time in ten years I was travelling in a passenger train looking out with interest through an unbarred window. On stations we were allowed to leave the carriage and talk to free people. I felt strange on first contact, indeed our clothing did not differ from theirs except that in a number of places we had darker patches of the original colour which for some five years had been covered by our numbers.

The local people looked at us as if we came from a different world, observing us with suspicion and interest. It appears that years of a different life had left our faces and movements with tell tale signs. They would approach us hesitantly and ask, 'from which labour camp' or 'from which prison'. We would reel off replies, 'Karaganda, Workuta, Tajshet, Magadan.' They would then pull out their tobacco pouches and treat us with hospitality, keeping an eye on what our guards were doing. I also looked at them as people from a different world, feeling strongly that there was a barrier between us. I knew it would take some time before that barrier would disappear.

We stopped at one small station where, as usual, the locals were selling food to passengers. Those who had money were buying whatever they could afford. I had not a 'kopeck' to my name but I looked with interest at the delicious spread which

274

included homemade soup, hot milk, eggs and piping hot potatoes. My face must have reflected my craving since one of the women selling food approached me, pulled out from her basket five hot potatoes, filled a mug with milk and said, 'Here you are, eat it. You probably don't have money to buy this. I hope that someone one day will give my daughter a piece of bread. It is seven years since she was taken from home and I have not heard of her since.'

I tried to console her saying that the girl was young and would cope with prison life, and it might not be long before she would see her loved one again. As the train started moving I looked with a heavy heart at the receding figure of the sad mother.

On the third day the train halted at a small stop in the taiga. Our commandant entered the carriage and ordered us to collect our possessions quickly and get out. This was the final destination for the occupants of my carriage, 151 men and nine women. The former prisoners in the second carriage continued their journey.

I was fully aware of the consequences of deportation to the taiga and yet as I left the train I felt happy and free. It was nearly the end of May, the day was sunny and emanating from the taiga was a strong scent of awakening spring. We were proceeding towards a large barn just beyond the railway stop and the men had no difficulty carrying their small bags, wooden boxes or nothing at all.

We women, as usual, were burdened with heavy luggage since, after all, everything can come in handy in time. In one hand I carried a fairly heavy sack made from German booty which had been 'looking for a good home' in a prison store and I got it specially for this very 'celebration of my freedom'. It contained my duvet, small pillow and a few pieces of cloth given to me by friends on my departure from my last camp. In my other hand I carried a sheep skin coat, a bag with my rations and a small kettle. It was rather heavy and uncomfortable and from time to time I had to stop and change the luggage from one hand to the other.

Suddenly I heard a voice from behind 'Madam, may I help you?' This caught me so much by surprise that I dropped my luggage. Who in the taiga could possibly call me 'Madam?'

Puzzled, I turned round and saw a pleasant looking, smiling Japanese man who respectfully bowed his head. 'If you would be so kind' I said 'and carry my things, you will help me greatly. Where are your things?'

Smiling continuously, he took from inside his jacket two books and said 'Here. What I had I left with my friends in the labour camp. Surely I am being set free. I have a profession, and will be able to earn money and buy what I need'.

He picked up my baggage and easily tossed it over his shoulder. I offered to carry his books which turned out to be textbooks on advanced mathematics. I commented that it was a perfect subject for the taiga. 'Oh yes, I very much like mathematics' he admitted happily.

Relieved of the heavy luggage I walked beside him, watched his agile movements and listened with a smile. He spoke with enthusiasm about his future 'professional' work. His Russian was reasonably good but he had naive ideas about life in communist Russia. I knew what 'professional' work was awaiting us here, but I would not interrupt and disillusion him in his enthusiastic planning. Soon we all reached the barn, dropped our belongings, and started to explore the taiga. From that moment Kacuya and I did not take any interest in anything or anybody else.

Not far away we found a large fallen tree covered in moss which we sat on. A curious thread of friendship and sympathy had woven us together from the instant that our eyes met. We talked like old acquaintances who have suddenly met after a very long separation.

'Do you know' he said to me 'I saw you for the first time in the Krasnoyarsk prison yard and when on the roll call your

name was called I involuntarily turned my eyes to the person I
expected to answer. It was you. I looked at you for some time
and suddenly as if a misty memory materialised, I felt close to
you and a strange longing for something that I cannot find
words to express. Where do I know you from? We have never
met before. From that moment I continuously thought of you
and impatiently awaited the morning and evening roll calls so I
could see you. How good it is that destiny has sent us to the
same place, together. I feel I am no longer lonely'

'Believe me, Kacuya,' I said to him 'as I look at you I get the
same feeling that we have met somewhere before. For me it is
also a feeling which I do not comprehend'.

Sitting on this ancient tree trunk we related to each other
events from our past lives. I felt as if he was my brother, and he
felt as if I was his sister. We were happy and content. It got
slightly darker at midnight and we parted company. I went to
join the women in one of the office rooms and he joined the
men sleeping on the barn floor.

CHAPTER 22

Long Bridge, Krasnoyarsk
Region 1952

We settled in a small wooden cabin on the outskirts of the village with the wood just behind and, one afternoon, Alma visited us.

Thin and always hungry, Alma was a dog without a name and without an owner. She wondered all over Long Bridge, our small Siberian settlement, scavenging for food. Sometimes someone would throw her a bone, or throw a stick at her to chase her away. She sat down quite a long distance from us, looking apprehensively in all directions and, from time to time, got up to sniff out the area around her. She was particularly interested in the front door but did not have enough courage to approach. She was obviously trying to size up the new occupants and wondered if they would throw her some food or chase her away with a stick.

I watched her through the window and then, after a while, went to open the door. The creak of the opening door frightened her and she retreated further back, settled down and watched my every movement. I threw her a potato but the most persuading words and inviting tone had no effect. We repeated this ritual for a few more days and each day she would come nearer as if gaining confidence and trust. One day 'the ice broke' and she came to the door. I named her Alma and we became friends.

Alma was an elegant and good looking dog and I have not met another one like her in Siberia or elsewhere. Most likely she was a mixture of Griffon and Setter. She had attractive wavy hair with a beautiful silky shine, the light and dark golden colours mixing in perfect harmony. She was well built, neat and full of grace, but her greatest asset was her eyes, also of a golden shade and capable of clearly communicating her thoughts. It would have taken a really wicked person to chase her away or to harm her. Looking into her eyes I would sometimes think what a very intelligent dog she was, or even that she had wisdom and humility, and was full of understanding and pity.

In the mornings when I opened the outside door, Alma would be waiting there to welcome me with her expressive eyes. Her movements and looks were hesitant as if she thought that her presence was causing me trouble. However, her wagging tail was saying, 'I like you very much'.

I knew that she was hungry, so I would give her a bowl of potatoes but she would never touch it without my encouragement. She would sit by the bowl with dignity and glance at it from time to time before turning her head away. I had to tell her, 'Alma it is for you. Eat it!' Only then would she slowly get up and gracefully, unhurriedly start to eat. I don't know where she acquired such graces. She never belonged to anyone before and knew no home since her mother abandoned her during the biting Siberian frosts.

She was so thin I could count her ribs and bones when stroking her. I was very sad for her and would whisper into her ear 'I am ashamed that I cannot feed you better, and that you have to continue to scrounge for your food. It is my first winter after ten years in prison. We only have what we are clothed in and our store is empty, but soon we will grow more prosperous. Spring will arrive and Kacuya and I will plant potatoes and vegetables. They will grow and when we harvest them we will be rich. You will no longer have to go round and beg for food.'

I often used to talk to her about one thing or another. She

would look at me sympathetically, open her mouth to make little sounds or lick my hand.

Alma was always apprehensive when entering our hut. During the severe frosts I wanted to keep her in during the night but after a few minutes she would go to the door and strenuously beg to be let out. I did not know at the time that Siberian dogs never spend the night indoors. She was, on the whole, moderate in displaying pleasure except, when at dusk, I started to get ready to fetch water. Her immediate response was frenzied at the chance to keep me company on the way to the well some 300 metres away. On the way there she would dash onwards and then back, wallowing in the snow and shaking it from her coat with a joyful whine, or chase her tail in a circular dance.

It has always been the custom in small Siberian settlements for women to collect water from a deep well using a long, wooden crane. It was an opportunity for a chat and to exchange daily news. Most women brought their dogs with them and they had the opportunity to sniff each other, fight or play. Alma never joined the other dogs in their frivolities. She would sit patiently by my two buckets and, with a show of teeth, fend off any intruders. On the way back she would once again go through the ritual of her 'pirouette'. She always watched with fascination when Kacuya was sawing logs for the stove or when I was stacking them against the wall. Together, the three of us survived the long Siberian winter.

It may be difficult for me to describe objectively the events in the deportees' settlements and the free collective farms leading to Stalin's death, on 6th March, 1953. I will try to relate them as impartially as I can.

Everyone in the settlement followed with great interest the progress of Stalin's short illness. Friends would surreptitiously pass the latest news to each other. Information in the papers and on the radio was scanty, more interesting were the tidings brought by visitors, family members from Moscow and other large cities who were visiting relatives.

When the official news of his death was announced, no one wanted to be the first to pass it on or talk about it in case their feelings betrayed them. Throughout my long time in Russia I found most people when pronouncing Stalin's name lowered their voice and looked over their shoulder to make sure they were not being overheard. Occasionally they would even go so far as to mimic his manners like curling a moustache or stroking one's hair.

Following a few days of indecision, the district authorities started to organise general meetings where speakers repeated well rehearsed phrases such as 'Our sun is extinguished and our benevolent father has died.' Everyone, obviously, attended the meetings and then quietly dispersed as if they were completely uninterested. Men, in the evening after work, drank a little more vodka than usual in the local canteen. At the buffet table, normally the centre of loud talk and discussions, there was silence. Women in the bread queues, in the public baths, or by the wells drawing water, talked a lot as was usual, but not about Stalin's death although this was the news which affected every one of us and in which we were all so deeply interested.

We women do not like to keep our thoughts to ourselves for long and we probably have more courage in expressing ourselves than men. In the company of trusted friends one would limit oneself to saying that one would have expected him to live much longer, after all he was from Georgia and a lot of them lived to be a hundred. He was so strong and fit, or, thank God he did not suffer too long. Day followed day and there was not much change in our lives.

The names of Malenkov, Beria and Molotov would crop up frequently in the papers but they did not mean much to the local population who were unlikely to experience much of a difference. One devil is as bad as another. We, foreigners, were more hopeful and felt that a basic change must occur.

Molotov was clearly disliked for his stubbornness in policy and in the intelligentsia circles he was given the nick name of 'Stone' (abbreviated from 'Stone Buttocks'). Beria was hated and everyone knew why. A little later Zukov's name began to circulate in furtive whispers to start with and then gradually louder and even with joy. Zukov was a national hero to the Russians and after the war his popularity was wide, particularly with soldiers. They often extolled his wartime achievements, particularly the high esteem with which he was regarded abroad. The Russians had been puzzled and downhearted when soon after the war Stalin had demoted him to a minor post.

Eventually, in May, completely unexpected news reached us that Beria had been arrested and swiftly executed as an enemy of the state. Previously unexpressed enthusiasm and joy galvanised everyone, both free and prisoners, but not the NKVD. Observing them I noticed that they were frightened. Those who had behaved badly to us avoided us altogether, not knowing how to adjust to the news. They used to walk through the settlement with arrogance and conceit but now you could not see them anywhere. Those who were more human and friendly towards us, and there were some, particularly the ones who fought on the war front, became more open and talked more freely about the fast changing events in Moscow.

The demeanour of the inmates in all the nearby encampments suddenly changed. They walked with a spring in their step, eager to listen to news and, more importantly, started to express their true thoughts. The local canteens were crowded. Men drank even more vodka and in this merry state nothing would stop them from expressing joy about Stalin's and Beria's deaths. In our district there were two incidents when people tore down Stalin's portrait and trampled on it. These were ignored by the authorities.

Zukov's name eventually gave way to Khrushchev's when

he took charge of the federal government. It was a sad surprise to people in the Krasnoyarsk region where most inhabitants were deported from various Soviet Republics and from occupied territories like Estonia, Lithuania, Latvia, Poland, Ukraine, Finland and Germany. They all remembered that Khrushchev had been in charge of the deportations and had been blindly obedient to Stalin.

On taking charge Khrushchev issued a directive reducing the tax burden on the collective farms. It was a great help to the peasants who had to pay their taxes in kind leaving very little for themselves. They even had to deliver a quota of eggs to the government although they may not have kept any hens. This gained Khrushchev some popularity among the collective farms but soon afterwards another decree, known as 'Celina' called for the colonisation of Kazakhstan. In it he requested the 'enthusiastic and voluntary' migration of young people as well as whole families from towns and cities. This did not go down well and led to stealthy talk and dissatisfaction.

Shops, characterised in the past by glaring emptiness, began that autumn to fill with goods, particularly food. It was now possible to buy frozen or dried fish, marinated herring, oil, and substitute coffees and tea. Clothing and materials that had been manufactured mainly in Poland and Hungary began to arrive.

In the following spring a new bar was opened where at certain times one could buy some rolls, tinned fish, and sometimes even sausages. There were still considerable shortages but one could begin to feel more relaxed and more confident.

In Siberia, spring, summer and autumn pass in a quick succession. Speed is imperative in order to finish digging, sowing and harvesting in four months. I had mountains of work preparing the soil, planting potatoes, sowing vegetables, weeding, watering and storing the produce for the winter.

During my work in the garden, Alma would sit by the wooden fence and observe my every movement. From time to time I would take a rest and sit down by her for another chat.

'You see,' I would tell her, 'soon a miracle will take place and the little kernels buried in the soil will wake up and with incredible strength they will fight their way to the surface. To the sun! To the sun! There is nothing that can stop them. Yet the little seedlings will be weak and vulnerable. Our neighbours' hens are waiting for just that moment. Our fencing is not high enough or good enough to keep them out. It will be your task to chase them and other intruders away.'

Alma seemed to understand and, when the tiny, light green rows started to appear, she took her position in the garden and with indefatigable resolve guarded our produce. Neither a hen nor a bird ever managed to devour our fledgling plants. I still find it difficult to understand how Alma instinctively knew later when the plants were sufficiently grown and no longer needed her protection. She then stopped her constant vigil and the hens were then able to come in and scratch around for worms.

As autumn was drawing to a close one had to hurry and gather in the potatoes and vegetables before the frosts suddenly arrived. That year the harvest was phenomenal. Out of one bucket of seed potatoes we collected on average thirty buckets. Vegetables also gave us very generous returns. When all the produce was carefully and safely stored in the cellar Kacuya and I burst with joy into triumphal song, Kacuya in delightful baritone and me in soprano. Alma joined in with a howl, whine and whimper. I am sure that she realised that we would not go hungry in the fast approaching winter. She stopped scavenging in the neighbours' back yards, no longer hungry and looking more beautiful.

It was already December when one day I was walking through the settlement and noticed a group of people watching and laughing at something. I came nearer and saw a large black dog with yellow patches lying on a handful of hay and Alma's head resting on his chest. To every one's astonishment, the dog put his paw round her body and cuddled her warmly. There were other dogs around but, whenever one of them wanted to come nearer, her beloved mate would flash his teeth and the intruder would shy away.

For weeks to come she would stay faithful to him until she disappeared one day towards the end January. We both became very concerned. What could have happened to her? I went to a lot of trouble to prepare a comfortable place for her and her puppies, but this she scorned. It was only later that I was told that Siberian bitches have their puppies in solitude and at some distance. And so we were waiting until, at long last, she appeared one morning at the doorstep, thin, miserable and hesitant. Immediately I cooked a bowl of potatoes and added some milk. As soon as she had finished eating, she disappeared in a flash and we did not see her again for several days.

One day Kacuya discovered where Alma secretly disappeared to, dug his way to the bottom of the cave and brought me one puppy carefully carried under his body warmer. We named him Mamataro and he became our joy.

This 'Mamataro'* is not the hero in the old Japanese legend who was born one warm morning in the land of the 'flowering cherry tree' from the kernel of a peach and became a joy to two old folk. This Mamataro was my dog, born in the taiga during a crackling Siberian frost, deep in an enormous haystack just outside the settlement for the 'lifelong deportees'. Alma, his beautiful mother, when she felt that her time was coming, dug a deep hollow in the haystack and brought into the world seven vigorous pups.

He was still very clumsy but day-by-day he became more

* The name of this hero from Japanese legend is usually spelt Momotaro but Urszula knows best the name of her puppy!

cute and brave. He had no fear of the hens or pigs that were also 'lodging' with us. While still unsteady on his feet he started chasing the hens and, when they started to peck at him, he was not the one to run away. I had to come to his rescue and bring him inside.

I had never previously come across a more gluttonous dog. Before I even had a chance to put a bowl of food in front of him, he was pushing his mouth into it with all the strength he could muster, and whining loudly. Once he started to gobble his tune changed to a warning growl and, when the bowl was well licked, he would drag it in his mouth along the floor until I forcibly retrieved it. After the meal, swollen like a ball, he would lie on his back and joyfully turn from side to side. Eventually he would crawl to his place by the stove.

Mamataro grew fast as if fed on yeast. When two months old he looked like a six month old puppy and I no longer had to protect him when he was guarding the garden from intruders. He was very devoted to Kacuya, who trained him in numerous tricks, and was intelligent enough to learn after only two or three tries. He also displayed a characteristic of some Siberian dogs in that when he lived in the kitchen he would collect items fallen on the floor, or drag them from a bench, and place them in his corner. When looking for something, I soon learnt to go to his store where I would find the missing item.

After he got his outside kennel he would bring our neighbours' possessions and store them in a hole behind the log cabin. There was not only a variety of hand tools but also a selection of clothing. Neighbours, knowledgeable of the weakness of such dogs, would come happily to collect their 'stolen' belongings.

It gave us great joy to have him and to see him daily getting stronger and more handsome. His bark in guarding the property was enough to chase away unwelcome guests such as hens, pigs or even horses. At night even the drunks were kept away from the property. We were very proud of our Mamataro.

Mamataro did not enjoy Kacuya's company for long. At the end of the winter in 1954, a year after Stalin's death, there came a ukase from Moscow allowing some Japanese citizens to return home from their lifelong sentence and Kacuya was lucky to be one of them. It was the first joyful news on this earth that we had for a long time and hope was lit in the minds of all the foreign prisoners that we would soon be allowed to return home.

Kacuya was liked in the settlement. He was honourable and always willing to help others. We were all genuinely glad to see him return home. But Mamataro did not share this joy with us. He did not touch his food for three days after Kacuya's departure. Instead he would sit on the doorstep and whine with sadness. On a few occasions I even noticed tears in his eyes. In time the longing passed away. He started to eat and he became even more attached to me.

CHAPTER 23
Fugitives on the taiga

In the spring I volunteered for summer work in the north of the region and was very sad to leave Mamataro behind, but not knowing the conditions I had no alternative. In the evening before my departure I took him to my neighbour who promised to look after him until my return and he was chained, for the first time ever, to his kennel. I petted him and told him not to fret for I would be back in a few months. I left him quickly unable to look back as he was whining and trying to free himself.

Early next morning I went to the collection point where a tractor with a trailer was waiting for us. A tractor was the best means of travelling in the taiga particularly at this time of the year when the roads were sodden with thawing winter snow. Lorries or horse carts were useless for longer journeys.

Provided the weather permitted, the tractor left Long Bridge once a week to take people and mail to the many small settlements scattered across the taiga where political ex-prisoners were condemned to work for the rest of their lives. We had all settled ourselves as comfortably as possible, sitting on our possessions, when I began to think with sadness of my dog. The driver started the tractor and we were about to move when suddenly a barking dog jumped on the crowded trailer, frightening everyone as it might be mad with rabies. It forced its way through all those present and with joy stopped at my knees, my Mamataro. I removed his chain, cuddled him and we started on our journey together.

The tractor entered the taiga just outside the settlement

perimeter. Thick, mature fir trees and bearded cedars with thick undergrowth stretched endlessly on both sides of the track. We were making our way slowly through the succession of muddy humps and water filled hollows.

It was a beautiful sunny day with clear, refreshing air fragrant with the "scent" of the taiga and, from time to time, the tractor would stop to leave mail at prearranged points. On odd occasions there was a messenger waiting for us and at some stops one or two of our travelling passengers would disembark. More often we stopped to cut overhanging branches and lay them on the track to provide a better 'road surface'.

Mamataro enjoyed the stops. He was not used to being tossed about on such a rough ride and did not feel well most of the time. By the evening, at long last, we reached the old Siberian track. The road surface was firmer and the potholes were fewer. We were seized with memories and filled with emotions.

From time immemorial the rulers and tsars of Russia sent endless convoys of political and criminal deportees for penal servitude along this route to the most distant outback in their country. They walked along the route chained together or were transported on sledges in the winter. Along the way we passed derelict barns or feeding posts where the condemned had found shelter for the night and basic food to sustain them. One could not help but think 'how little it all has changed', and yet, in some ways, there was a change. The taiga, as always silent and vast, had now more tracks and roads on which big and powerful tractors could carry even more political prisoners, and there were now thousands of clearances created for settlements where millions condemned for life worked very hard.

We travelled all night. As dawn came up, more and more light penetrated through the wood and, soon after, the tractor came to a halt. We were on the high bank of a river and near a large Collective. On the other side was a small settlement for the deported. This was journey's end for the tractor and we all disembarked with our possessions, settling on the bank to await the ferry. Mamataro, delighted with the end of the journey, ran around barking with joy. It was not long before he found an accessible place and jumped into the river for a quick swim. We followed his example. The water was icy but it had the most desirable effect. I felt invigorated and refreshed. We bought some eggs, milk and fresh fish from the locals, started a bonfire and soon settled down to a sumptuous breakfast.

The River Biryusa, which originates in Mongolia, displayed a most unusual scene. Across its full width of some 350 metres, metre long creatures that were neither long worms nor huge leeches swam about, bumping into each other, turning round and hurriedly disappearing down the stream. The river was simply boiling with them. Its disturbed rhythm changed into a strange roar and left us with a feeling of anxiety.

Later on I witnessed another sight that I had never seen before. The river was full, from one bank to the other, with logs floating down the stream in a single, unbroken mass. This was the wood that the deportees living in the local settlements had felled in the surrounding taiga, dumping them into the river so that the stream would transport them to the Yeniseysk sawmills downstream. It took some hours for the logs to pass and then a small floating island came into view.

It was an enormous raft with long and strong logs tied firmly together and it carried the living quarters, kitchen, stores and the commander's office. There must have been more than a hundred people living on that raft. All of them, bar the commander, were ex-prisoners forcibly settled in the taiga. Their main task was to ensure an even flow of the logs. To do this they had small boats and paddled about releasing logs jammed along the riverbanks or small islands. It took them weeks to accomplish the journey. They also faced many dangers when crossing the rapids and falls.

When this floating island passed, the ferry came and took us across the river to my place of work for the next few months, a small settlement populated by ex-prisoners except for the chief and the commandant. Most of the ex-prisoners were political and they belonged to the working Soviet intelligentsia. A few of them worked in the office, predominantly the older men not able to face hard physical work. The rest felled trees and were building more log cabins for the settlement.

My job was to cook for the local workers and the returning 'floaters' as they made their way upriver. I was also in charge of the dining hall that had an adjacent small shop. I was hopeful that, working in the kitchen, I would be able to find enough scraps to feed Mamataro. Unfortunately this was not the case. The supply of food was very limited and Mamataro had to supplement his rations by hunting. After a few weeks he established himself as 'top dog" and the others respected him and kept out of his way.

From his mother Alma he inherited an attractive mouth and nose as well as soft, curly and brownish underbelly hair. He looked very much like a Siberian dog. He had a large, wide chest with glistening black fur, and intelligent eyes that expressed courage and authority. In the settlement Mamataro was known to everyone and admired by all. He was welcomed in most log cabins and this was a great incentive for him to develop a wandering habit which included excursions to the taiga.

At the same time I was so busy in my work that I was unable to devote much time to him. He did spend late evenings with me and slept by the door guarding the cabin. At sunrise he was always there to accompany me to work. I remember one night two drunk men tried to make their way into my cabin but Mamataro made so much noise attacking them that neighbours were wakened and the men fled.

Mamataro often hunted in the taiga, but also hunted in the settlement to my regret, embarrassment and annoyance. He knew where hens' nests were, ate their eggs and sometimes carefully even carried them in his mouth to his 'store'. Once he gave me a 'present' of a dead hen. In the settlement there were a dozen or so couples cultivating gardens with a few domestic animals and, for them, Mamataro was a real plague. Something had to be done.

I asked an acquaintance living on the other side of the river to take care of him and now, whenever he could escape from the attention of his carers, he would dash through the woods and jump on the ferry as it cast off to start his rummaging in the settlement again.

One day he got to the riverbank just as the ferry was casting off. He jumped into the river and attempted to catch up with it but the strong current carried him to the middle and then downstream. I happened to be standing with some others waiting for the ferry when we noticed a black spot floating downstream but it was too far away to recognise. It was not long before the ferry docked and the passengers told us what had happened while everyone watched the ever-decreasing black spot until it disappeared round a bend. The fate of Mamataro became a talking point throughout the settlement. Many recalled previous and similar happenings and some took bets on Mamataro's chances of surviving.

The hours were passing slowly by and I constantly glanced at the river through the kitchen window, asking it to save my dog. To Mamataro I was sending thoughts of strength and courage. Well after dark had set in Mamataro arrived back breathing heavily and with his tongue hanging out. I immediately prepared food for him and he started to eat hesitantly.

The news of his return spread like wild fire. Well-wishers even brought their children to greet him and admire his fighting spirit and the ones who won their bets drank to

Mamataro's health. From then on he stayed with me in the settlement.

During this period I was sent to a tiny settlement to cook for a small number of former prisoners sent during the summer months into the depth of the taiga to collect the resin which oozed out of the pine trees.

One can hardly describe the place as a settlement. Just one log cabin built with tree trunks, the gaps between them filled with moss, and still fragrant with resin. There was a low door and two small, crooked windows. Outside there was a well and a tool shed. That was all and, when the workers departed at sunrise, I was left with only the gentle sound of swaying branches and the buzz of mosquitoes. Sometimes an animal would come out of the woods but, frightened by the presence of humans, it would disappear quietly and quickly.

I did not come here to collect resin. My job was to look after the twelve workers, keep the cabin clean, and cook for them. They would return at sunset tired but in good spirits. After all, they were 'free'. I would light a small oil lamp for them and in its paltry light they would take off their sticky clothing covered with resin and wash, passing the soap to each other and using it very frugally.

The supper was served to them outside on tree stumps. There was silence in the taiga at this time of the day. The only noise came from their hurried eating, the rasp of wooden spoons on enamelled plates and their occasional swearing at invisible but biting mosquitoes. After supper they had their smoke, carefully rolling their tobacco into small pieces of newspaper and, in silence, taking pleasure in inhaling the strong smoke. One day more was gone and they had one day less to live through.

Sometimes one would make a comment, or another one would recollect something from his happy past and help to bring back memories of their country and dear ones, but soon tiredness and sleep overcame them and one by one they made their way to the cabin. The lucky ones who possessed boots would take them off. The others would remove the rags wrapped round their feet and throw themselves onto the hard, communal plank beds where overpowering, deep sleep knocked them out. Yet, like animals, the slightest unfriendly sound would instantly awaken them. Darkness and peace slowly enfolded the cabin.

Watching them asleep, the only blessing that prisoners shared with free men, always created in me a feeling of sadness and pity. Men in their prime, some of them very young, professional, with ambitions and bright thoughts for their future, were here transformed under the pressure of the Soviet system into robots retaining only the basic, superficial features and characteristics of humans.

The men treated me well, but we were no strangers. We were united by the same years of poverty, the same feel of hunger and yearning, and the same reaction to a life of misery and neglect. Everyone experienced it, and everyone was equally resigned. Though we might have just met, we immediately felt we knew each other well and trust developed quickly.

My plank bed was separate from the others, and was just by the door. I always fell asleep quickly and was always vigilant, just like them, so when one night the door was quietly pushed open, I woke up instantly. On the doorstep were two dimly seen figures.

'Who are you?' I asked.

After a second or two came the quiet answer. 'Don't be frightened. We are yours'.

'We are yours' could only mean one thing.

The men wakened and I lit the oil lamp. Only one young Lithuanian continued to sleep. He had come here after a relatively short sentence and the animal instinct of awareness had not yet come to dominate his being.

I could just see the arrivals in the spare light of the oil lamp. They must have been on the road for a very long time, their clothing was torn, their faces were emaciated and their restless eyes surveyed the room to see if the people there were sympathetic or worse than the wolves in the woods. It was obvious that intense hunger had taken the upper hand and forced them to approach this settlement.

Seeing the men lying on their communal beds and me covered in the rag that I used as a dressing gown, the anxiety in their eyes subsided, but their feelings of hunger and desperation remained. We looked at each other for a while in silence. We guessed who they were, and they soon realised who we were. It took a few moments before one of them spoke.

'Greetings, do you have any bread and tobacco?' he asked.

'Please can you share some,' said the other, almost before the first one finished.

None of us had any bread to spare but the men, without a word, reached into the bags where they kept their daily ration. I went round from one to another and collected their offerings. Some gave a slice, some gave half a slice, and some gave even the quarter loaf that was their daily ration. Each one gave a pinch or two of tobacco and it all happened without a word being spoken, as if in a silent film.

The strangers put the bread into their bag and collected the tobacco, rolling two cigarettes and lighting up. A trace of smile appeared on their faces and their eyes showed satisfaction and gratitude. They took great pleasure in inhaling the smoke and then delayed exhaling it for as long as their lungs could possibly hold out. Finally they said 'thanks' and walked out in silence.

In the room nobody stirred or made so much as a move to satisfy their curiosity as to which direction the men had gone before being enveloped by the wood. I, under an impulse which even the experience of years of imprisonment could not suppress, ran out and called after them, 'May God protect you.'

'Thank you. May he protect you too,' they replied.

I did not know from which direction the reply had come, but it was better for them and better for us not to know. Not once but many times I had seen those in the camps who had not succeeded in escaping. They had resembled nothing more than a bloodied pulp in which there was just enough life left for them not to be put into a rubbish bag and thrown into a pit. Instead they were kept in public view in a cell to warn other prisoners of the consequences of escape.

On my return to the cabin I could still see the faces of our nocturnal visitors, faces that expressed the humiliation and pain of a defeated animal, and all the way to my hard bed I whispered, 'may they succeed, may they succeed'. The men had similar thoughts but there was silence in the room. They did not know who the two were nor where they were heading. They knew only where they were escaping from. This was enough not to refuse help and not to ask questions. I continued to whisper 'may they succeed', when someone shouted 'you woman, shut your mouth and don't keep other people awake.'

There was no spite or malice in the voice. It was only a merciful caution, which he may not have fully appreciated himself, to warn me against converting my thoughts into words. The call for self preservation, stronger than the ties of blood, bound them with a chain of silence. Only the young Lithuanian continued to sleep without interruption.

In the morning I lit the fire as usual so that the men could refresh themselves with a drink of boiled water. No one said anything about the interruption in the night to the sleep of tired men. There was no mention of it in the evening either, though no one could have thought of anything else all day.

In the approaching darkness the men settled in front of the cabin for their evening meal and the rituals of smoking. They had to be economical with the tobacco so that it would last until new rations were distributed. Soon it was time to go to bed and the room was covered in complete darkness.

It must have been about midnight when the door was thrown wide open, this time accompanied by a lot of noise. On the doorstep we recognised the broad shouldered silhouette of the local NKVD informer. I did not even have time to ask, 'Who is it?' when he yelled 'light the lamp!'

The men were fully awake in an instant but no one was eager to greet him. I put on my rag dressing gown and in my own time lit the oil lamp. Time passes by at its own speed and no one can hurry it. If you do it may gall you. What you want to pass quickly may turn out to last painfully long, so I was not in a hurry. Eventually I lit the lamp.

The informer was well dressed, round faced, of reddish complexion, and with thick, strong arms. He was well fed. The sound of barking dogs came from afar and soon another bundle of meat entered the cabin shouting aggressively as to why nobody was getting up. The men, as if just wakened, raised their heads but made no other moves and remained silent. Not, this time, because of mercy and charity but because of stubbornness. We realised immediately that someone had betrayed us. It was also obvious that the NKVD had lost the fugitives trail and failed to apprehend them. That was why they came here to question us. This supposition added to our self-confidence.

The second man spread himself on the bench, took a small bag of tobacco from his pocket, untied it, took out from it neatly cut pieces of newspaper and skilfully rolled a long cigarette. He bent one end to resemble the shape of a pipe and lit it. Only then did he take a good look round the room.

'Well, how are you men?' he asked in a cheerful voice, although one could detect in it a fearful significance.

'We thank you, somehow we are surviving,' they replied together.

'And you, Caretaker?' he said to me. 'Are you lonesome being all the day on your own, or do you have visitors? Did you have any visitors by any chance last night?'

In such situations it is not seconds that matter but fractions of seconds. The lips may shiver or the face may suddenly change colour and your inquisitor will discover at once what he is seeking. I turned towards him with a glazed look so that he could not read anything from my face, pointed to my plank bed and replied with a Ukrainian proverb. 'My house is on the outer boundary of the village and I don't know anything.'

He laughed but could not conceal his annoyance. 'Ho, ho,' he said. 'Look how clever she is.'

I replied with a faint smile. 'I have completed ten years at the Prison Camp University and what I have learned has not been wasted. You should rejoice that your effort and money has not been squandered.'

He had enough of this comedy and felt that his time was being wasted. He knew that under the darkness of night the fugitives were making good progress and their capture was becoming less likely. He had no time to waste. He jumped up and shouted, 'Why did you not inform the commandant? You should have informed him immediately and stopped to tie up the escaping men. Such is your duty. You know very well what an honest Soviet citizen should do when he meets an escaping prisoner. And what do you do? Help escaping bandits but not the lawful authorities!'

He would have shouted longer had it not been for the loud voices in the hut waking the young Lithuanian who sat up on the bed and looked round in disbelief. The men's questioning grew, 'Escapees? What escapees? There were some people who got lost in the dark and just wanted a short rest'.

'Which way did they leave?' shouted the frustrated official. 'Devil with them,' replied the men. 'Nobody is going to dash out in the darkness of the night and watch which way some strange people are going.'

'You should have informed the authorities immediately,' shouted the dog handler

In reply the men chanted with increasing annoyance. 'Do we

have time? It is a long way from here to the commissar. We are in the middle of a very busy season. Resin is oozing out of the trees and must be collected promptly. We have targets to meet and we are not here to take joy walks to the commissar. If one of us is lucky enough to join the NKVD, then he will have time to chase fugitives, but not now.'

The increasing din of mutual accusations got too much for the officials and, swearing profusely at everything on the earth, they left empty-handed. One could still hear their swearing as they walked away into the darkness of the night. We waited awhile and when the barking of the dogs grew fainter, we burst into spontaneous and uncontrollable laughter.

It was laughter straight from the heart, an expression of achievement and victory. It was also a sign that what the men had been silent about all day remained very much in their hearts. It is true that thoughts can oppress and putting them into words can bring a welcome relief, but words can also kill. Hopefully our night visitors had made enough progress to be out of range of the pursuing guards.

None of us had known either of them, and nobody even wanted to take a good look at them, and yet they suddenly became our dearest friends. One had tremendous admiration for prisoners who decided to escape against all odds of success and the appalling consequences of failure. The instinct of such a prisoner is not all that different to that of an animal caught in a snare that bites off its foot to escape.

I was still laughing as I made my way back to my plank bed. At the same time another thought came into my mind. 'Who could have informed the authorities about the night visitors? What was the likely motive or the intended gain?'

In the eyes of your fellow prisoners betraying brings vile contempt, but silence is rewarded with noble regard. Who could have stooped so low as to betray, or was it just careless talk in an unguarded moment?

In The Soviet Union it is not easy to make friends. One can

never tell what will motivate people when they are under stress. Even the most trusted friends could prove to be moral cowards whose ill-gotten reward could be a reduction in their sentence.

I returned to Long Bridge in the autumn and immediately began to search for Alma. None of my acquaintances were able to help and I drew a complete blank. One day I went to fetch water from the well and met a local Siberian, Ivanov Petrovich. He was wearing his old dog hide coat, in which he permanently lived, and beautiful fur gloves of an old gold colour.

After exchanging the usual pleasantries I asked him 'Ivan Petrovich, where did you get the beautiful gloves from?'

With a look of surprise and disbelief he answered. 'Don't you recognise them? They are made out of the hide of your bitch which you fattened up so well. I have one pair left and you can have them at a discount'.

It left me dumbfounded and speechless. After a few moments I turned away, picked up my buckets and left.

CHAPTER 24

I become a free citizen

Sometime between 10th December 1955 and the 1st of January 1956, there was a train travelling on the line between Krasnoyarsk and Przemysl that you might say was the most joyful and happiest of trains speeding over the whole of this globe. Returning home from 'permanent settlement in Siberia' there were in the train about 800 Polish citizens travelling in Pullman coaches without a care for tomorrow.

Krasnoyarsk is situated on the line between Moscow and Vladivostok and was one of the assembly points for the returning prisoners. We had travelled from the numerous outlying areas of this vast Siberian region to the nearest rail station to take a train to Krasnoyarsk. We were accompanied by one or two NKVD men, and journeyed hundreds of kilometres on sledges, trailers pulled by snow tractors, lorries, and sometimes even by bus. Yenisieysk and Norilsk were completely isolated by ice and snow and the prisoners from there were transported by air. Each group, as they eventually arrived at the Krasnoyarsk station, was greeted by the chief of the NKVD and allocated places in the train scheduled to take us home.

There was a continuous arrival of small groups of ex-prisoners in the three days of my waiting in Krasnoyarsk. Many experienced some of their most emotional moments since being taken prisoner when they met friends, or members of their own families, about whose lives they knew nothing after being parted in prisons or labour camps many years earlier. I was astonished and surprised when I met Father Kapusta among of my old friends.

The Long Bridge

For the last 13 years I had often thought of him and was happy to assume that he was free and abroad. Instead, he told me, that in 1943 when he was due to be released and deported to Iran where the Polish Forces were stationed, diplomatic relations were broken between Moscow and the Polish government in London. He was kept in a Moscow prison for a year and then was sent to Komi labour camp to serve a ten year sentence. On completion he was deported to the Krasnoyarsk region for life.

Some of us, with the guards' permission, managed to take occasional trips to the town while we were waiting for the departure of our train. The name Krasnoyarsk, the name of the town and the region, is derived from the red tint in the soil. The town is one of the oldest Siberian settlements along the River Yenisey.

In the days of the tsars there were Cossack outposts protecting the territory as well as the new Russian settlers. Krasnoyarsk, like all the Siberian towns, spreads over a wide area. The houses are made of wood with large balconies running the full width of the dwelling. Here and there one comes across modern houses built in brick for government officials. Food shops were mainly empty and deliveries were instantly sold to the quickly formed queues. Shops selling ornaments and local crafts were well stocked with high quality products largely made of native wood. Women were dressed modestly but often had beautiful garments of silver fox fur.

In the local museum, from which there was a breathtaking view of the river, I was perusing with great interest the local exhibits. Among them was a large meteor that fell in this area and a large mammoth that had been excavated in the vicinity. There was a very interesting ethnographic section about local tribes and races, particularly about Evenks and Samoyedic people with plenty of exhibits. The museum was well looked after and the staff were kind to us.

After a few days the train started on its journey. We all burst into the Polish national anthem and with joy bid farewell to the land of Krasnoyarsk.

In the middle of the train there was a coach for officials who were escorting us. It also contained a sick bay and medical staff whose duty was to deliver us safely into the hands of the Polish authorities. From time to time the commandant of the train would come round and ask about our wishes. He soon learned that our greatest wish was to be with our relatives as soon as possible.

Arrangements were made along the route to have hot food awaiting our arrival at the railway stations. Every day I had white bread with butter, drank tea with sugar and ate food I had not seen for 16 years. On the journey each of us received 300 roubles as pocket money and those of us clothed in rags were given better clothing.

On the whole no one was worried about their shabby dresses but the authorities, obviously, did not want us to arrive home in the appalling state in which we had lived in the prisons and camps. I was returning without an overcoat because I had left my endlessly patched and mended fur coat to a friend in Long Bridge whose need was greater than mine. I knew that once I got home and found my family they would re-clothe me from head to foot.

The train journey was to all of us the first opportunity to have a rest after many years of forced labour. The thought that we were returning home and would be reunited with our families filled us with tremendous joy. Sadness and worry completely disappeared. There was singing in every railway carriage. People walked the length of the train looking for members of their family or friends.

New friendships were developing and there was no end to the exchanging of stories and experiences. There were a lot of young men who as boys had served in the Polish Underground Army and who had been deported in 1945 and 1946 to the

Soviet labour camps. They were eager to meet Polish girls and new friendships quickly developed. There were even some engagements. There were, therefore, many good reasons for celebrations and drinking.

Most of us had been isolated in the camps and settlements either individually or in groups of two or three, and one had not heard one's native language for many years. Consequently the prevailing talk was a mixture of Polish and Russian and sometimes it was difficult to determine what language was being used. We consistently corrected each other and after a few days there was a noticeable improvement in the use of our native tongue.

There were two carriages occupied by married couples and their families. They were mostly of mixed marriage and speaking the Russian language, but with fathers making strenuous efforts to teach their wives and children a few basic words in Polish.

We were allowed to leave the train at longer stops and to talk to the local people. It is customary in Russia for the locals to sell to the travelling public hot, home cooked meals. One may even find stalls selling provisions. I also noticed that now people were better supplied with goods and though the rouble kept a steady value, there was still a lot of barter taking place. Everyone seemed to be better dressed than 16 years earlier and, when they learned who we were and where we were going, they shared our joy and wished us good fortunes.

Our train made very slow progress and sometimes we spent hours waiting at stations or on sidings. I was travelling with a very good friend of mine, M. I first met her in one of the prison camps and we came across each other later in the taiga. It occurred to us how pleasant it would be if we could meet up with some of our Russian friends who lived in Moscow and whom we got to know in prison camps and in the settlements.

I become a free citizen

They had been released a few months before us a result of the general amnesty for Soviet citizens following Stalin's death. It would also give us an opportunity to see round Moscow.

I borrowed the best overcoat I could and we secretly left the train in Kazan. We hid in the most remote part of the station and only came out after our train had left. We bought tickets and boarded the next train for Moscow. We overtook our original train standing at one of the stations and next day arrived in Moscow.

We had an impressive view from the station of the tower blocks dominating the City and made for the Metro which took us to our friends. On the way we admired the beautiful station of which the Muscovites are so proud.

Our Russian friends gave us an emotional and affectionate welcome. We were delighted that their lives had returned to normal. Rehabilitated fully, most of them had got their old jobs back. Some had even managed to get their own flats but others had problems in finding accommodation.

One couple, who owned a car, took us on a sightseeing tour on which I managed to get a superficial impression of Moscow. Modern and impressive buildings stood next to old and neglected houses and, on the whole, the city was clean and bursting with life.

Pedestrians were well drilled in the traffic laws. People on the whole were dressed simply and monotonously. Most women had scarves or shawls over their heads and many of them had fur coats though they were poorly cut and made. We visited the large government store, GUM, which occupied a complete block with internal, suspended bridges connecting the various shops. All those that sold articles of daily need had long queues but jewellery and fur shops, on the other hand, were deserted and I was able to view at length fantastic but expensive fur coats. I decided to buy a pair of slippers and alternating with my friend to keep a place in the queue, it took us four hours to get to the sales counter. When we got there we found that I could only buy slippers one size too large because that was the size they were selling that day.

We walked a good deal and saw the Kremlin from the outside, admired the splendid Orthodox churches, and visited Red Square.

We ran into some difficulties trying to find out when and at which station our train would be arriving. One of our dear friends took the trouble to locate it for us and, after thirty hours in Moscow, we found it on the outskirts of the city at a goods station. When we got into the carriage we found that some people were asleep while others waited for our return. Also waiting for us were the guards who managed to find out about our escapades. Surprisingly they met us without a reprimand and I think that, in fact, they were relieved that we had managed to return in time.

When we left Moscow we made our way to Kiev and I found myself travelling along the route that had taken me into the depth of Russia at the beginning of 1940 when I was in a sealed goods wagon with my two very young children and all of us filled with terror and anxiety.

Now I was travelling in the opposite direction, returning home.

Fourteen years had passed since I last saw my children. To start with I had yearned for them intensely and had a burning desire to know what was happening to them. Years of isolation and helplessness had caused my inquisitiveness to diminish and eventually to vanish. I felt so united with them in my thoughts that they were always near to me. I no longer worried about them and it had ceased to matter any longer where they were, be it on this or the other side of Life. Every day I sent my prayers to God wishing all would be well with them. I believed that good thoughts that come from the depth of one's heart must always help and could never vanish without trace.

Travelling now in comfort and without anxiety, I was able to run my thoughts through the years spent in this country, dwelling on some events longer than others, analysing and rationalising. My daughter's voice was always in my ears.

I was now returning alone, without my children, without a home to go to, carrying with me the rich but heavy burden of sixteen years in a multitude of prisons and labour camps. My mind was at peace and I had an objective view of the events I had lived through.

I do not possess any special education or qualification. I am an average woman, like millions of others, except perhaps more inquisitive about the inner life than its external form. Life itself has taught me to base my views on the facts of my own experiences as well as those of my friends in adversity.

The relationship of man to man is not antagonistic. We helped each other and showed sympathy and compassion in the face of personal discomfort, sacrifice and repression by the authorities. Neither is this the privilege of one particular nation or race. Every person is capable of friendship and providing help. I have not met evil people in my life. If some appeared to be wicked then their evil was their own misfortune and affliction. As to others, very often we were guilty of adopting false attitudes and seeking in them an odiousness that was not there. The evil resided in the brutality of the NKVD system. It placed adversities and obstacles at every step of the way that we had to fight, very often at high cost to ourselves.

From the moment of my arrest the thread that connects and binds one human being to another was severed and, in its place, there appeared a wild and savage force. The NKVD officers considered us to be something that has to be oppressed with brutality devoid of human consideration, and yet many prisoners during their long incarcerations met with quiet compassion and even material help from those who worked for that brutal force.

I know of cases where the commandants or the guards secretly passed on letters from prisoners to their families.

307

There were even instances where NKVD men, during their holidays, visited prisoners' families and gave the relatives a first-hand account of the fate of the loved one. There were also guard's wives who secretly passed bread to prisoners with an encouraging word. Such deeds when discovered not only led to loss of position but also severe punishments and repressions.

It is, therefore, a 'blind force' that manipulates millions of innocent prisoners and forces them to submit to oppression and gross injustice.

Women, on the whole, responded to and coped better with this 'other life' in the prisons than men did. They were not broken down so easily and the death rate was minimal.

Many women told me that before their loss of freedom they were physically and psychologically very weak. They were not involved in hard work and were not engaged in sporting activities. A relatively short walk on an outing or a more strenuous physical effort would soon bring on tiredness and various aches and pains. Likewise, minor day to day problems or unfulfilled desires would soon result in a bad mood, or a feeling that tragedy had struck. Now they survived long marches while hungry and cold, digging in the fields, and collecting stones, in addition to coping with the trauma of separation from children, loved ones and loss of personal freedom. Often one would recollect some 'tragic experiences' from one's previous life that now appeared insignificant and almost laughable.

Painful and dramatic changes in one's life bring forth energies which we do not realise are latent within us.

Women prisoners adapted to the new surroundings more quickly than men. They found friends more easily and developed trust more quickly though it took time to be sure who your real friends were. Friendship helped to assuage the sadness of losing contact with those one had so dearly loved and proved a welcome relief in our difficult life. Equally our relationship and attitude to surrounding nature was different to that of the men. Nowhere more so than in the taiga where through our nearness to nature we were able to strengthen men's resolve and reinforce their belief in a better tomorrow. I also learned here how strong a woman is in coping with adversity and how beneficial and helpful friendship can be.

I was crossing the very wide River Dniepr when suddenly I remembered a dream I had sixteen years earlier. It was the first time that I had recalled it. Now, here I was about to cross this 'Long Bridge' of my life. What a strange coincidence to be also returning home over a long bridge and coming from a settlement called Long Bridge. At the far end of the bridge was a small but very intense light. Today this light is still shining brightly in my heart fuelled by human friendships and an ardent belief in people, God in me and my neighbour.

I sent a telegram from Tarnopol to my sister warning her of my arrival, though I did not know at which station. We arrived in Lwow the following night and were enthusiastically greeted at the station by many Poles who still lived there. I was very moved by this reception and by the beautiful night silhouette of the city where I had spent my school days. Next day in the afternoon we crossed the new Polish-Soviet border and very soon arrived in Przemysl. It was the end of our journey on the wide gauge Soviet train.

Many of my fellow passengers, when they stepped out of the train, knelt and kissed the Sacred Native Earth. My sisters were waiting at the station and it was with great joy and deep emotions that we hugged each other. The Polish authorities gave me permission to leave the group. My sisters wrapped me in a blanket and took me to their home, and so at last I became a free citizen.

CHAPTER 25
The circle closes

The composition of the prisoners changed constantly. Familiar faces disappeared as group after group was transferred to other, often very distant, camps. New faces were always appearing, long term convicts, in many cases from Arctic camps or from thousands of miles away in the Far East. An experienced newcomer always entered a camp as if he or she had just left it. The conditions of life and the housing were always exactly the same. Personalities became smoothed out, but moral traits remained unchanged and were a constant point of contact.

Summers, springs and winters were invariably passed amidst a large group of prisoners, women for the most part, and I closely observed relations between the convicts, their inner and external reactions to their sufferings and those of others. Wandering from land to land, a pilgrim perceives variety and differences though the road winds its way over one and the same world.

For sixteen years I was such a pilgrim, though what I observed were the hearts and souls of people. After many years of suffering and dire experiences, as these hearts disrobed and laid themselves bare, I invariably found them identical or at least very similar to one another.

It needed great determination and will power not to lose one's real being amidst these frightful conditions, and to attain a consciousness of one's real self. On this pilgrim's progress of one's own experiences and those of others, it was possible to acquire a profound and lasting knowledge which facilitated work and co-existence with others. Ineradicable was the profound understanding gained about forms that must pass, and a great fellow-feeling for all.

All our faults and virtues were fully revealed. None of us sought to present herself as any better or worse than she really was. We used to say, 'Our souls lie on the table for all to see.'

From the most hidden crannies of mind and heart we extracted all that brought us pain or joy, whatever had been concealed even from ourselves when we had still been free. Good or evil, noble or base, all was said and revealed. Our individual thoughts were expounded in sincerity and willingness, yet I never heard sharp clashes in discussion. Agreement to agree or disagree was the rule and in no wise affected co-existence. Nobody expressed surprise or was shocked, and nobody ever condemned anybody else.

It was at first embarrassing, even painful to bare oneself in this way, particularly for those whose shielding clung so closely as to become second nature though often imposed, ill-fitted to the wearer and clashing with the environment. This outer shell did most to stifle and cramp our real inner being. It took some people years to rid themselves of this accretion and they suffered as, withal, they considered it to be their real ego.

The prisoners were comprised of every conceivable class and intellectual level, from the most hardened and brutal criminals to the highest and most intellectual grades of the political prisoners. Suffering was what united the varied hearts of all these people and brought them resurrection.

Our heart to heart talks, or rather confessions of souls, provided a powerful sense of internal freedom as if to compensate for the loss of physical liberty. In this sense we no longer felt imprisoned. Mere oppression cannot imprison thought.

When the first few years of disquiet, distrust and sheer fright had passed, a calmer period set in. We changed our judgement about the forms of treatment applied by the strong to the weak. Our attitude now sprang from an inner impulse, a deeper and calmer one. We feared neither the camp commandants nor Moscow, nor the repressions they imposed on us. We regarded them as a transient evil, a physical, brutal power which must sooner or later wither away.

These currents still flow through the enormous sea of humanity, sanctioned in brutality, carried along by its imperialistic lust with utter disregard for the millions of victims it produces. All in vain! In the depths, there is still the human heart, good and noble souls, and these must win the final victory.

It is not true that the struggle for life is typified, as many think, by the stronger snatching a piece of bread from the weaker. He merely has temporarily improved his conditions of living. How often have I seen the so-called 'strong' types perish more quickly than the weak. It is not physical strength which endures, but that tiny, unassuming spark of inner strength often contained within a weak body which, properly cherished, becomes a real power and works miracles. In these strange circumstances, only when one has passed the test and realisation of the real inner being has been attained, is it possible to rise above all.

External joys were rare among us and even these were relative. We were glad when spring approached because we could cast off our heavy rags, but with spring came hard labour and a longer working day. Sometimes an encouraging rumour – of an amnesty or of some improvement in our living conditions – would gladden us for a while only to prove unfounded. It would seem that a letter from home should be a joyous occasion but, no, only as long as one held it unopened in the hand. Reading such a letter, regardless of its content, the recipient would often become sad and burst into tears. Sometimes a concert organised by the prisoners would soothe our melancholy for a time, only later to increase it.

After some years of this life with companions in misfortune, new joys would arise, different ones yielded by calm and lasting inner satisfactions. What joy was it when one 'acquired' without detriment to the others, some extra food and shared it. It warmed the heart when you returned to the hut after a long, hard day's work, tired out and cold, and found your pannikin of soup still hot because some kind heart had tucked it away in your bunk and carefully wrapped it in a rug. The kind heart belonging to the woman excused from work this morning by the doctor. Or, you come back from work and are wet through so you take off all your clothes to get them dried and stand about naked – because you have nothing else to put on. Something is thrown down on your bunk and somebody says, 'Here, put that on.'

You are digging in the fields or carrying heavy stones, and too tired to complete your quota. A strong young bandit moll comes up and says, 'Have a rest, Auntie, I will finish it off.' You are shivering with a bout of malaria and other women pile all their rugs and wadded jackets on you. All this is done in a matter of fact way, without unnecessary words. You feel you are not alone when there are so many kind hearts around, and you try to be still better and help others with even greater zeal. One feels as if strong in shining armour, able to arouse others, to reinforce their strength and give them further courage to endure.

Once this armour is buckled on it will never be laid aside or lose its potent force. You will go through life with faith in humanity, with deep understanding, firm in the knowledge that in every land and amidst every people there is much good and fellow feeling.

In those Soviet concentration camps, really great human friendships were born, friendships not based on material gain but on inner values, and on experiences common to us all. We are now separated by time and space. Our life together has ended, but its friendships last and will endure to the end of our mortal days, perhaps even beyond them, regardless whether my companions were Europeans or Asians: Christians, Buddhists, Muslims, Jews, or non-believers.

From Poland I established contact with my son and daughter who were living in England and, soon after, started my application to leave for the UK. The political situation in Poland at that time made this virtually impossible, but changes were taking place and when Gomulka took over the Government of Poland, in October 1956, he liberalised the laws and I received my permission to leave in the following year.

One happy day I flew from Warszawa to London to find two grownups awaiting me at the airport. I did not immediately recognise them but my son and daughter spotted me immediately, and it was not long before I saw in their faces the small but unforgettable features which I knew so well and which I had treasured so much in my memory.

When I hugged my daughter, she started to cry quietly. I said to her, 'Don't cry, I have returned'.

She smiled and replied 'They are the tears of happiness, Mother'. She then placed on my finger the wedding ring that I had given her for safekeeping 15 years earlier as the NKVD officers were taking me off to prison.

Postscript

Urszula Latawiec was born in 1903, the seventh of ten children in a wealthy family living in Rawa Ruska. She received a good education and was brought up within the Catholic Church in a town where there were also many Jews and Greek Orthodox. As a young woman she met and married Wladyslaw Muskus, a forest manager living near the village of Hrebenne, about 6 kilometres from her home.

Wladyslaw managed a privately owned forest, roughly 50 kilometres in diameter, which was under the control of the Polish Government. Five years older than Urszula he was the eldest of eleven children. His parents had one of the larger farms in the village of Przychojec near Lezajsk. Wladyslaw attended Lwow University where he studied forestry and surveying, financing his studies by tutoring other students in mathematics.

During the Polish–Russian War of 1918-1921, local fighting broke out between Poles and Ukrainians in Lwow. Most of the city's population was of Polish descent, but in the surrounding countryside most were Ukrainian. There was street fighting between solders, partisans and students. The Poles were the first to organize a regular army unit which arrived by train and took control of the city. This is mentioned in Urszula's story. Wladyslaw graduated from student to an officer in the Polish force that pushed the Red Army all the way to Odessa. There he fell sick with typhus and the Polish army retreated without him to the new agreed border.

The family gave him up for dead, except his father who

insisted that he was still alive and would turn up one day. Miraculously he arrived home after walking hundreds of kilometres, mostly at night, unable to risk contact with the mainly Ukrainian population. He arrived in a shocking condition, having lost all his hair, and collapsed at the gate unable to manage another step. He convalesced for many weeks before regaining his health. My father remembers hearing this account, not only from Urszula, but also from his grandfather.

My father, Zbigniew (known as Clive in the UK), was born in 1925 while his parents were living near Hrebenne. Soon afterwards they moved in with Urszula's family in Rawa Ruska and from there Wladyslaw became a self employed forestry surveyor. A daughter Grazyna was born three years later. My father remembers living in a big extended family with his grandparents and various aunts, uncles and cousins until he was ten years old.

For a month each autumn Wladyslaw took his family by train to Lezajsk to help with the harvest on his parents' farm. He is remembered by his nephews and nieces as a generous man who always produced a large bag of sweets. The family must have enjoyed relative wealth since my father was the only child in the village to own a bicycle.

In 1935 the construction of a block of apartments was completed by Wladyslaw in the centre of Rawa Ruska, almost opposite the town house. The building was very much a family effort with one of Urszula's brothers in direct charge. It contained six flats and a basement in which the caretaker lived. It is in a top floor flat of this building that we find my grandparents living with their children at the beginning of The Long Bridge. At that time Urszula was living a happy family life in comfortable circumstances that were soon to change.

In her story Urszula recounts the last time she saw her husband at Rawa Ruska railway station. For many years my family assumed that Wladyslaw had been shot in the Katyn woods massacre by the Russians. However, following the collapse of Communism records became available, and in 1995 Polski Memorial unearthed the facts. Listed as a lieutenant in the Polish reserve army Wladyslaw was transferred to the Zamarstynon Prison in Lwow where he was shot on 5th March 1940, along with 3435 others in this prison alone. His NKVD number was 71/1-55. Wladyslaw is listed as number 2022 on the Ukrainian Government's list of Poles executed in the Ukraine.

Historical records now suggest that in Kresy, eastern Poland controlled by the USSR, any Poles who fought against the Bolsheviks in the 1918-1921 war were hunted down and executed or sent to labour camps. Wladyslaw would have been in this category.

The first time that I met my grandmother was in our hallway, the day after her arrival at London airport. I was only five and a half years of age, but still remember her as she was that day, a warm and affectionate woman who wore soft woollen clothes and, unlike my mother, used plenty of perfume. My father had prompted my sister, Ann, and I to call her *Babka*, but his Polish was rusty and *Babka* rather bluntly means 'old woman', or a type of Easter cake. The more usual word is *Babcia*. However we settled on Babusia which, I have since learned, is an older word for grandmother.

Babusia lived for most of her remaining years in a bedsit in her daughter's home in London, a three hour drive from the village where we lived. When my father's work took him to London during my school holidays I would go with him to visit Babusia. I remember that when she visited us she liked to cook Polish dishes, pierogi, little pastry envelopes filled with meat and cheese in a sauce, and my favourite, golumpki, a mixture of rice and bacon wrapped in cabbage leaves. She baked cakes that were especially rich in eggs and butter and would get the whole kitchen, every available surface, in a terrible clutter of dishes and spilled ingredients, which my mother found difficult to cope with.

In the years before World War II she was accustomed to having a full time housekeeper while she involved herself in charitable work around the town of Rawa-Ruska. This might explain the mess.

We children were acutely aware of how she did not like to see food wasted or left on our plates. Babusia even ate fish skins. During the preparation of this book Ann reminded me in a note how '. . . old ways die hard. Just as in the camps a little spare bread would be kept close "just in case", in London or Lincoln there was always a piece of oven-dried bread under the large, Polish-style pillow on her bed'.

Her experiences over sixteen years in the Soviet prison system made her outlook and values rather different from that of the people around us. My sister remembers:-

'Babusia was a happy person who seemed to have managed to overcome and conquer her past experiences. I remember her teaching me Polish dances on the driveway at home, sometimes early in the morning in her dressing gown, much to my father's embarrassment. She would take me with her as we went each morning to greet the apple trees in the back garden. How she loved the apple blossom!'

In her bedsit she pinned charts of the night sky to the walls. Babusia loved to look at the stars. It was only much later, when reading her book, that I received my first inkling of their spiritual importance to her. She loved country walks, and the seaside when she holidayed with us in Cornwall. Anything to do with the environment was important to her; she felt a need to be close to nature, a need that has continued in me here on the croft.

Ann also reminds me how, '. . . she thoroughly enjoyed sixties London. Like many Polish women she enjoyed getting dressed up, wearing make-up and plenty of perfume. I particularly remember she loved to dress in purple with the long beads and metal pendants that were popular then. The physical freedom which she had finally gained mirrored the mood of the sixties and very early seventies. I have always described my grandmother as the youngest person I have ever met.'

In London she made many friends and developed an extensive social life. At a sewing class Urszula met the wife of a Japanese diplomat. With her help an advertisment was placed in a newspaper to make contact with Kacuya. Seeing the advert he replied saying that he was well and living with his wife, and that he did not want any further contact.

In the Hammersmith Polish Centre she met with Dr Maurice Frydman, a Pole who spent much of his life in India at the Ashram of Sri Ramana Maharshi. This was very much in the spirit of the times, but Sri Ramana also confirmed ways of living, thinking and being which were compatible with her experiences on the steppe.

Urszula had her first small heart attack in 1959. It was discovered that she had high blood pressure and very high cholesterol. White globules of cholesterol could be seen in the palms of her hands. The doctors carried out extra studies on her because they were surprised by this condition after all her years of malnourishment.

In a small notebook, in Babusia's own hand, I had discovered a list of the names of her nine brothers and sisters, and also the ten of my grandfather. In 2005 my wife and I travelled to Poland for the first time, where we met fifty out of some two hundred surviving relatives.

During this visit we travelled to Rawa Ruska, where Babusia's book begins and which is now in the Ukraine. Here we were introduced by chance to an old lady called Luba. She had been a friend of Grazyna when they were children and produced a class photo in which I could easily recognize my aunt. Luba had received no news of Grazyna since 1942 when she had heard that she had escaped to Persia. A bottle of Russian champagne was produced and we were given a generous meal in a very simple home, hospitality I shall never forget. On my return home I posted her a copy of the Polish version of Babusia's book.

Urszula, Babusia to Ann and me, stopped typing in mid sentence in Hayling Island and went to bed to die in her sleep. She had wanted a bright and cheerful funeral, and the priest was not well pleased that she had requested the involvement of two friends, a Rabbi and a Buddhist. Her body slipped away into the crematorium to the rousing sound of Sibelius's Finlandia.

While in captivity Urszula knew that her son had enlisted in General Anders army and had left Russia with one of his uncles. He sailed across the Caspian Sea to Persia, leaving Russia on 13th March 1942, exactly two years after their deportation from Poland. The army stopped in Tehran for several months to recuperate because conditions in Russia had left them in no fit state to fight.

From there my father continued to Palestine with the British Army where, ambitious to become a pilot, he volunteered for the Polish Air Force which was based in the U.K. He boarded the liner Aquitania in Port Said as one of the guards for 2000 prisoners from Rommel's Africa Corps. Feelings by this time ran so high that the British feared that the Poles might shoot the Germans, and so issued only one rifle for each guard on duty with only five rounds each. At the end of each duty the guards had to get out sight of the prisoners to hand the rifle to the next guard.

They sailed through the Suez Canal and around Africa before heading for the United States. In mid Atlantic they found themselves in the midst of a large German fleet spread over their horizons. Sailing under full power they zigzagged between the German warships for three days and my father has no idea how, with four funnels, they were not recognized. Leaving the prisoners in Boston he sailed to Manhattan Island, New York and, from there, north to Halifax, eventually arriving in Liverpool in the autumn of 1942.

On joining the Polish Air Force father was not allowed to fly because he was still under eighteen. Instead he began training on Radio Direction Finding equipment, known as radar, and was stationed at RAF Bolt Head near Hope Cove in Devon in late 1944. The station was reduced to a skeleton staff as fighting moved nearer Germany, but was kept on alert to watch for enemy planes or ships. There were no raids, it was a very relaxed posting and it was here that he met my mother. In September 1945 he was responsible for closing the radar station down, padlocking the gate and sending the keys to Group 60 Command. He continued to work with radar in the electronics industry, rising to be Manager of GEC's Lincoln division.

Retiring early he then ran a successful guest house in North Wales with his second wife before retiring to Lanzarote in the late nineties. At the age of 80 he was doing two years voluntary work in Ecuador, plumbing and building in a seminary and wiring in a new school at 4000m in the mountains. His good health lasted until after his 83rd birthday. He died following a short illness in Lanzarote in 2009.

Urszula described how she prized open the grip of her daughter's hand when they were separated by her arrest. What she did not know was that the thirteen year old went to the prison every day demanding to see her mother. When the soldiers started saying, 'What's a nice girl like you doing in a place like this?' Grazyna realized that it had become too dangerous to return.

Grazyna was lucky to meet an old friend of her mother's who was gathering orphans to transport them out of Russia and, in October 1942, they travelled across the Caspian Sea to Tehran. Within the refugee convoy Grazyna made friends with an older girl who had a little brother. Much later she told me that, in her hunger and naivety, she had traded a heavy gold chain for an ice cream. In Tehran she did not meet her brother. In that year more than 100,000 Polish people found their way to Iran, then known as Persia, many dying and being buried in a special Polish cemetery located in Tehran.

On the voyage from Iran her friend died from tuberculosis and Grazyna adopted the little boy as her own brother. They landed in Tanganyika, in East Africa, travelling to the foothills of Mt. Meru where they were settled in a refugee camp built by the Red Cross. About two thousand Poles, mostly women and children, lived in circular mud huts with banana leaf roofs.

A high standard of teaching was provided by refugee Polish teachers. A Franciscan monk from America taught English. One of these teachers knew Urszula from Rawa Ruska and gave a home to Grazyna, the little boy and two other children.

When my aunt passed her matriculation in 1948 she was faced with the choice of returning to Poland or emigrating to America, Australia, New Zealand or the UK. She flew to England, and in 1949 was met by her brother at the airport. She went to live with one of her mother's brothers in London and studied pharmacy at an evening class. Through all the years that Grazyna was separated from her mother she wrote to her every month through the Red Cross, but Urszula did not receive a single letter.

Together again, Zbigniew and Grazyna had no news of their mother until they received the letter from Walter, the German POW who Urszula met in the gulags. It was forwarded to them by General Anders' office in London in May 1950.

Postscript

11th May 1950.
General Anders,
Polish Expeditionary Corps,
London.

Sir,

Having just returned home from a soviet forced-labour camp in Middle-Asia I consider it my foremost duty to render a service of friendship and to comply with the wish of a real friend.

In summer 1948 I met in a camp in Kasachstan / Middle Asia/ Mrs. Urszula Muscus with whom I was, in spite of great difficulties, narrowly connected on account of common social and mental views in a company of the most depraved criminals of the world. I had the highest respect in connection with Mrs. Muscus for her wonderful bearing in spite of the most adverse circumstances and I admired her energy, courage and high spirit which never left her. She never ceased to be a lady. Mrs. Muscus told me that she was your secretary before in Akmolensk in 1941, she was sentenced to 10 years forced labour for espionage. She asked me to look for her son Zbigniew, who in all probability was a member of your forces and trasmit to him her greetings. I was for a considerable time separated from Mrs. Muscus, but heard from a friend 3 weeks ago – at the moment of my departure in Middle Asia – that at that time she safe and sound arrived in Karabas / Kasachstan/, the camp from where I was sent home. Unfortunately, I had no more opportunity of seeing her.

I am at your disposal, should any further questions arise, my be at a personal conversation on the occasion of a visit to London.

In the meantime, I remain
truly yours,
Walter S.

The Long Bridge

Grazyna has lived the rest of her life in London, she married and has one son. The later part of her life has been dogged by ill health and she is now living in a nursing home.

Photographs and further details are on my website at http://www.hiddenglen.co.uk/long_bridge.htm If my domain should change over the years try a web search.

Peter Muskus

APPENDIX 1

Timeline – Urszula Muskus

23.10.1903   Born seventh of ten children into the Latawiec family living in Rawa Ruska near Lvov in south east Poland. Her father was a wealthy livestock dealer.

1914–18   World War I. Violent revolution in Russia in November 1917 leads to the formation of the USSR.

18.03.21   Treaty of Riga signed after Poland repels Bolshevik invasion and established a new border further east in territory with a majority Ukrainian population. Some claim that Stalin took revenge for this defeat in 1940 when the Soviets executed many Poles, including those in the Katyn massacre, who fought against the Bolsheviks 20 years earlier.

25.10.24   Married Wladyslaw Muskus a forestry consultant and veteran of the 1920 Polish-Bolshevik war.

18.10.25   Birth of son Zbigniew.

21.10.28   Birth of daughter Grazyna.

1934   NKVD (People's Commissariat for State Security) reformed into a pan Soviet security force under Yagoda. Responsible for the network of labour camps known as the Gulag.

23.11.38   Stalin appoints Beria head of NKVD in place of Yezhov.

23.08.39   Ribbentrop-Molotov Pact: This non-aggression pact between the German Reich and the USSR included a secret protocol which divided Poland (and other parts of eastern Europe) between them to re-establish the common frontier which had existed throughout the

19th century. This was approximately along the line of the rivers Vistula, Narew and San.

01.09.39 A group of German convicts were dressed in Polish uniforms and forced to attack a German radio station near the Polish border. They were then shot by their SS minders as the Nazi news service announced an unprovoked attack on the Third Reich. Poland is invaded with no declaration of war.

03.09.39 Britain declares war on Germany.

28.09.39 German-Soviet Treaty of Friendship, Cooperation and Demarcation: Going much further than the pact of five weeks before it redrew the demarcation line. It contained another secret protocol which envisaged joint action against Polish 'agitation' and was put into place as the Polish Government escaped into exile and Warsaw surrendered. Large numbers of Polish troops took to the woods, or fled abroad. The final capitulation took place on 4 October, when Hitler arrived in Warsaw.

1939/41 In the Soviet Zone the population felt the full force of the Stalinist terror. Some forty categories of people, from policemen to philatelists, were selected for instant arrest and deportation. By summer of 1941 between 1 and 2 million individuals had been transported either to the Arctic camps or to forced exile in Central Asia. The Terror was directed at all former Polish state officials, down to village teachers and foresters.

06.01.40 Husband Wladyslaw arrested by NKVD.

05.03.40 Unknown to Urszula, Wladyslaw executed by NKVD in Lwow prison.

13.03.40 Urszula and her children Zbigniew (14) and Grazyna (11) are arrested and transported to Kazakhstan, travelling for thirteen days locked in a goods wagon over 2700km. Forced labour on collective farms.

15.03.40 Katyn Massacres: Stalin authorised the massacre of 26,000 prisoners of war who had been captured in Poland the previous autumn. Nearly all were Polish

326

reserve officers, doctors, lawyers, professors, engineers, policemen and priests. When the massacres came to light they were variously blamed on the Germans and the Soviets. The UK Government sidestepped the issue to avoid upsetting the Soviets and the British public who would have been distressed that they were allied to the perpetrators. In the 1950s a US Congressional Committee put the full blame on the Soviets. The British Foreign Office was still claiming it was unclear in 1989.

Autumn 1940 Urszula and her children move to the town of Aktyubinsk where she founds a knitting cooperative.

22.06.41 Germany attacks the USSR: The initial German advance east was rapid and by 1942/43 the Germans controlled the area west of the line between Leningrad and Stalingrad. Urszula and other Polish citizens forcibly moved out of towns and back to collective farms.

Jul 1941 Soviet Polish Military Convention and Political Treaty: The German attack resulted in an alliance between the USSR, the UK and Poland. An 'amnesty' was granted to the millions of innocent Polish deportees and prisoners in the USSR and a Polish army commanded by General Anders, released from the Lyubianka prison in Moscow, was formed in Russia.

Summer 1941 Urszula visits General Anders and starts relief work for Polish POWs.

07.12.41 Japan attacks American naval base at Pearl Harbour bringing the US into World War II.

13.03.42 Son Zbigniew leaves the USSR for Persia, in the company of his uncle, as part of General Anders army.

22.05.42 Urszula is arrested, separated from her 13 year old daughter Grazyna, and transported to Alma-Ata for interrogation. A 2100km train journey, this time in a seated passenger compartment.

July 42 Grazyna leaves USSR for Tanganyika with a group of orphans.

Nov/Dec.42	A 3000km rail journey in harsh conditions takes Urszula to the transit centre at Karabas followed by a forced march to Shakhan, her first gulag.
Spring.43	A two day march to a gulag at Berazniki.
16.05.43	The Warsaw Ghetto uprising crushed after almost a month of resistance.
28.11.43	Roosevelt, Churchill and Stalin meet in Teheran to discuss the progress and objectives of the war. They could not agree over Poland, but the Western leaders conceded that Poland's eastern border should be moved to the west, at Germany's expense, to appease Stalin. This was kept secret from the Poles.
1944/45	Transfer to Volkovsk complex including settlements at Karadzar, Kirgitaz and Zavod.
27.01.45	Soviet troops enter Auschwitz.
04.02.45	Yalta Conference: Roosevelt, Churchill and Stalin agree that there should be 'free and unfettered elections' in Poland, and that a Provisional Government should draw its members both from Stalin's Lubin Committee and from the London Poles.
08.05.45	VE Day: Victory in Europe.
17.07.45	At the Potsdam Conference the victorious Allied leaders (Truman, Stalin, Churchill and Atlee) agreed a Polish frontier on the Oder-Neisse line. All Germans living east of the new frontier were to be expelled.
06.08.45	After six months of intensively firebombing 57 Japanese cities, the US explodes the first atomic bomb (Fat Boy) over Hiroshima. Exploding the second (Fat Man) over Nagasaki three days later effectively ends the war in the east.
1946	General Anders and his Polish Army had fought their way into northern Italy when the war ended. The men and their dependants, whose homes had been seized by the USSR, were brought to the UK where they were added to the Polish Resettlement Corps for retraining and assimilation. Few returned home.

Timeline – Urszula Muskus

1948/49	A two day march to Karabas, three days in a crowded rail wagon and a lorry transfer takes her to Kingir, a gulag near Dzhezkazgan.
11.05.50	Letter from Walter, the German officier released from the gulags, sent to General Anders, informs Zbigniew and Grazyna of their mother's survival.
Summer 50	Urszula returns to Karabas by train and is transferred by lorry to a gulag at Spask.
May 52	Her ten year sentence ends and Urszula is sent into 'eternal exile'. A 2400km rail journey takes her to the Siberian settlement of Long Bridge. She meets and lives with a Japanese ex-prisoner named Kacuya.
05.03.53	Stalin dies and is replaced by Beria, head of the NKVD, who is assassinated at the first Politburo meeting. The NKVD is reorganised as the KGB. Over the following three years collective leadership gave way to the personal supremacy of Khrushchev.
Spring 54	Kacuya allowed to return home with other Japanese citizens.
10.12.55	Urszula begins her journey home to Poland. A very happy 5300km rail journey which takes 22 days.
Early 57	Urszula is allowed to travel to London to be reunited with her now adult children.
1962	'One Day in the Life of Ivan Denisovich' by Aleksandr Solzhenitsyn published in Novy Mir.
08.04.72	Urszula dies in her sleep in the UK aged 69.
1975	Urszula's family and friends organise the printing, in London, of a limited number of the Polish version of The Long Bridge – Dlugi Most. Poland is still part of the Soviet Bloc and copies of the book must be smuggled in.

APPENDIX 2

Place names in The Long Bridge

	URSZULA'S SPELLING	DESCRIPTION	PRESENT NAME
	Rawa Ruska	Home town near Lwow in SE Poland	Rava-Rus'ka, Ukraine
	Lwow	Historic city in Polish and Ukrainian culture	L'viv, Ukraine
	Tomaszow	Town near Rawa Ruska	Tomaszow, Poland
	Zhovkva	Town near Rawa Ruska	Zhovkva, Ukraine
	Warszawa	Polish capital city	Warsaw
	Podwoloczyska	1939 Polish/Ukrainian border town	Pidvolochys'k, Ukraine
	Kuybyshev	City on the River Volga	Samara
	Orenburg-Czkalow	City in eastern Russia	Orenburg
13	Alga	Town in western Kazakhstan	Alga
14	Tok-Man-Say	Collective farm near Alga	
19	Maxim Gorky	Collective farm near Aktyubinsk	
20	Aktyubinsk	City in western Kazakhstan	Aktobe
	Totskoye	Site of POW camp where Polish Army mustered.	Totskoye Village, Orenburg District
25	Buzuluk	City in southern Urals, Gen Anders HQ	Buzuluk

31	Arys	Station 70km West Of Chimkent	Arys
31	Chimkent	City in southern Kazakhstan	Shymkent
32	Tian-Shan	Mountain range	Tian Shan
32	Alma-Ata	Capital of Kazakhstan in 1942	Almaty
39	Semipalatinsk	City near Soviet atomic test site from 1949	Semey
	Novosibirsk	Largest city in Siberia	Novosibirsk
	Omsk	City on Trans-Siberian railway	Omsk
	Petropavlovsk	City in northern Kazakhstan	Petropavl
	Karabas	Gulag rail transit point near Karaganda	Karabas
41	Karaganda	City at hub of Kazakhstan gulags	Karagandy
69	Temirtau	City 30km North Of Karaganda	Temirtau
86	River Nura	Flows into Lake Tengiz which has no outflow	River Nura
118	Dzhezkazgan	Central Kazakhstan city on River Kara-Kengir	Jezkazgan
141	Krasnoyarsk	Siberian city	Krasnoyarsk
144	Dlugi Most (Polish) or Long Bridge	Settlement 250km ENE of Krasnoyarsk	Dolgiy Most (Russian)
151	River Biryusa	Flows north from Sayan Mountains for 1012km	River Biryusa
	Tarnopol	Major city founded as a Polish military base in 1540	Ternopil, Ukraine
	Przemysl	City in SE Poland	Przemysl
	Yeniseysk *	Remote settlement 270km north of Krasnoyarsk	Yeniseysk
	Norilsk	Remote settlement 1500km north of Krasnoyarsk	Norilsk
	Kazan	Capital city of Tatarstan	Kazan
	River Dniepr	Ukrainian river, fourth longest in Europe.	River Dniepr
	KIEV	Ukraine	